Sarfraz Manzoor is a journ [...] en-writer. His journalism has [...] the *Observer, The Times, The Sun* [...] *ork Times.* He has written and pre [...] umentaries for BBC Radio and frequently appears as a critic and commentator on television. His first book, *Greetings from Bury Park*, was published in 2007 and adapted into the feature film *Blinded by the Light*, which was co-written by Manzoor and released in 2019.

Follow him on Twitter and Instagram @sarfrazmanzoor

He lives in London with his wife Bridget, daughter Laila, son Ezra and cat Socks.

Praise for *THEY*:

'A deeply personal and wonderful journey around identity, on who we are and wish to be: evocative, timely, powerful, superb'
Philippe Sands

'A must-read for anyone who wants to know why multiculturalism appears to have failed so many Muslims' **George Alagiah**

'Sarfraz Manzoor made me laugh, cry and broke my heart a little as he took me on an eye opening journey through a world I'd only ever glanced at as an outsider' **Shappi Khorsandi**

'Authentic, brave and powerful storytelling' **Sayeeda Warsi**

'Compelling, optimistic and intensely personal. Hope is ever present in what is simply a must-read' **Sajid Javid**

'This is not another book about the relationship between Muslims and non-Muslims. It is THE book' **Matthew d'Ancona**

'An absolutely essential and inspiring read. This excellent book is filled with stories of hope and optimism we rarely hear but which need to be told' **Nazir Afzal**

Sarfraz Manzoor

THEY

وہ لوگ

What Muslims and Non-Muslims
Get Wrong About Each Other

WILDFIRE

All the people like us are We,
And every one else is They.
And They live over the sea,
While We live over the way,
But – would you believe it? – They look upon We
As only a sort of They!

'We and They', Rudyard Kipling

First published in 2021 by
WILDFIRE
an imprint of HEADLINE PUBLISHING GROUP

First published in paperback in 2022 by
WILDFIRE
an imprint of HEADLINE PUBLISHING GROUP

1

Cataloguing in Publication Data is available from the British Library

ISBN 978 1 4722 6684 2

Typeset in Scala by CC Book Production

Printed and bound in Great Britain by Clays Ltd, Elcograf S.p.A.

Headline's policy is to use papers that are natural, renewable and recyclable products
and made from wood grown in well-managed forests and other controlled sources.
The logging and manufacturing processes are expected to conform to
the environmental regulations of the country of origin.

HEADLINE PUBLISHING GROUP
An Hachette UK Company
Carmelite House
50 Victoria Embankment
London EC4Y 0DZ

www.headline.co.uk
www.hachette.co.uk

For Bridget, Laila and Ezra: may they always know
how much they are loved.

CONTENTS

PROLOGUE: FATHER, PART ONE   1

AUTHOR'S NOTE   9

1: THEY . . . DON'T WANT TO LIVE AMONG US   11

2: THEY . . . DON'T MARRY OUTSIDE THEIR OWN   49

3: THEY . . . DON'T TREAT MEN AND WOMEN AS EQUALS   105

4: THEY . . . FOLLOW A VIOLENT RELIGION   155

5: THEY . . . FOLLOW A RELIGION THAT HATES JEWS   193

6: THEY . . . BELIEVE HOMOSEXUALITY IS A SIN   229

7: THEY . . . LOOK DOWN ON WHITE GIRLS   269

8: THEY . . . WANT TO TAKE OVER OUR COUNTRY   309

9: THEY . . . DON'T BELIEVE IN OUR VALUES   345

10: THEY . . . DON'T LOVE OUR COUNTRY   385

EPILOGUE: FATHER, PART TWO   413

ENDNOTES   423

ACKNOWLEDGEMENTS   435

Where there is ruin, there is hope for a treasure.

Jalāl ad-Dīn Muhammad Rūmī, Persian poet,
30 September 1207 – 17 December 1273

When I was a boy and I would see scary things in the news, my mother would say to me, 'Look for the helpers. You will always find people who are helping.'

Fred Rogers, US children's television presenter,
20 March 1928 – 27 February 2003

FATHER, PART ONE

I am searching for my father. It is a cold, late January morning, and I am wrapped in a long black coat on a train that I boarded at London's St Pancras heading to Luton. My memories begin in this town. I was born in Pakistan but arrived in Britain in May 1974, one month shy of my third birthday. My father, Mohammed Manzoor, left Pakistan in January 1963, leaving behind his wife and two children – my older sister was one and my older brother had been born the previous month. My father promised my mother, Rasool Bibi Manzoor, that he was only going to be away for five years; he was going to work and save money and he would then return home. He did return, but only for visits; in the eleven years my parents were apart my father visited Pakistan three times – most significantly for me in 1970, when I was conceived. It was never a permanent return. Britain was becoming his home and, in the spring of 1974, it became mine. My younger sister was born the following year. We lived in Luton where my father worked on the production line of the Vauxhall car factory and my mother as a seamstress at home. I went to school and college in Luton but left first to study in Manchester and later to live and work in London. I left Luton at the age of eighteen, it is my past. But the past is never over – it is not even past.

I get off the train and hail a taxi. The Muslim taxi driver asks me where I'm from. I tell him Luton. 'Yes, but where are you *really* from?' he asks. I stare out of the window in anticipation and guilt. I do not visit my father often enough. The taxi reaches its destination and I take a deep breath and step out. A light rain is falling and my footsteps are heavy as I walk towards him. I stop in front of him and say: *'As-salāmu 'alaykum Abu-ji'*. Hello, Dad. The marble tombstone in front of me reads: 'Mohammed Manzoor 1933–1995'.

My father died from a sudden and unexpected heart attack in June 1995, three days before I turned twenty-four. He lies buried in the Vale Cemetery and Crematorium in a section reserved for the Muslim dead. Mohammed Manzoor is buried as he lived – among his own. My family's origins are in the villages of rural northern Pakistan. There is no record of where or when my grandparents were born and no documents that detail their lives. There are no certificates that record their births and no memorials that reveal where they are buried. The lives of my grandparents are a mystery but the early life of my parents is scarcely more distinct. My parents married around 1960 – there are no photographs of the wedding and my mother cannot recall the precise date. I remember as a teenager being filled with an aching envy at seeing my White friends' family albums: photographs of grandparents' weddings, grandfathers in military uniforms, and scenes of parents as small children. My friends took these things for granted but I was acutely aware of the impact of not having such images. The years my mother spent in Pakistan without my father went undocumented. There are no letters and no photographs. There are photographs, though, of my father's time in Britain during the sixties and early seventies, living in a succession of houses he shared with fellow Pakistani men. They offer tantalising glimpses of him, not as a father but as a man. I can see him standing by a cooker stirring a pot. He is wearing an apron over his shirt and tie, while another man, more casually dressed, looks on. I can see him seated at a table, again in a tie, preparing to eat with three other men. I see him gazing at the camera in sunglasses, his hands casually slipped into the pockets of a cream suit. He doesn't look like a newly arrived immigrant working in a poorly paid manual job: he has an unruffled dignity that transcends his humble surroundings. In these photographs my father seems a sociable fellow. He is usually in the company of other men but never any women. These were my father's friends but I have no idea who they are, or what happened to them.*

---

* I always hoped that writing about my father in the newspapers and making *Blinded by the Light*, a film about my relationship with him, would prompt some of his old friends or their children to get in touch. Sadly no one has ever contacted me.

Why do the faces in the photographs from my father's early life in Britain haunt me? In part, it is because photographs can help flesh out and provide colour and detail to our understanding of the past. Relatives who are long dead, or whom we view only through a rigid parental prism, or through the fog of distant memory, are revealed as fully-fleshed, vital human beings. It is not easy to feel rooted when one is drowning in a sea of unknowns. I stare hard at the grass under which his coffin is buried, and I swear the ground seems to move gently up and down as if the dead are still breathing. There is a space set aside next to my father's grave for my mother. I should come to see him more often.

I leave my father and order another taxi to take me into town. The driver is Muslim. 'The difference between what *they* are like and what we are like,' he says, 'is that they cry about their parents when they're dead, but they treat them like crap when they're alive.' I say nothing and look busy on my phone until the taxi arrives in Bury Park. It does not look special – just another two-bedroom terraced house on a narrow street in the heart of the Asian part of town. But this was my first family home and where I spent my first five years in Britain. It was from this house that my father would leave for work. My mother would pack his lunch – chapattis, lentil curry – in a blue tiffin box. She would then take us to school before taking her place behind a black, iron Singer sewing machine. I weigh up knocking on the door but decide against it. What would I say? 'I used to live here forty years ago – would you mind if I took a look around?'

4

When my father arrived in Britain in 1963, I imagine he came filled with hopes and fears. He would not have left Pakistan unless he believed in Britain, believed that it was a land of promise. In the years since he died there have been many times that I have wondered how he would feel about that promise – was it delivered, or has it been betrayed?

My father died in 1995. I got married in 2010, my daughter was born in 2011 and my son joined us in 2016. This same period has also seen the rise of Islamist and far-right extremism. There have many occasions when I have felt despondent about the times we are living in and what might be coming next. My father never lived to see me build a career; he never had the chance to meet my wife or his grand-children. He also never lived to see a British-Pakistani mayor of London, a British-Pakistani Chancellor of the Exchequer, a British-Pakistani presenter of the *Today* programme or a British feature film about a Pakistani teenager growing up in eighties Luton. He didn't witness the terror attacks in the United States on 9/11, the terror attacks in London on 7/7, the Manchester Arena bombing, the London Bridge stab-bings, the rise of Islamic State or the reports of Pakistani grooming gangs. He never lived to see fascists back on the streets of Luton.

Luton is my hometown but for many Bury Park and Luton have long been shorthand for many of the ills associated with Muslims and multiculturalism: extremism, segregation and a sense that such Muslim-dominated neighbourhoods resemble a foreign land more than England. When I was growing up in Luton, I was raised by my parents to believe that *they* were different to us. *They* had different values, *they* had a different culture, *they* were a threat to our way of life, and *they* would never accept us. *They* were White people. In recent years I have heard the same accusations repeated: *they* are different, *they* have a different culture, *they* are a threat to our way of life, and *they* will never accept us, but now it is far-right groups such as the English Defence League (EDL) – founded in Luton – and Britain First, as well as hate preachers in the national press and on social media, making the accusation, and now *they* are Muslims.

My ambition with this book is to honestly confront the fears some people have about Muslims. Why do *they* live in segregated communities? Why do *they* not treat women the same as men? Why do *they* wear the niqab? How much should *they* be held responsible for Islamist extremism? Why are *they* so over-represented in child sex street gangs? Why don't *they* show more loyalty to this country? I want a book that is clear-eyed not rose-tinted. Whatever your preconceptions and prejudices, I hope there are moments when they are challenged, and you occasionally feel uncomfortable when forced to confront what you thought you believed. This book is for anyone who is interested in knowing why we became so divided, and how we might yet become more united.

The Muslim population in Britain is estimated to be around 2.71 million. Muslims in this country have arrived from Kosovo and Kenya, Somalia and Saudi Arabia, Morocco,

Nigeria, Iran and Iraq, but the focus of this book is the 60 per cent of British Muslims whose origins lie, like my own, in the Indian subcontinent. 'You are not a drop in the ocean,' wrote Jalāl ad-Dīn Muhammad Rūmī, 'you are the entire ocean, in a drop'. It is impossible for any individual's story to represent the entirety of the British Muslim experience, but I believe that human tales of hope and love, rage and loss can reveal a greater story. 'The fight against dehumanisation,' suggests Turkish writer Elif Shafak, 'needs to start with words. Stories. It is easier to make sweeping generalisations about others if we know close to nothing about them; if they remain an abstraction. To move forward, we need to reverse the process: start by rehumanising those who have been dehumanised. And for that we need the art of storytelling.'[1]

This is a story in which my father, my family and I are all characters. It is my contribution to that effort of rehumanising, of trying to build a bridge of empathy and understanding. When Muslims and non-Muslims see the other as 'they', the danger is that they stop seeing each other as individuals, with each side dehumanising the other. At times it has been tempting to succumb to hopelessness, to accept that the divisions are too wide to bridge. But I cannot yield to despair – as the father of two young children, I have to believe that a better future is reachable, to believe Britain can still be a promised land.

My ambition for this book is that it reveals a story that is ultimately inspiring, optimistic and hopeful as it illuminates a path that helps lead from *they* to *us*.

AUTHOR'S NOTE

Some names have been changed to allow those interviewees who were nervous about their identities being made public to be able to speak honestly and share their stories.

ONE

THEY . . . DON'T WANT TO LIVE AMONG US

'You should all just leave, leave the country, I don't want you here, in the room or in my country. Listen to me, man, I think we should vote for Enoch Powell. Enoch's our man. We should send them all back.'

Eric Clapton, rock star, drunk
and on stage in Birmingham, 1976

'You ain't English. No, you ain't English either. You ain't English. None of you's fucking English. It's nothing now. Britain is nothing now. My Britain is fuck all now.'

Emma West, dental nurse, drunk and
on crowded tram in Croydon, 2011

This is Britain, but it could almost be Pakistan. I am walking along a street lined with halal restaurants, Islamic book stores and jewellery shops, and travel companies offering Hajj pilgrimage tours. I can see the moss-green dome of a mosque in the distance as a woman in a niqab hurries past me. This is Whalley Range in Blackburn and I have come here because it is arguably the most Pakistani place in Britain – only 7.8 per cent of the population is White British in what is one of the most segregated towns in the country. This is Blackburn but I could be in Manningham in Bradford or Small Heath in Birmingham or Glodwick in Oldham. I could be in Bury Park in Luton. White Britons are a minority in Leicester, Slough and Birmingham, and Luton will follow suit by the end of this decade. Britain is becoming more divided and more segregated.

I grew up in a segregated community and I know the impact it had on my own life. I want to know how and why so many Muslims came to live in segregated communities. Is it through choice or is it the consequence of circumstances outside their control? I also want to know what can be done to encourage such communities to integrate and ask whether that is a reasonable aspiration. In trying to investigate these questions I will chart the stories of a group of men who landed in this country predominantly in the 1960s, and follow the journeys of these men, their wives, children and grandchildren over successive chapters. It is a story that begins in the early sixties on the streets that I am standing on.

1962. It was the year of The Beatles and it was the year of the Stones. The Rolling Stones played their first ever gig on 12 July at the Marquee Jazz Club in London and three months later, on 5 October, The Beatles released their first single, 'Love Me Do'. It was the year of JFK and the Cuban

Missile Crisis and Harold Macmillan and the Night of the Long Knives. It was the year *Dr. No*, the first James Bond film, was released and the year the first episode of the BBC sitcom *Steptoe and Son* was broadcast. England was in the grip of the Big Freeze, one of the coldest winters on record, with London shrouded in fog when Abbas Hakim arrived in Britain. He was the son of a blacksmith who left India in the early 1920s for Zanzibar. Abbas landed in London but travelled to Blackburn, where his younger brother had settled two years earlier. He rented a house and started working in the cotton mills, where fellow workers nicknamed him Smiley because of his sunny personality. When he wasn't working, Smiley would dress in sharp suits and winklepicker shoes and buy rock-and-roll records. His neighbours grew accustomed to hearing Elvis Presley blasting from his home.

Abdul Ghani arrived in Britain the previous year, landing at Heathrow with a £1 note in his pocket. His friends told him to spend one night in London and then travel north – the further north you go, they told him, the more likely you are to find work. He got to Birmingham and stayed a few nights with a friend who told him he should travel even further north until he reached towns with mills. Abdul ended up in Rochdale, where he worked at the mills before getting a job on the buses. He worked as a driver and conductor doing day and night shifts. The other bus drivers called him Mr Night and Day.

Mohammed Karmani arrived the same year but settled in Bradford. He too started working in the mills. The mills operated twenty-four hours a day and Karmani lived in a shared house with other Pakistani men – some would sleep during the day while others worked and later those men would sleep while the night workers began their shifts. Karmani left the mills and, like Abdul, became a bus driver.

Mohammed Afzal also arrived in Britain in 1961. He had worked as a caterer for the British Army during the Second World War and served in Burma and Cyprus. The only other Pakistani he knew was in Birmingham, so Afzal travelled to Birmingham and worked in a factory that made construction vehicles.

These men joined those who had already arrived in the country – men like Habib Ullah, who had left East Pakistan in 1956 and moved to Manchester. He found work in factories before running a restaurant – the Selina Indian Restaurant – named after his daughter.

In *The Infidel Within*, his meticulously researched history of Muslims in Britain, Humayun Ansari writes that 'Muslim workers . . . arrived in response to the rising demand for cheap labour . . . In the 1950s and 1960s they formed part of the broader migration from the former colonies to satisfy the need for replacement labour, both in growth industries, where a labour shortage had developed, and in declining ones which were in the process of being deserted by indigenous workers because of low pay and poor conditions, and which therefore came to rely on immigrant labour. Migrants moved in order to work and indeed their movement itself showed where the demand for their labour was strongest.'[1]

My father was among those who chose to leave the Indian subcontinent in the early 1960s. He was an economic migrant – he made the decision to come to Britain in search of a better life for his family. My father worked in a factory during my childhood, but at weekends, and later when he was unemployed after being made redundant, he would dress as if he was a Conservative politician. He would wake up and put on a dark blue woollen pin-striped suit invariably over a pale blue shirt with a white collar. He dressed as if he was heading to Parliament when in fact he was going to the newsagents, or the job centre. He was not alone: across Britain working-class Pakistani men in low-skilled manual jobs were dressing in sharp suits. In the photographs of my father from the sixties he is always impeccably dressed. In the photographs of the men from that same time, they too are invariably dressed in sober suits and ties. I had assumed my father's pathological fanaticism for dressing smartly was a charming character quirk, but I now suspect his choice of clothing was freighted with greater significance. His suit was a response to his class and circumstances, it was a plea for respect, and it signalled that he believed he was worth more than his factory job implied.

It was not only the demand for cheap labour that drew migrants from the subcontinent towards Britain. When Pakistan gained independence from India in 1947, the settlement left Pakistan without adequate access to water. It was this that prompted the construction of the Mangla Dam in the Mirpur district of Kashmir in northern Pakistan.

The dam was constructed in the mid-1960s and led to the flooding of Mirpur and surrounding villages. The dam dislocated 485 villages and over 100,000 people were left homeless. Some of those displaced were offered financial compensation as well as passports, which before then had been difficult for rural people to obtain. Many men used the compensation and the offered passport to seek a new life in Britain – more than half the population of some villages moved to settle in British industrial towns.

In 1948 the non-White population of Britain was estimated to be 30,000, but thanks to the 1948 Nationality Act, which granted colonial and ex-colonial subjects in India and Pakistan the same national status as native Britons, by 1962 the figure – including migrants from the subcontinent and Caribbean – had risen to 500,000.[2] The men who came from the subcontinent at this time had certain things in common. They were ambitious – usually economic migrants or students coming to Britain in search of a better life through work or education. They tended to be young, in their twenties or early thirties, and unmarried. Those who were married – like my father – left their wives back home.

Abbas had been in Blackburn five years when he received a phone call from his father telling him that he was sending a photograph in the mail – it was of a woman he was expected to marry. She flew in to Heathrow and Abbas arrived at the airport holding the photograph and trying to recognise her among the passengers. He met her, they were married the next day, and they went on to have seven children. This was a story repeated across the country during the late sixties and early seventies as existing wives and potential wives (and children) came to join their husbands and fathers. Between 1955 and 1968, net immigration increased by 345,000, and by the late sixties areas like Whalley Range, Small Heath, Manningham and Bury Park looked very different than they had at the start of the decade.

The native White population did not always welcome this change. 1967 – the year Abbas got married – saw the birth of the National Front, the far-right political party whose initial policy platform advocated the repatriation of all settled non-White immigrants to their ancestral nations. In April 1968, Conservative politician Enoch Powell delivered a speech to a Conservative Association in Birmingham in which he quoted what 'a middle-aged, quite ordinary working man' had told him. 'In this country in fifteen or twenty years' time,' the man apparently told Powell, 'the Black man will have the whip hand over the White man.' Powell went on to predict that by the year 2000 'whole areas, towns and parts of towns across England will be occupied by sections of the immigrant and immigrant-descended population . . . those whom the gods wish to destroy, they first make mad. We must be mad, literally mad, as a nation to be permitting the annual inflow of some 50,000 dependents . . . it is like watching a nation busily engaged in heaping up its own funeral pyre . . . as I look ahead, I am filled with foreboding; like the Roman, I seem to see "the River Tiber foaming with much blood."'[3] Surveys suggested that 74 per cent of the British population agreed with Powell, and in London dockers carrying placards that read 'We Back Enoch' marched in support.[4]

In the summer of 1969, one year after Powell's 'Rivers of Blood' speech, journalist Jeremy Seabrook travelled to Blackburn and spent two months talking to residents. He spoke to a Mrs Frost who lived on Altom Street in Whalley Range – making her a close neighbour of Abbas. 'I'm living slap bang among all these Pakistanis,' she complained. 'Most of us are getting very alarmed at the amount of numbers [sic] that are being allowed to congregate. In the street that I live there's forty-two houses of which only seventeen are occupied by White people – the rest have been driven out. We shall be swamped, there's no doubt about it. In a few years the way they're breeding they'll take over.'[5]

One can quibble with Mrs Frost's tone but not the accuracy of her prediction. In 1961 the families on Altom Street had names such as Heaton, Murray and King. By 1971 they were joined by the Kiwalas and Patels and in 1981 the street was overwhelmingly populated by families with surnames such as Desai, Munshi and Ahmed. The Heatons and the Kings had moved on. In 1961 there were 116 names listed on the electoral roll for Inkerman Street – where the Hakim family would later move – and every one was English. By 2019 there were 175 names and not a single one was English. 'It was really quick,' recalls Abbas' son Aziz, 'when we moved to Whalley Range, there were White people and then there weren't. It was like a switch had been flicked.'

Blackburn was not the only place where the switch was flicked. In Birmingham, Mohammed Afzal was one of the first south Asian immigrants in 1961 but, his son Nazir recalls, 'during the next few years others started coming from the subcontinent and, seeking some safety in numbers, they also chose Small Heath. Suddenly you had ten houses occupied by people from the same village in Pakistan.'

The arrival of Muslim immigrants led to pubs converting to halal cafes, local theatres becoming mosques and entire ecosystems developing that catered for Muslims. 'These communities came together and started looking at their concerns and their needs,' says Humayun Ansari, 'cultural, social and economic, and then they began to develop those institutions such as halal butchers that would satisfy those needs.' In Rochdale, where Abdul Ghani owned a corner store, by the early 1970s there were already twenty Pakistani-owned grocery, butcher and drapery stores, three Pakistani banks and seven Pakistani cafes. Motoring schools, launderettes, radio and television shops and cinemas were also owned by Pakistanis to provide services to their community. There were also six Pakistani GPs, two mosques and four centres for children to learn Urdu and receive religious instruction after school. 'Participation in ethnic activities and utilisation of exclusive institutions increases the Pakistani's identification with their religion, traditional culture, language and national origin,' observes the academic Mohammed Anwar, 'and is an expression of their ethnicity in this country. Consequently, this increases Pakistani "encapsulation" and reduces the chances of interpersonal relations across ethnic boundaries.'[6]

This 'encapsulation' revolved around an awareness that their religion and culture made Pakistani children different. There were similar scenes across the country. In Birmingham, Nazir Afzal was attending mosque after school. 'It taught me discipline,' he recalls, 'but it didn't actually teach me anything about my faith.' In Rochdale, Abdul Ghani's son Sajid attended mosque every day, including Saturdays. 'The imam had a long bamboo stick,' he recalls. 'I'd mainly get whacked if I was mispronouncing a word from the Qur'an or chatting to my brother or friends. It was mostly whacks on the hands.' In Blackburn, Aziz visited the mosque on Altom Street – the same street that Mrs Frost lived on – for two hours of Qur'an study after school each evening.

One day in 1975, Aziz was playing on the street with his friends when they were approached by a teenage White boy with a camera. Roger Bracewell was on the streets of Whalley Range taking photographs for a school competition. He noticed Aziz and his brother playing and asked if he could take a photograph. The black-and-white photographs he took that day, which remained lost in his files for more than four decades, are mesmerising.[7] Aziz leans in the right of the frame in a buttoned-up jacket and flared trousers that hover above his ankles. There are no parents in any images, just a bunch of young children playing unsupervised. 'We were just street urchins,' Aziz says. 'We would spend hours playing.' Whalley Range was, recalls one long-time resident, 'a mix of all cultures – you had the Hindu community, the African

Hindus and the Indian Hindus, the African Pakistanis, the Pakistani Pakistanis (recent arrivals who had been born in Pakistan), the Muslim Indians, the Sikh Indians: it was the United Nations of Asians.' Were there any White people in this United Nations, I asked. 'Very, very few,' he says.[*]

Even as the United Nations of Asians was out on the streets of Whalley Range, elsewhere in Blackburn – and across the country – there was growing antipathy towards the increasingly visible and vocal immigrant community. Blackburn was becoming a stronghold of the National Front and, later, its spin-off National Party. Two hundred people attended a far-right meeting in Blackburn in 1976 to hear the NF's Martin Webster tell them that 'the decision before you in the next decade or so is do you want the British race to survive, or do you want this country to become occupied by a load of khaki-coloured multiracial bastards?' The National Party leader John Kingsley Read declared that 'we do not want to mix with blacks, we do not want to marry blacks, we do not want miscegenation and we damn well are not going to have a multiracial society . . . we will have our country back.'[8] In the 1973 local

---

[*] In 2012, Jacqueline Woodhouse, a forty-two-year-old former secretary, was jailed after being filmed launching a drunken racist outburst on her fellow passengers on the London Underground. Woodhouse turned to her passengers and began to ask: 'Where do you come from? Where do you come from? Where do you come from? All over the world, fucking jokers. Fucking country's a fucking joke. Fucking jokers taking the fucking piss. I used to live in England and now I live in the United Nations.'

elections, the party gained 23 per cent and 16.8 per cent of the vote in two Blackburn wards. The number of people voting for racist parties trebled in three years and, in 1976, Blackburn elected two councillors for the National Party. In Rochdale, the National Front candidates and their supporters intimidated and harassed Pakistani voters. 'Their agents challenged almost every Pakistani voter in the afternoon. It was observed that this created panic, and the result was that a number of Pakistani voters, particularly women, did not come to vote at all after hearing about the NF's bullying tactics.'[9]

Racism was a daily reality for many young Asian children during the seventies and eighties. It is striking how many recall running from racists when they were children. This was a time of macro, not microaggressions. Everyone was running. In Birmingham, a young Nazir was running from skinheads. 'It was horrific,' he remembers. 'If you weren't sworn at, you were spat at, if you weren't spat at, you were treated with disdain. I lived within sight of the Birmingham City football ground, so you never went out on the weekend because fans would be going in and out and they'd shout and scream in your face.' In Rochdale, Sajid was running to avoid skinheads shouting 'Paki bastard' at him on his way to school. His parents owned a store that was regularly sprayed with racist graffiti. 'My dad would spend hours trying to take it off with a sponge,' he recalls. 'I would sit there, ten, eleven years old, and I would be thinking, "Why would someone do this? This is our business. We're trying to earn a living. Why would people be so cruel to each other?"' In Blackburn, a pregnant young woman called Zubaida Patel answered the front door one evening and was confronted by a White man who punched her in the face before running into the night. I saw the young Zubaida recount the incident in a 1976 *World in Action* documentary on the rise of the far right in Blackburn, which I watched during the course of research for this book.[10]

The racist backlash to growing numbers of Asian immigrants continued during the seventies and into the eighties. In 1985, the travel writer Dervla Murphy visited Bradford. She met a man at a bus stop who 'swung his arms around in a gesture encompassing all of Manningham and said, quite quietly, "I'd shoot them all, men, women and children. Here they're all around us, every street like a sewer full of rats. [Enoch] Powell was right. He said the people of England would not endure it. And he understood why we shouldn't endure it, why we should take England back for the English ... if you gave me an armoured car and some ammo I'd clean this place up overnight. And if I don't, my sons and grandsons will."' [11]

Mohammed Karmani moved from Bradford to south London in the eighties and his son Alyas started school in Tooting. 'My only experience of growing up that I really remember was racism,' Alyas tells me. '"Paki this, Paki that." It would happen every day from kids in school, teachers and people in public. I was always made to feel like the outsider, like I was not part of the mainstream.' He tells me a story about the time when, at the height of the Falklands War, he started singing 'Don't Cry for Me Argentina' in the classroom. 'Every single one of the White boys jumped me and laid into me,' he says. 'These kids would come into our school with copies of *Bulldog*. This was a National Front cartoon magazine for kids. It had comic strip caricatures of Black people and Asian people. You can imagine the stereotypes and overt racist language – and these are the kids in my class.'

I was luckier than some in that I never suffered violence at the hands of racists. I do remember frequently running home from school. I would see a skinhead and, rather than risk confrontation, I would break into a sprint. However, my childhood was still often overshadowed by fear of what might happen should I find myself cornered and outnumbered. I often dreamt that I was walking through an underpass and a gang of skinheads blocked my path. I remember being around six or seven, walking along a street in Bury Park and having an older boy – possibly a teenager, I can still see his long sandy hair – turn towards me and spit in my face. I remember sitting at a table in the school library and a White boy walking up behind me, wrapping his arm around my neck and starting to strangle me. I must have wriggled and wrestled, and he eventually released me and walked away. I remember the boy at our school who routinely spat in the face of the Asian boys – he made an exception for me because we shared a few friends. Young White boys urinated through the letterbox of my Sikh friend's home.

In Manchester, Habib Ullah's son Ahmed was a pupil at Burnage High School in the south of the city. It was autumn 1986 and Ahmed was an outgoing popular boy who was rarely harassed but often stood up for others. 'His natural instinct was to step in and defend,' recalls his sister Selina, 'that's just what he did.' On Wednesday, 17 September, Ahmed headed to school as usual. It was around 9 a.m. when the phone rang. There had been an incident and the school wanted his family to go to the hospital. 'We didn't think it was serious,' Selina says, 'but maybe he needed blood and that was why there was such a sense of urgency.' When they arrived, the family were taken to a side room. An Asian boy was being attacked in the school playground and Ahmed had stepped into defend him. Ahmed had been stabbed in the stomach with a kitchen knife by one of the gang. An ambulance arrived forty-five minutes after the incident, but Ahmed was dead on arrival at the hospital. 'It was hard to comprehend,' says Selina. 'I just remember kicking the bin. My parents started crying, they were completely broken and saying, "He's gone, he's gone."' Even thirty-four years after her brother was murdered, Selina says: 'There is always that sense of loss. We will never know what impact he would have made if he had lived.' Darren Coulburn was convicted of murder and sentenced to be detained at Her Majesty's pleasure. A report of a committee of enquiry found that the murder would not have happened if Ahmed had been White or of some other ethnic origin. It concluded: 'racism was one of the vital ingredients that brought the two boys together.'[12]

I was fifteen when Ahmed was murdered, and I remember his killing vividly. I must have read about it in the newspaper – the murder made national news – and I remember an overpowering sensation of powerlessness. It was a draining awareness that the colour of my skin would determine my future more than how hard I studied or worked. These were not fears I could share with my parents or my friends, so I poured my anxieties into poetry that I kept hidden. I kept these teenage poems, and while I make no claims as to their literary merit, reading them is a reminder of how it felt to be a Pakistani teenager in the eighties:

WHAT'S THE VALUE OF EDUCATION?

What's the value of education
with all this racial discrimination
Is there any point in ambition
if you happen to be an Asian

What's the value of education
if you are treated as an inferior relation
What point is there in qualifications
when you will not get the desired occupation

What's the value of education
when you don't belong to any nation
Long ago we left our country behind
respect and acceptance we have yet to find

What's the value of education
Do we not regret our creation
for the dream we have searched for
will not be realised til after my cremation.*

---

* Muslims are not actually cremated, but the sixteen-year-old me did not know this, which for the purposes of the poem is just as well.

The children who endured racism and the threat of violence rarely revealed their fears to their parents. That was the other shared experience among my generation: our relationship with our fathers. These were men who had typically left the subcontinent in their twenties, returned to get married or – as in my father's case – spent a decade on their own, before bringing their wives and children to Britain. They were not fathers who read stories at bedtime or knew how to play with or even talk to their children. They were rarely physically demonstrative. These were men who believed their role was to work and to earn money. 'Dad went out to work,' says Zulfi Karim, who was a young boy in Bradford during the seventies, 'there was no connectivity whatsoever – it was stiff upper lip. It was almost a Victorian style of parenting: he went to work, came home, went to work and came home.' 'He was always working,' says Sajid about his father, Abdul Ghani. 'That's something I'll always remember. You've got to work. You've got to work. If you don't work, you don't get anywhere in life.' Abdul was bald but would wear a wig he attached to his head with double-sided sticky tape. 'Growing up as kids, if someone wanted Sellotape and you couldn't find it in the house, you'd think there is always Dad's tape in the bathroom,' he recalls. 'We would get it and forget to put it back. I remember some mornings where he'd say, "Where's my Sellotape? Who's got my Sellotape? I can't put my hair on! I've got to get to work!"'

There were occasional moments of lightness with my father during my childhood, but my overriding memory is of frustration – his and mine. My father, like so many of the men who migrated from the subcontinent, was a frustrated man. He believed, rightly, that he was capable of more than working on a factory production line. Parenthood did not come naturally to him. He was married to a woman from whom he had spent more than a decade apart. These were not the ideal conditions for a loving family, and it explains why he so often seemed angry at the world.

Their wives and children might have borne the brunt of these men's anger and frustration, but the true target was White people. It was White people that our parents feared and sometimes despised. When the academic Mohammad Anwar talked to Pakistanis in Rochdale in the early seventies, scepticism and fear of White culture was already palpable. 'I would like to see the children getting education,' one man tells Anwar, 'but having no social mixing with British people at an individual level.'[13] This sounds exactly like my father, who was also wildly ambivalent about Britain – admiring the education and opportunities but wary of how its culture might infect his children. 'I regret bringing my children to this country,' a man complains to Anwar, 'it is very difficult to keep control. I make sure that my children go straight to school and return straight home from school. They also go for religious instruction. But how could we stop what they learn and see? I brought them here so that they could get a good education, but schools do not have any control. I have a feeling that they would be spoiled irrespective of our precautionary measures, as some situations are out of our control; that is why I am seriously thinking of taking them back to Pakistan before they are too old.' One respondent told Anwar that 'the only way to keep ourselves Muslims and Pakistanis is to avoid contact with English people and stick to our religion and our own people – this is needed to protect our values and culture in this progressive society.' This desire to protect Pakistani culture recorded forty years ago, and the sense of viewing White people as *they*, have not disappeared, and remain potent reasons why some Muslims choose to segregate themselves.

I can see why the first immigrant generation wanted to live amidst their community – when you are far from home it is entirely understandable you might wish to live among your own. I am not at all convinced that this argument can be sustained sixty years on. Dilwar Hussain is the founding chair of a charity called New Horizons in British Islam, which works on Muslim identity, integration and reform. He told me of an imam he knew who lived in a northern town. 'He was very proudly talking about how he never had to meet anybody who's not Muslim in the course of his daily life,' he says. 'He had bought the house next door to the mosque and he works as the imam, so he doesn't have to go very far. His children go to a Muslim school and his wife does all the shopping! And he's very proud of this.'

This lack of integration does not strike me as anything of which to feel proud. My view is that segregation is a Bad Thing and my life has been immeasurably enriched by leaving segregated Luton for integrated London. As someone who appears, by all outward appearances, to be a poster boy for integration – or a grim reminder of the consequences of assimilation, opinion is divided on the matter – it is unsurprising that I would advocate for greater integration and mingling of communities. However, one of my intentions in writing this book is to ask hard questions about my own prejudices and preconceptions. So, is it really true that I no longer live in a segregated community? I live in north London and the vast majority of my friends – if not all of them – share the same broadly liberal worldview: they read the *Guardian*,* they listen to BBC 6 Music and Radio 4, they own the same cookbooks by Yotam Ottolenghi and Anna Jones and discuss the same Netflix shows. I don't recall an instance when I have had friends over for dinner and someone has complained that it might be nice to have a true-blue Tory, or someone who is still working class, around the table for the sake of diversity. In my present world *they* could refer to anyone who takes their children to eat at McDonald's. If segregation refers to living in a self-reinforcing bubble, then maybe I do live in a segregated community – one that is, on the whole, White, well-educated and well-to-do.

Until recently I lived close to Stamford Hill in Hackney, home to the ultra-orthodox Jewish Haredi community. They too live segregated lives; I would see Haredi men in their

---

* I was on contract with the *Guardian* until 2013 and then went freelance. It was striking how many of my more casual acquaintances, who only read the *Guardian*, assumed I had left journalism. Some *Guardian* readers may have presumed I had died.

long black coats and black hats with wives in monochromatic clothes ferrying small armies of children, but in the seven years that we lived there I did not have a single conversation with any of them. The criticisms levelled at Muslim communities about outdated attitudes and a failure to integrate could equally be aimed at the Haredi, but few bother to aim. During the coronavirus pandemic, British Muslims were criticised for flouting lockdown rules and blamed for spikes in infections. They 'are just not taking the pandemic seriously enough', the Conservative MP Craig Whittaker told a radio station in August 2020 and, when asked if he was talking about the Muslim population, Whittaker replied: 'Of course.'[14] Needless to say Whittaker was wrong. 'When we look at the local authorities with a significant spike in cases and the ones without,' noted Stephen Bush in the *New Statesman*, 'the presence or absence of a large ethnic minority community, or of a specifically Muslim one, has no bearing on the coronavirus picture.'[15] These inconvenient facts did little to prevent the narrative spreading that it was British Muslims' irresponsibility that was driving up infections. The revelation, in February 2021, that the infection rate in Stamford Hill was nine times higher than the UK average and among the highest reported anywhere in the world failed to attract the same level of interest and attention.[16]

The complaint I sometimes heard from Muslims in Blackburn was that they were not harming anyone else, so what business was it of outsiders how they lived or whether they integrated or not – the implication was that Muslims are judged by a higher standard than other communities. I have some sympathy for this argument – there is certainly less clamour for ultra-orthodox Jews or middle-class White liberals to integrate more. It is also possible to believe that segregation is harmful while not placing the blame entirely on the segregated communities. 'Many people were confused and adrift in the back streets of Britain,' writes David Goodhart in *The British Dream* about immigrants who arrived in the fifties and sixties. 'The authorities did little to help them ... Britain should have at least provided them with language lessons and some idea of the country that they were to make their home. The failure to do this drove people deeper into their protective family and clan networks and has contributed to the segregated communities.'

This effect of this failure of the state was reinforced by White flight. 'There are parts of Blackburn where you used to only have White people living,' says one local Pakistani man, 'but since the Asians started moving in it's become a predominantly Asian area.' The reason this happened, he suggests, was that White people who contemplated staying worried 'We might be able to take them, but my friends aren't going to come and see me, my sons and daughters aren't going to see me – we don't know what these people are like.' In Manchester, Selina Ullah witnessed the same phenomenon. 'An Asian family moves into a nice area and the neighbours immediately start selling their homes,' she says, 'and it becomes a self-fulfilling prophecy and eventually the whole area becomes brown.'

I can see why it might feel unfair to single out Muslims in places like Whalley Range and Bury Park or to suggest that they all intentionally ended up living in segregated communities. I am not, however, ultimately persuaded by the claim that there is no difference between living in the sort of community in north London where I live now and the community in Bury Park where I was raised. I think back to my childhood in Luton, and particularly the early days in Bury Park, and wonder how different my life might have been had my parents remained there rather than moving to a Whiter part of town. It is impossible to say for sure, but in this hypothetical scenario I would have remained at a school that was almost entirely Muslim rather attending one that was almost entirely White. In this alternate universe there is much less chance I would have been exposed to the Western music, television and films that my White friends introduced me to. We would have lived closer to the mosque, so rather than my mother teaching me Arabic, I would probably have attended mosque after school and cultural expectations and pressures would have pressed harder on my family and me as a result of living in the heart of the community. Those pressures might have led me to remain in Luton rather than travelling hundreds of miles to study in Manchester. I would have missed out on the freedoms and pleasures of living away from home: I would not have gone to so many concerts, I would not have had the courage to get dreadlocks, I would not have had so many memorable nights dancing in nightclubs and I would not have had the chance to have relationships so easily.

It was by leaving that I found myself. In my experience, segregation can suffocate the potential for individual growth, it can stifle the opportunity to dream differently, and it can allow stereotypes about what *they* are like to thrive. I was fed my share of stereotypes about White people: that *they* treat dogs better than their children, that *they* have dubious standards of hygiene and *they* don't give a damn about their parents. These stereotypes persist and are amplified by mutual ignorance, and that ignorance can have negative consequences for social cohesion. Ignorance descends into distrust and distrust morphs into hostility.

In the summer of 2001, rioting raged through towns near Blackburn, including Burnley, Oldham and Bradford. A government-ordered report by Ted Cantle, chairman of the Community Cohesion Review Team, said most of the White communities were living parallel, quite separate, lives from minority Asian and Black groups. Cantle wrote that segregation manifested in separate schools, communal and voluntary organisations, employment, places of worship and cultural activities. He concluded a lack of contact between races 'fuels fear and suspicion that is easily exploited by extremists ... the team was particularly struck by the depth of polarisation in our towns and cities. The extent to which this physical division was compounded by so many other aspects of our daily lives was very evident. This means that many communities operate on the basis of a series of parallel lives.'[17]

In 2016, a study of community cohesion commissioned by the government and led by Louise Casey warned that segregation and social exclusion were at 'worrying levels' and were fuelling inequality in some areas of Britain. The Casey Review said there was a sense that people from different backgrounds got on well together at a general level, but community cohesion 'did not feel universally strong across the country'. Casey found 'high levels of social and economic isolation in some places, and cultural and religious practices in communities that are not only holding some of our citizens back, but run contrary to British values and sometimes our laws'.[18] Two years later five councils – Bradford, Blackburn, Peterborough, Walsall and Waltham Forest in London – were selected for special funding to tackle segregation. The government's Integrated Communities Strategy would see £50 million invested in schemes to improve community relations over the next two years. The proposals included extra support for English language classes, help to improve economic opportunities – particularly for women – in segregated communities, schemes to encourage school pupils to form lasting relationships with those from different backgrounds and an increased take up of the National Citizen Service – a project launched by David Cameron that saw groups of sixteen- and seventeen-year-olds carry out community projects. I have seen in my own family the importance of lasting school friendships between those of different backgrounds. I have also seen the impact not being able to speak English has had on my mother.

Rasool Bibi Manzoor arrived in Britain in the early seventies and spent the next three decades at home raising four children. My father dealt with everything that necessitated speaking English; while he was having meetings with bank managers and estate agents, my mother remained mostly at home. When she did venture out it was to Bury Park, where fellow Pakistanis who spoke her language owned the grocers, butchers and fabric shops she patronised. She never learnt English and was never encouraged to by the state or my father. So, following his sudden death in 1995, my mother became completely dependent on her children. She needs us to manage running her home and to translate when any doctor cannot speak Urdu. It means my mother has not read a single I word I have written. She cannot understand any of the television programmes, films and songs that have influenced and shaped my life and her inability to understand them means she has never had the opportunity to fully understand me. Since my father's death, my mother's world has shrunk, and it is tragic to witness. I wonder how different her life might be now had things been different back then. If my father had encouraged her to learn English or if the state had demanded that she do so. What new worlds might she have explored, what new friends might she have made if she had the means to communicate? It breaks my heart to know that the trajectory of my life has been one where I have had the opportunity to be creatively curious but the person whose hard work enabled my good fortune was effectively prevented from fulfilling or even discovering her potential. The fact that we were working class is significant in explaining this, but it is also the fact that my mother lived a segregated life where she did not need to learn English to survive – and because she did not have to, she never did.

I am wary of segregation because I see what it did to my mother. It isn't only about learning English; it is also about having someone to speak English with in everyday life. When I talked to Ted Cantle, he suggested that rather than learning English in a class with other non-native speakers, each person should be buddied up with a native White British speaker with whom they could meet for a cup of tea once a week. That meeting would be both an English lesson but also a chance to interact with someone from a different community. It would be a way of building friendships and breaking down walls.

Those walls start in childhood and, when parents are fearful of the consequences of integration, those fears shape how they raise their children. In Oldham I attended a women-only English class, and I asked the women whether their children had any White friends. 'I tell my children make friends but make sure they are Asian friends and not White ones,' one woman told me. 'Why? Because they have a different culture – the open one – they go out at night on their own, their girls get boyfriends, we don't want them to forget their roots because if the children forget their roots they will be neither British nor Pakistani.' This was all told to me in Urdu.

Oldham, like Blackburn, has some of the most segregated schools in Britain. When school catchment areas are geographically determined, schools can become segregated simply because the communities pupils are drawn from are segregated. This was recognised as far back as the seventies when eleven local authorities installed a policy of bussing, where Black and Brown children were bussed out of their local areas to attend majority White schools in the hope that it would help them integrate. Blackburn was one of the councils that adopted the policy, as were Luton and Bradford.

Zulfi Karim was living in the Manningham district of Bradford and one of the children who was bussed. 'I just remember a long bus journey to a White school on a council estate,' he says, 'and then we were put into different year groups – two or three would go into each classroom.' The White children bullied Zulfi. 'Nobody would play with me,' he recalls. 'It would just be me and my two Pakistani friends in the school yard and we would be scared shitless that someone was going to come over and hassle us.' He remembers eating alone at lunchtime as some White children threw pieces of bacon and ham at him. The bussing scheme was well intentioned, but for Zulfi it was a failure and an unhappy time in his childhood. Bradford became the last place in Britain to phase out bussing in 1980. It was the last serious attempt to enforce an integrated intake in schools in multi-ethnic areas for more than three decades.

The Schools Linking Programme was established in Blackburn in 2017 but has been running in Luton since 2009. I attended an event in Luton in 2011. Pupils from two schools – one White majority and the other Muslim majority

– were meeting for the first time. We were in a brightly lit
hall of the Carnival Arts Centre and there were thirty pupils
– all year five pupils at William Austin junior school – sat in
neat rows. Apart from one boy, who was Black, they were all
Asian. In an adjoining room there were thirty pupils from
St Joseph's, a Catholic junior school located close to William
Austin, where the vast majority of the pupils were White.
The children had been building up to this moment since
the previous September, sending letters and photographs to
one another about themselves. As their teachers looked on,
students from St Joseph's filed into the main hall and took
their seats. The woman leading the linking project asked the
children to put their hands up if they had pizza for dinner
and to join the others who had had the same meal. There
were other questions – who liked football? Who was nervous
about coming this morning? And with each question the
group was reordered. Hassan from William Austin told me
he was a bit nervous at the start of the day because he had
'never really met any Christians'. He was surprised to learn
the children from St Joseph's were more similar to him than
he had imagined. 'I thought they'd be totally different – like
a different kind of person,' he says, 'but actually they like the
same football teams and the same food.' Jenna, who attended
St Joseph's, said she enjoyed having the opportunity to ask
questions about other religions: 'I've always wanted to ask a
Muslim how often they go to mosque because I know I go
to church every Sunday,' she says. 'I've looked in books, but
I never get the right answer, but today I could ask someone

who was Muslim.' There were some Muslims living near her home, she says, 'but they are not very sociable.' I remember feeling sad and shocked that children who were so geographically close could feel so distant from each other. But that isn't my most vivid memory of my day. I remember talking to two children and asking them to offer examples of what was different about the other person. It was a long time ago, but I seem to remember that one suggested they were wearing different makes of trainers and the other that they supported different football teams. Instead of thinking these were perfectly valid responses, I pushed them to think of other differences. They mentioned how they had different coloured hair. I ended up becoming frustrated and said something along the lines of 'and what about the fact one of you has white skin and the other has brown skin?' They looked at me as if they genuinely hadn't noticed this. At the time I felt as if this suggested the children were a little dim or had worryingly low powers of observation. This was before I had children of my own.

I am now a father and look back at the way I pressed those children with guilt. I think those children really did not see skin colour, or if they did they assigned it less significance than football-team allegiance and trainer brands. That is actually rather hopeful and beautiful, but I could not see it then – a reminder that sometimes children are wiser than the supposed adults. Linking schools projects can play a part in encouraging integration but there is a danger that the entire exercise is a little anthropological. The way to more meaningful integration is by having a mixed school population, but how do you achieve that without bussing?

In 2015 a new school opened in Birmingham on part of the University of Birmingham's estate in Selly Oak. If the intake was drawn from the local catchment area, the school's pupils would have been 100 per cent White, but Professor James Arthur from the university's school of education, and the founder of the school, had a different vision. The Casey Review listed Birmingham as one of the top ten areas for segregated schools in the country. In Selly Oak, where the school is based, 71.8 per cent of the population is White, 11 per cent is Asian and 5.8 per cent is Black. 'We wanted a school that reflected the city,' Professor Arthur tells me, 'so we had to think how we would get children from across the city to come to the school.' The solution he came up with was simple but revolutionary: rather than having one catchment area, the school would have four from different parts of Birmingham. Admission would be determined by how close families lived to four 'nodes': Selly Oak, Small Heath, Hall Green and the Jewellery Quarter. White students make up 42 per cent of the school's population, Asian students 26 per cent and Black students 16 per cent. 'We deliberately did that to attract pupils that reflected the city as a whole,' Professor Arthur told me, 'it was to bring a diversity of students into the school.' The nodes are all train stations connected to Birmingham New Street so that pupils can travel to the school, and a fund was set up to pay the fares of children who could not otherwise afford the cost. I asked

Professor Arthur what he thought the practical benefits of having a genuinely diverse school population were for the children. 'It opens their horizons,' he tells me. 'One of the things we discovered was that children from a Pakistani Muslim origin in Small Heath hardly ever went into the city. They knew their local area, but they never ventured very far. I think that's a disadvantage because that closes their horizons to the world – to not meet anybody else forces them into a bubble, and that's not good for their growth. At this school they experience other people who are different to them, they make friends with children that they would never ever have met, and that also goes for the White kids. That wouldn't have happened if this school didn't exist.'

The University of Birmingham School is, Professor Arthur believes, the only school of its kind in the country. I found this surprising given that it is the most oversubscribed school in Birmingham. As segregation in education is an issue for many towns and cities, why aren't more schools considering a nodal approach to admission? 'Because that would be incredibly brave,' says Rebecca Tigue, headteacher of the school. 'It is beautiful and utopian and, of course, it's what should happen, but you'd have to change everything. You'd take away that consumerist choice of where to send your child and have to convince every parent of the benefits.' Despite these apparent challenges, Professor Arthur tells me that he has been talking to education advisers in Downing Street about the possibility of introducing a nodal admission approach for schools in other towns and cities with large Muslim populations. 'The trouble is some people say it's a bit like bussing kids in,' he admits, 'and there is an element of truth in that.'

I believe in the power of the individual to embody hope and encourage change, which is why I want to highlight two people who both live in Blackburn and give me reasons to feel hopeful in very different ways. Laura Butterworth is the deputy head of a large primary school in the centre of Blackburn. She is in her early thirties and one of those people with a ready smile and an irresistible enthusiasm for their work. When she is not helping run the school, Laura has a passion: she loves clog dancing. 'I have been clog dancing for four and half years,' she told me when I visited the school. 'Clog dancing has a really important place in Blackburn's history and it's a dying art form. I am not young, I'm thirty-two, but I am the youngest performing dancer in our group in the north-west ... so, if we don't promote areas of our own culture and heritage, if things aren't passed on to the next generation, they will disappear.' This desire to keep clog dancing alive inspired Laura to start teaching it to her pupils. 'The children love it,' she tells me. 'We teach it as part of our PE curriculum, and we send letters to all parents at the beginning of term explaining what the children will be doing, and each child will receive a set of clogs in their size. We've had no complaints at all from parents. They've been really supportive. We've had one or two girls – the boys have thrown themselves into it – who are nervous about the dancing because dancing is not promoted in their homes.'

In anticipation of my visit, Laura arranged for the children to demonstrate their clog dancing. The class lined up in rows and as the music started they began dancing, the percussive sound of the clogs echoing around the hall. The children were White and Brown, but they all wore the same costumes and were all dancing in time, mostly. 'We do a big event with other schools at King George's Hall,' Laura tells me, 'and the last time we went we were the only school who did clog dancing. We did it to live music and the hall just went silent because nobody had seen anything like it before.' I found Laura's clog-dancing passion inspiring – there are now ten schools in Blackburn learning Lancashire clog dancing – and it shows how one person can make a difference. 'When the children perform they all have something in common,' she says. 'They've all learned the same routine. They're all as good as each other. They all do it to the same music. It's a really good way of just bringing everyone together where there isn't any kind of difference between the children.' The fact that it's clog dancing – rather than, say, Bollywood dancing – is also significant for Laura because it is an acknowledgement of the children's shared Blackburn present, even if their families' origins might lie elsewhere. 'I do think that it's really good for a sense of identity for the children,' Laura says. 'We do a lot of celebrating their own cultures . . . but we actually don't teach them much about where they currently live and as great as it is to appreciate the children's heritage, I think it's also really good for them to appreciate the heritage of the place where they live now, because they are citizens of Blackburn.'

Faz Patel's grandfather, Musa Khan, was one of the generation of immigrants who arrived from the subcontinent
in the early sixties, and his family settled in the Shear Brow
area of Blackburn. 'It was a very dense Muslim Asian community,' Faz recalls. 'I had no English friends when I was
growing up.' One day, around twenty years ago, Musa called
him. The clocks were going back that weekend and Musa
was nervous. He had a clock on the wall and was worried
about falling from the stepladder while trying to change it.
Faz told him not to worry – he would come and change the
clock. Afterwards, Musa told him that many of his friends
had the same worries. 'There were no smart technology
clocks, there were no gadgets or digital clocks,' Faz recalls,
'and so I changed one, and then the next time I changed a
handful, and the following year I changed ten, twenty. Now
I do about sixty houses. They now call me the Clock Man.' It
began with Musa's fellow Muslims but Faz decided he also
wanted to help the local elderly White community. 'People
now actually contact me,' he says, 'and last year I went to a
lady's house in a predominantly White area. And she was
a lovely White lady in her seventies. I went to change her
clocks, and she was lovely, chatting to me. So now she's my
good friend.' This elderly White woman would not ordinarily
have become friends with a Pakistani man in his forties and
vice versa, but the changing of the clocks enabled interaction
and friendship.

Faz has been involved in community cohesion work for
the past twenty-five years. It is clearly a passion for him,

and he told me that he was inspired to work in community cohesion because of something his mother experienced in 1976, while she was pregnant with him. There was a knock on the door one night and his mother answered and was confronted by a White man who punched her in the face before running into the night. 'Hang on,' I say, 'is your mother Zubaida – the woman in that *World in Action* documentary?' Faz nodded. He told me that knowing what had happened to his mother had influenced him when he was deciding what to do with his life. It was a barely believable coincidence – I watched the documentary during the course of researching this book but never suspected the young woman standing on the doorstep was Faz's mother. It is a hopeful coda to a rather grim story – light emerging from the darkness, a reminder that progress is possible, and that one person can make a difference.

In my life, the person who made the difference, who changed the course of my life, was my father. It was his decision to come to Britain in the early sixties that opened the doors of possibility for my siblings and me. My father, like so many of the men who arrived from the subcontinent at the same time, chose to live among people he considered his own. The reasons, as we have seen, were understandable and justifiable at the time. Over the following decades a combination of factors, including the failure of successive governments to adequately support these communities, the phenomenon of White flight and a nervousness among some in the Muslim community about the consequences of greater integration, has led to a worrying level of segregation. While I do not believe that British Muslims are wholly responsible for the emergence of these segregated communities, I am also convinced that living in Britain but trying to replicate Pakistan is neither healthy nor desirable. When Muslims and non-Muslims live separately and apart from each other there is a greater danger each will view the other as *they*. Segregation can breed greater fear and anxiety, which can be exploited by those with extremist religious or political agendas. I have outlined some examples of how to tackle segregation – intervening in how schools choose pupils, using English language lessons as a way of bringing communities together – but I strongly believe that promoting integration is also in the power and responsibility of people alongside politicians and policy makers. My father's choice to come to Britain opened a door of opportunity for his family but it also opened a door to conflict and confusion, as I struggled to reconcile the expectations of my parents with the reality of my own dreams of freedom, and love.

THEY . . . DON'T MARRY OUTSIDE THEIR OWN

'Seventy per cent of those questioned said "most White people would mind if a close relative married a Muslim."'

British Social Attitudes Survey, 2017

'Asians will mix socially with White people and some will even date White women, but they won't go so far as marrying them because they don't trust them enough.'

Yaseen, Blackburn, 2020

One evening in the winter of 1988, my father called me to his bedroom. I was seventeen and my biggest preoccupation was passing my A levels with sufficient grades to leave Luton and attend university in Manchester. I switched off the cassette player, took off my headphones and reluctantly sat

at the side of the bed. These conversations were never fun.
I didn't know what he wanted to talk about but, based on
precedent, it was unlikely to be anything I wanted to hear. My
father started by reminding me that I would soon be eighteen
and it was important to start thinking and acting like a man
and not a boy. This was a familiar opening preamble, and
it offered few clues as to the main purpose of that night's
conversation-cum-lecture. My father then started get to the
point. There was a girl back in Pakistan, from Paharang, the
same village I had been born. She was still young, around
ten or eleven, but she was attractive, and my father thought
I should consider marrying her. It is hard to convey fully the
combination of terror and bafflement that washed over me
when I heard my father patiently make his case. I was still
only seventeen and the prospect of marriage was so far in
the distance it wasn't visible to the naked eye. I said nothing
at first – struck dumb by shock – prompting my father to
clarify that he was not suggesting I marry an eleven-year-old
girl – we weren't that backward for God's sake! What he had
in mind was that I give my broad assent, which he could
then convey to the girl's family. The actual marriage could
wait until after I graduated. This didn't feel sufficiently in
the future to allay my gloom. I was still living at home and
leaving to go to university felt daunting enough without
adding a wedding into the bargain. My father explained that
the problem was that this particular girl was very attractive
and thus in high demand. If we didn't signal our intent she
would be snapped up – so we had to, in effect, buy now but

pick up later. I must have gone very quiet because my father agreed that I did not have to decide that evening, but he did warn me that time was not on my side. I went to bed in a state of panic and sadness.

One of the dispiriting consequences of growing up in a working-class Muslim Pakistani family during the eighties was the awareness that my parents would dictate the script of my life. I was resigned to this reality and could imagine no other. I had internalised my powerlessness and assumed that the only choice I had was *when* the inevitable happened not *if*. This was one of the reasons why, as a young boy, I dreaded adulthood. I did not associate it with freedom: adulthood was when my lack of freedom would be most starkly revealed. The most brutal instance of this, for me, was the understanding that I would not be choosing who I would spend the rest of my life with. I knew that *we* had arranged marriages and *they* had love marriages and our way was, of course, superior. There was no question that I would end up marrying a fellow Pakistani Muslim, but I had assumed I would not need to confront this reality for a few years. I was yet to be kissed or fall in love, and here I was being asked to commit my life to a stranger in a faraway country. I had no one I could confide in, which was why I wrote poems and kept a diary:

6 December 1988
I must admit that I have begun to strongly dislike my parents, particularly Dad. I really do not have any positive feelings about him at all these days. I don't even speak to

him unless there is a purpose. It is not their arrogance or bigotry. I am almost used to that, it's just the way they happily decide all our lives. I know everyone says that parents do what is best for you but I am not sure this applies to Dad.

Why should I let my life be decided by Dad when they know me least well? Their idea of a good bride is probably diametrically opposed to mine, and since it is my life why should I go with their choice.

The individual does not matter in our society. It is the family, it is status and I hate it.

The thing that I get most irritated about is that my parents' decisions have a direct bearing on my life. I don't want a relationship like Mum and Dad and yet they probably think it's a good marriage. But it isn't: Dad is allowed to do virtually nothing, Mum does so much and yet it is my Dad who hogs the sympathy and wields the power. What the hell is going on? It is really disconcerting to see that here I am intellectually rationalising out all my thoughts and it does not make a blind bit of difference.

I sometimes get really naive and think why can't life be like Scott and Charlene.* I know it sounds stupid but why can't a guy meet a girl who is compatible and their families approve?'

---

* I remember watching the television show *Neighbours* and seeing the wedding between Scott and Charlene – played by Jason Donovan and Kylie Minogue – and their love seemed so pure and true. It clearly affected me a lot.

I rarely revisit my diary, but when I read that entry I am struck by how clearly I recognised and articulated my problem and placed it in a larger context. My impotent frustration is so palpable: it was as if I was tied to the railway tracks and it was only a matter of time until the oncoming train came hurtling towards me. I got lucky. I deflected and dodged through the winter, spring and summer, and the following autumn I left Luton for Manchester, but I never stopped worrying about or expecting that oncoming train. The train, in this rather tortuous metaphor, represents an arranged marriage with a Muslim who would have been chosen by my parents. I could imagine no other destination for my life and in this I was entirely typical of British Muslims growing up in the seventies. In this chapter I want to follow the journeys of some of the sons of the men introduced in the previous chapter, focusing on the pressures we all faced to marry 'suitable' girls and the related intense pressure exerted to ensure that under no circumstances should we believe in the possibility of marrying anyone who was not Muslim. These were pressures that I myself experienced, which is why this will be the most personal chapter in the book. I am not usually an advocate of gender segregation, but in this chapter I am going to focus on male stories. This is because the experience of the fathers, husbands and sons often varies so dramatically from the mothers, wives and daughters that I felt it better to focus the following chapter more fully on female stories.

Alyas was living in Tooting in south London with his bus driver father, Mohammed. 'My dad was embarrassed that he was working class,' he says. 'This is a culture about status and about power and about position and about materialism. My dad was low down – he wanted to mix with doctors and professionals, but he was a bus driver, and he had a feeling of insecurity amongst his peers.' That insecurity was accompanied by powerlessness – the sense that he lacked the power to change his situation – and alongside that was the daily racism he endured. Alyas paid the price for his father's frustrations. 'He would beat me,' recalls Alyas, 'and I would hear him tell me: "I hate you. I hate everything about you. I detest you and what you're about." It leaves real scars, and it leaves real anger.' The violence continued until Alyas was fourteen. 'There comes a point,' he says, 'where you realise that your dad's punches don't hurt any more.' He remembers his father hitting him and turning round and saying to him: 'Is that it? Is that all you've got? Punch me harder.' The moment his father realised that Alyas could take the beatings, he stopped hitting him.

Having passed his A levels, Alyas left London to study in Glasgow. 'I went there because it was the furthest I could get from home,' he says. 'I was running away from home.' Meanwhile, in Birmingham, Nazir – who we last saw running from skinheads in Small Heath – was excelling in his studies. He was consistently at the top of the class, which meant that his parents gave him the freedom to pursue his studies free from worry about an impending arranged marriage. 'I am very fortunate,' he says. 'The comments I would hear from my father were "Keep Nazir away from this. Let him study – he is going in a different direction so let him be".' Nazir ended up sitting six A levels – three that could lead to a medical career and three others. His grades were not good enough to pursue medicine, so he decided to study law.

By leaving home for university, Alyas, Nazir and I all managed to buy ourselves time. After being bussed to a White school, Zulfi Karim returned to his local schools, and by the time he was seventeen he was looking forward to leaving Bradford and attending university. 'I had so many ambitions,' he tells me. One day Zulfi was returning home from his part-time job at Halfords when his mother told him she had some news. She had arranged his marriage to his first cousin and the girl was flying in from Pakistan the following week. 'It came massively out the blue,' recalls Zulfi. 'It was just absolute shock. I was only seventeen – to be told that there is this bride, and I am going to Heathrow to pick her up, and we are going to get married – none of it was registering.' The following week Zulfi took a van with his family to Heathrow. 'I think there were three hundred girls on the plane,' he says, laughing, 'a few grooms but mostly brides.' He approached the immigration desk and was asked to pick out his bride-to-be. 'I remember saying to the immigration official: "I've never seen her!" Well, you can just imagine what she probably thought. And she took me over and said, "Here she is." She stood me right opposite her and she said, "Right. You can go now."' Zulfi walked out with the girl, who couldn't speak English, and they were married a few months later.

This was a story endlessly repeated for the generation growing up in the seventies and eighties. When Ansar Ali was four years old and living in Pakistan, his brother was eight and their mother promised her sister that her eldest son would marry her sister's daughter. But the eldest boy died, and it was agreed that the marriage would be passed on to Ansar. Ansar grew up and moved from Pakistan to Bradford, but always knowing that he had been promised to his cousin. By the time he was eighteen, his parents began to demand that promise be fulfilled. 'I was a teenager, I had discovered girls and was going to discos,' says Ansar, 'so the last thing on my mind was getting married, but the conversations got heavier and heavier, and the family tried every trick in the book.' He was told that if he refused the marriage no parents would offer their daughters to his other brothers. Ansar started coming back later and later in the hope that his parents would be in bed. He would go out with his friends to nightclubs in Wakefield and Bradford where they would have dance offs listening to soul and disco. But no matter what time he got back, his parents would be waiting, and the conversation would start again. Eventually Ansar agreed to the marriage. His uncle and some of his uncle's friends drove him to Heathrow. When he arrived he heard a message on the loudspeaker saying that his cousin had landed and was waiting for him. 'The immigration officer called me over and there was a group of girls lined up behind him,' he recalls. 'He said: "Which one is your fiancée?" I said: "I haven't got a clue, mate. I don't know what she looks like."

He said to me, "It's that pretty one with the pink scarf."' Ansar and his fiancée travelled back to Bradford and were married the following week.

Aziz Hakim was nineteen and still living in Whalley Range. He had left school and started working for his dad in his plumbing company. He had also started to get involved in petty crime. 'I was off the rails,' he recalls. 'I had started to wheel and deal, handling stolen goods just for the thrill of it. You would work all day and seek thrills elsewhere. I was getting into fights just for the rush.' He got home one evening and his father said he had to get married. Aziz was put on a plane to Nairobi and, on arriving in Kenya, he was introduced to a girl. 'They wanted a decision quite quick,' he says. 'I thought there was nothing wrong with her, so I said yes.' They were married the following day. That same year Aziz's brother came home one evening to find their father standing in the kitchen with a photograph in his hand. 'He put the photo on the table and said: "That's your wife." It was the daughter of his cousin who lived in Zanzibar.' He also agreed to the marriage. 'I just had to do it,' he says, 'I did it to please him.'

After their wedding, Ansar and his new wife went home, but he refused to let her sleep in his bed. 'I said: "This is my bedroom and nobody else sleeps here but me," and she said: "But we are married now, and I am going to sleep there." So, I picked up the mattress and threw it down the stairs and said: "There's your bed."' That must have been incredibly hard on her, I say, she must have been so vulnerable and far from home. 'I didn't really appreciate that at the time because I didn't have the maturity,' Ansar says. 'But when I think about it now, she was more of a victim than I was because, for me, life went on. I didn't spend much time at home, and I started working, so I would leave the house in the morning, come home and then be out again in less than half an hour. We never consummated the marriage or even slept in the same bed.'

Ansar and Zulfi were raised by parents who were themselves brought up to believe that being engaged as children, marrying their cousins and arranged marriages were the norm. When they moved to Britain, they brought those attitudes with them and assumed they would be able to retain them. They believed that this was how one preserved the culture and protected it from the way that *they* did things. There were also practical advantages to arranging for your son or daughter to marry their cousin. The families already knew each other, and it could be a way of helping the extended family. When I was growing up, my father constantly impressed upon me how lucky we were that he had left Pakistan to come to Britain (this was when he was not declaring that the worst mistake he had made was coming to Britain – he was somewhat conflicted on this question) and that great stroke of good fortune carried a responsibility towards those left behind. Using your son or daughter to help bring a cousin to Britain was a way of sharing that good fortune, even if it came at the price of those getting married being desperately unhappy. It might seem utterly bizarre, and it often did to those being married off, but the parents did not think they were being heavy-handed, they did not think they were destroying their children's lives. They believed they were doing the right thing, and, by their values, they were.

It is also important to note that even though the prospect of an arranged marriage horrified me when I was young, that does not mean that all arranged marriages were inevitably unhappy or unfulfilling. Abdul in Rotherham had an arranged marriage to his cousin when he was twenty-one. 'The way I see it, when you marry someone in a love marriage you already know that person,' he says. 'With someone you don't know right well, you've got all your life ahead of you to get to know each other.' Aziz in Blackburn got married in 1990 and, more than thirty years later, he and his wife are still together. 'It is possible to fall in love after you have gotten married,' he says. 'You learn to accept each other's likes – sometimes reluctantly – just to get by in life without fussing and fighting.' This does not sound hugely different from the compromises involved in any marriage.

Arranged marriages are these days most often associated with the south Asian community, but they were common around the world until the eighteenth century. They have been part of south Asian culture since the fourth century and were seen as a way of uniting and maintaining upper caste families. The system then spread to the lower caste, where it was used for the same purpose. Muslim parents often see it as their responsibility to provide for the marriage of their children.* When my father sat me down to tell me about the girl in Pakistan, he believed he was fulfilling his religious duty. I remember being teased and quizzed about the possibility of having an arranged marriage, and I would feel deeply self-conscious because arranged marriages were one of the things that everyone associated with Asians. I did not know then that, in fact, European royal families, including the British royal family, had historically not only had arranged marriages but also marriages between cousins. The Queen and Prince Philip, for instance, were cousins who shared the same bloodline, being both directly related to Queen Victoria, who was married to Prince Albert, who was her first cousin.[1] 'The notion of anyone wedding for love would not only have been laughed at, it would have been ignored,' notes Leslie Carroll, author of *Notorious Royal Marriages*. 'If you have a complaint about not being loved or appreciated in this marriage,' Prince Charles tells Diana in the television drama *The Crown*, 'I suggest you take it up with the people who arranged it.'

I escaped to study in Manchester in the autumn of 1989 and, after graduating, I chose to remain there rather than return to Luton. I was struggling with the conflict between the life I was enjoying and the one that was expected of me. I was

---

* I am not suggesting that this is exclusive to Muslim parents. It appears to be a particularly strong impulse among Muslims, but that is not to suggest it is not also true among parents of other faiths or none.

hundreds of miles from home and the distance felt liberating. I was going to nightclubs and it was almost possible, when I was in the middle of the dance floor shaking my dreadlocks*[2] and dancing to 'Are You Gonna Go My Way', to forget about the real world and the oncoming train. I had a series of relationships with White girls but none of them lasted, in part because I knew they *couldn't* last. An arranged marriage always felt as if it was going to be my final destination. The best I could hope for was a scenic and distracting journey. I would imagine how it might feel to be in a relationship that had potential, to marry someone I truly loved, and sometimes, when I was feeling especially sad, I would write poems that tried to capture how I imagined true love might feel.

STATE OF BLISS

Outside the world is still aching
And inside I am far from free
But tonight I can't keep from shaking

From what you said to me
Suddenly all is clear and vivid
When before it was shapeless mist
You took me bleary eyed and stumbling
And led me to a state of bliss

---

* See *Greetings from Bury Park*, p. 44, for the full story on the dreadlocks.

All this time I had been searching
Along a long and lonely trail
Seeking answers to questions
Locked in a battle I knew I would fail

Last night it was all forgotten
Meaning returned as we kissed
And I was sent spinning
Towards a state of bliss

Even back when I just existed
On the fringes observing the dance
Even then I kept insisting
I could be more if I had the chance

Last night I stopped preaching
There is more to life than this
For the nirvana I was reaching
Came in a state of bliss.

Three months after the sudden death of my father in the summer of 1995, I returned to Manchester. I stayed for a year before returning home to Luton and, one year later, I moved to London. I was away from home but there was no escaping the expectation that the marriage train was heading towards me. There was the palpable sense that I was disappointing my mother. With my father no longer alive, the responsibility of arranging my marriage fell solely on her and this frustrated her. It was as if she had been given a role she had never asked to play, but she was compelled to do her duty. In an ideal world it would have been my father who would have been tasked with finding me a wife but he was no longer around. My mother believed she would be failing as a Muslim, as a mother and as a wife if she did not arrange my marriage.

The years passed, thirty came and went, and my mother became ever more desperate. I would tell her not to worry, that in this country men in their thirties do not expect their mothers to find them a wife, but my mother is from another country and another time. I was plagued with a nagging suspicion that no matter how successful I was in other parts of my life, the fact that I was unmarried overshadowed everything. I have never relished open conflict and so rather than engaging in loud arguments with my family where I could passionately make my case in favour of love, and where I could tell them why the idea of marrying a stranger horrified me, I avoided any discussion about marriage. I would not come home much, and when I did I would change the subject whenever my mum tried to raise it. It was painful for me, but I recognised that it was also heartbreaking for her. She had my best interests at heart. She would ask whether I had anyone to cook my meals for me and when I told her that I did all my own cooking and washing, she would look at me with sadness and pity. I felt pained by the seeming inevitability of what was to happen to me and my mother felt equally pained by the responsibility of ensuring that it did. It was a wearying and unhappy dance. I came to dread going back home because it was inevitable that at some point during my stay the question of my unmarried state would be raised. The question that would whirl around my head as I returned to London from these traumatising trips home was this: was it possible that there existed a woman I would desire and who could also secure my family's approval? My family's approval hinged on the woman being a Pakistani Muslim and, it often seemed, nothing much else. My mother might have been desperate to see me married but she was also at something of a loss when it came to identifying any potential wives. My late father had never been a particularly gregarious man and since his death our connections to the wider Pakistani community had further faded. It was not as if my mother was plugged into a large social network where she knew anyone who might know anyone who might be suitable, whatever that means.

I lost myself in work. My career was flying high: there were weeks when I had work published in the *Guardian*, a documentary broadcast on BBC Radio 4 and I was appearing on *Newsnight Review*. Work kept me busy and made me feel as if there was something at which I was successful even if I was a loser in love. In May 2008 I flew out to Los Angeles to interview Little Richard for a Radio 4 documentary.* When

---

* When we met he was wearing crushed velvet trousers, a bejewelled shirt and his face was heavily made up. After the interview I asked if I could get a photograph with him. He declined because, he said, he 'was not dressed up for it'.

I returned, I headed straight to Wales for the Hay Festival. I was presenting coverage of the festival for the *Guardian* and so, for ten days, I was immersed in the worlds of literature, culture and politics, which provided a welcome distraction from the fact I was single.

The last day of the festival was the first Sunday in June. It was a blazing hot day; the Hereford traffic was clogging the roads and it was looking as if I might miss the train back to London. The car pulled up at the station, I leapt out and, clutching my suitcase, I raced to the platform. The train doors were about to close when I jumped in, made a split-second decision to turn right, spotted an empty seat and collapsed into it. I was out of breath and sweaty. I lifted my head up, still panting, and it was then that I saw her. Sitting opposite me was the most beautiful woman I had ever seen. She had hair the colour of sunshine that ran past her shoulders and wild green eyes that were trained on a paperback copy of *Mary Barton*. I kept stealing glances at the woman and the thought that kept returning to my head was 'Who gets to be your friend? Who gets to know you?' She was – truth be told – way out of my league, and so for the first hour or so I was dutifully mute in the face of such beauty. The plain truth was that I never usually had this luck, and I didn't know what to do with it. I am not the sort who chats to strangers – ever – and yet something told me that if I didn't at least talk to this woman I would forever regret it. But the question was: what could be the ice-breaker that might persuade her to look up from her book and talk to me? And then I noticed it – a Hay Festival book bag. This meant that we had something in common and I had an opening line. So, I made a decision: I would talk to her. I asked her if she had been to the festival – she said yes – I said I had too, and before you knew it we were having an actual conversation.

Her name was Bridget, and she was a thirty-year-old Scottish speech and language therapist living in London. We talked about Hay, about books, and then about life and family and just about everything. If I had met Bridget in a more conventional location – a party or bar – I would not have been as relaxed as I was during the train journey. The fact I had not shaved for a few days and thus looked more like a vagrant than a journalist, and the fact that Bridget was so outrageously out of my league, plus the likelihood we would never see each other again meant I was looser, more relaxed and consequently better company than I would ordinarily have been. The conversation was surprisingly deep. I remember asking her, out of nowhere, what was missing in her life. She said that she didn't have any children, yet. The train rumbled towards Paddington and the closer we came to London, the more I inwardly began to panic. I did not want this to be just another brief encounter, an anecdote to uncork about that time I found myself sitting opposite the most gorgeous woman I had ever seen. I wanted to see her again, but I did not want to come across as a creep, so I took a risk. I said she could have *my* number, but I would not take hers – that way she could contact me, but I would have no way of contacting her. The only way we would talk again was if she initiated it. And that was how we left it as the train pulled up at the station.

It was two days before she texted me. She said she had enjoyed our chat and wanted to continue it, so we agreed to meet at the Tate Modern the following Saturday. That first date took place on 7 June 2008, two days before my thirty-seventh birthday. It led to another, and then another, and soon we were in a relationship that was both incredibly easy and hideously complicated. It was so easy being with Bridget; she was like sunshine in human form, that rare person who is beautiful both on the outside and inside. And yet even as I was falling in love with her, I was telling myself that this was not love, she was not the one. The idea that I could tell my family about her was unimaginable and the prospect of them accepting her as my wife was inconceivable. I did not have the courage or desire to burn all my bridges, not even for Bridget. It was easier, at first, to live two lives: be deliriously happy in my relationship with Bridget in London with occasional visits to Luton where my mother would bemoan her fate at having a son who was nearing forty (my mother's love of drama is greater than her numeric accuracy) and still unmarried. It was so tempting to get up and leap on the couch like a Pakistani Tom Cruise* and start yelling

---

* For younger readers, this is a reference to an infamous episode of *The Oprah Winfrey Show* from 2005, where Cruise leapt onto Oprah's couch in an allegedly spontaneous outburst of enthusiasm for his personal life. It was all very odd.

about how they didn't need to worry because I had found someone. I did no such thing. Instead, despite how much time we spent together, regardless of how well we got on, irrespective of how happy Bridget made me, I convinced myself that our relationship was doomed.

There were so many challenges. I was nervous about having mixed-race children and worried about my cultural heritage being lost rather than passed down. I also didn't want to become the clichéd middle-class ethnic minority who confirms their entry into the establishment by marrying White. I think my anxieties around this were related to issues around class, mainstream acceptance and the compromises one makes to be a success. I did not want to be accused of 'selling out' and, deep down, I must have associated those who married out as having in some ways betrayed who they 'really' were.* I also did not want anyone to think that the reason I wanted to be with Bridget was because I thought a White woman was somehow more desirable or worthy than a Pakistani one. I had not fallen in love with a 'White woman'; I had fallen in love with Bridget. When I revisit these anxieties from today's vantage point, it is striking how much what other people thought concerned me. Mostly, it was not

---

* While I was in the latter stages of working on this book, I received an email from a reader who had enjoyed my first book. She talked about how she had always seen me as 'the Asian guy who married a White woman' and how her best friend 'described you as turning your back on your community'.

random people's possible reactions that consumed me – it was the likely reaction of my family. I did not want to have to live with the scalding guilt of knowing I had let them down. I shared my doubts with Bridget, and she listened carefully before pointing out that I was talking rubbish. '*You* were born into a fully Pakistani family and look how you turned out,' she said. Despite my traditional upbringing, I had still grown into a reasonably well-integrated and Westernised adult. She also noted that my father had, in his own way, been a pioneer: the only one in his family to leave Pakistan for Britain. Was it so wrong to be have found someone I cared about, and who cared about me? The more I listened, the more Bridget began to make sense. If she, as a White, nominally Christian, Scottish woman, was not agonising about being with a Brown, vaguely Muslim, British-Pakistani man, why was I so nervous about being with her? Bridget had been planning to travel to India for seven months in the autumn, but she shortened her trip to four months and I went out to spend the last six weeks with her. We practically lived in each other's pockets and, on returning home, any doubts were gone. I felt certain that I loved her, but I was far from certain about how to respond to my feelings.

I used to joke to Bridget that she was my 'blonde distraction'. I thought I was making a light-hearted reference to the suggestion I often heard from other Asian guys that it was fine to have your fun with a White girl before settling down with someone more acceptably Asian. It is, in truth, an offensive mindset rooted in racism and misogyny. In referring to

Bridget in that way I thought I was mocking it, but the deeper I fell in love with her, the more the idea of her being just a 'blonde distraction' went from vaguely amusing to deeply terrifying. I tried to find reasons why she wasn't perfect to make the prospect of ending the relationship easier. But the longer our relationship lasted, the more perfect for me she was revealed to be, and the harder it became to reconcile the disparity between my London life and my Luton family. I did not want Bridget to be a dirty little secret, as she deserved better than that and it felt hugely disrespectful. There was no conscious decision made to tell my family, no date that I circled in the calendar as The Day. It happened almost by accident. I was visiting my mother and the conversation turned, as it always did, to my unmarried state. I had begun, during the previous few months, to drop hints about how I didn't expect any Pakistani Muslim girl to be interested in me now that I was the wrong side of thirty-five. I was in the midst of repeating this argument when my mother interrupted me to ask if I was seeing a White woman. In the past when she had asked such a question, I had immediately told her I was not, but, this time, some force urged me to tell the truth. And so I did.

I can picture the scene clearly as I write this: we were in the living room of my mother's Luton home; she was sitting in her armchair while I faced her. I remember the feeling of release and an awareness that, in admitting the truth, I could not deny it. The truth was now out there but whether it would set me free was as yet unknown. As soon as I had told her the most damaging detail – that the woman I was in love with was a *gori* (Urdu for White) – I tried to flood the conversation with evidence that Bridget's Whiteness should not be automatically disqualifying. I told my mother that Bridget worked with children, in a very Muslim part of London, that she could understand and even speak Urdu, and that she was very close to her parents and siblings. The inference was that she could almost be Pakistani. My mother seemed to hear all this and her response was more strategic than I had expected – she talked about how we would go about trying to persuade my older brother to give Bridget a chance. The implication was that she was on my side and was going in to bat for me. The encounter had gone much better than I could have predicted and I returned to London feeling somewhat elated. That didn't last long. Later that evening when I rang home, my brother answered and said that Mum would not come to the phone. She was now utterly furious and any notion I might have entertained that she was going to be fine with what I was doing was utterly misguided.

My family made it very clear that they vehemently opposed my relationship with Bridget. It would have been easier to never go home given that I knew what to expect. Every time I visited Luton I was roundly lambasted by my family. It was relentless and brutal, and I would go back to London and Bridget would be in tears. The message I would get from my family was that I was a terrible son and brother. I was cold-hearted and selfish because I was putting my happiness – or what I assumed would make me happy – ahead of what was right and proper. I would plead with them to give Bridget a chance. I would say that it was not right to assume all White people are the same or that just because she is White she is guilty of all the bad qualities *they* have. There were times when it felt like I was a trapped in a time-travel black-comedy-cum-horror movie. When I was in London my relationship with Bridget was utterly unremarkable, but travel thirty miles to Luton and I was transported to another time where what I was doing was dangerously transgressive. It would have been, technically at least, easier to cut off all communication with my family – to conclude that if they would not accept my life choices then I did not need to indulge their toxic presence in my life. But that never felt like an option to me.

When I contemplated life without my family, the over-riding emotion I felt was loneliness. My father was the only one in his family to make the journey from Pakistan to Britain and, since his death, there were only my two sisters, brother, my mother and me from my blood family. If I stopped all contact with them, there were no cousins or uncles or aunts with whom I could remain in touch, and that isolation felt worrying. What if my relationship faltered and failed? Where would that leave me if I burnt my bridges with my family? I would have nothing. I also knew that I would never be truly happy without some version of approval from my family. My dream, and it felt very much like a dream at the time, was to be sat around a dining table with my family and Bridget all eating together. This was all extremely challenging for Bridget. She had been used to the parents of past boyfriends actually liking her and mine wouldn't even deign to meet her. She was in a position of powerlessness – she could not *make* my family accept her and she obviously did not want to be the cause of me losing my family. These were very difficult days and, when I look back on them, I am always struck by how little I doubted what I was doing and how supportive Bridget was. She too was paying a price for being in the relationship, but she recognised and respected that I did not want to live a fragmented life. I wanted to keep fighting for that dream until I had no fight left in me. And so I kept visiting home, kept making the case for my family to at least meet Bridget, and progress was made. My mum relented, and so one Saturday afternoon Bridget and I took a train from London to Luton.

The night before we had war-gamed the meeting, rehearsing answers to anticipated questions with Bridget practising her Urdu.* I remember feeling deeply nervous as the taxi pulled up outside. Bridget had bought two bouquets of flowers – one for my mum and one for my brother and his wife. She presented them and we were led into the living room. My brother was not at home and the initial conversation was fairly pleasant and friendly. Bridget was nervous, but her sunny disposition, friendly and smiling nature seemed to be winning my family over. It was only

---

* When we had met on the train, Bridget had told me she had been attending Hindi classes and was surprisingly proficient. Hindi and Urdu – my mother's language – are very similar when spoken.

when my brother returned and we sat down for lunch that things changed, and the interrogation began. No one was directly rude to Bridget – the attacks were all directed at me: it was not her they were angry with, what angered them was what was wrong with me that I would choose to be with her. It was a deeply uncomfortable lunch – delicious food accompanied by a barrage of personal abuse. I was used to it, but this was new territory for Bridget. Eventually we left and, as Bridget stepped outside, she burst into tears. My hopes that actually meeting Bridget would change my family's minds had been exposed as wildly over-optimistic. I did not want to be a rebel and what I was seeking did not seem particularly extreme, but for my family, in the town they lived and the culture from which they came, it was not the done thing and there were few precedents.

Pakistani Muslim children who grew up in the seventies and eighties were told by our parents that not only should we not even think about marrying outside our race and religion, but that no one had ever previously done so. I did not know that there was a long history of mixed marriages. Englishmen returning from India in the late eighteenth century would sometimes bring Indian wives and their children back to Britain. Sake Dean Mohamed, who was born in 1759 in India to an elite Muslim family, arrived in Britain in 1784 and spent several years in Cork, where he met a young woman 'known to be fair and beautiful' called Jane Daly, with whom he eloped and had several children. Mohamed would later move to London, where he established the Hindoostanee

Coffee-House in 1810, which offered Indian dishes 'in the highest perfection . . . unequalled to any curries ever made in England'. He then moved to Brighton to open the Indian Vapour Baths and Shampooing Establishment and was later appointed Shampooing Surgeon to King George IV. Leap forward to 1857 and a report on the Asian working class and their relations with White women noted that 'it would surprise many people to see how extensively these dark classes are tincturing the colour of the rising race of children in the lowest haunts of this locality; and many of the young fallen females have a visible infusion of Asiatic or African blood in their veins. It is an instance of depraved taste, that many of our fallen ones prefer devoting themselves entirely to the dark race of men, and some who are not married to them have infants by them.'[3] White women who had relationships with Indian men were given nicknames like Lascar Sally and Calcutta Louise. By the late 1930s and 1940s, police in the Midlands were stressing that the 'numbers of young girls' associating with Indian men was a 'serious social evil' and voicing concern about 'half-caste' children and urging that women needed protection against 'their own foolishness'.[4]

Shafayat Khan arrived in Britain in the late forties and was working in the Lucas plastics factory when he met a fellow worker called Betty. Shafayat and Betty started a relationship and were married in 1949. They would go on to have a son named Munir. In my conversations with Muslims across Britain it was striking how many knew someone from my father's generation who had married or had a relationship with a White woman. Matloob Khan came to Britain after his village was displaced following the construction of the Mangla Dam. He started working for Boots the chemists in Nottingham. Tall, fair-skinned and charismatic, with a seventies footballer-style drooping moustache, Matloob enjoyed what his son describes as 'a playboy lifestyle – there were White girls, there were Black girls and he continued to have affairs after he got married. There were women that my mum had let into her life as friends and then my dad would be sneaking around behind her back and having dilly-dallies with them.' 'The thing is most of these men used to go clubbing and pubbing,' one Bradford man told me. 'That's the truth – one of my uncles, he's passed away now, was always very honest about it. He would say, "Yes we did." It was acceptable for our fathers when they were here alone to marry White women.' The difference between my father's generation and those that followed was that his generation were free from parents and relatives who would judge them.

I grew up knowing nothing about this history and so these stories, when I discovered them, felt like secrets that had been buried for too long. I remember as a boy religiously scanning the wedding page of the Luton *Herald* newspaper looking for mixed-race marriages. It wasn't so much that this was what I wanted but I just wanted to know what such a union might look like. In researching this book, I came across the online archive of the Belle Vue Studio in Bradford,[5] where there were many hypnotically compelling portraits of mixed-race couples dating back to the 1950s. The men, typically, are smart and bouffant-haired, sober-faced or with a nervous smile. In one photograph,[6] a White woman is dressed in traditional Asian clothes, a light dupatta draped over her head. Mixed-race relationships like this were still very rare and the couples who did it were outliers – the men were either already outsiders or particularly headstrong. These stories fascinate me because they reveal that the usual narrative of strict parents raising children who demanded more freedom choosing their partners is not the complete story. They hint at a more colourful life for the men of that first immigrant generation, but when these men had children the colour was drained and the choices presented would be in black and white. The children who dared to dream, to rebel, would pay a price.

Ansar in Bradford had been married four years when he started seeing another woman. She was a work colleague – her name was Julie and she was a White Roman Catholic. 'The relationship became more serious, but I didn't mention to Julie that I was married because in my head I wasn't,' says Ansar, 'and then one day I moved out of my wife's house and moved in with Julie.' Ansar and Julie were married in 1986 and his first wife returned to Pakistan. She never married again. I wondered if Ansar ever felt guilty about how he had treated her, and he told me how years later he met her again on a trip to Pakistan. 'I wanted to apologise to her,' he says. 'I wanted to go to Hajj and it was one of the things that was a black mark against me.' When he met her, Ansar told her that he had been young and hadn't known any better, and he asked her if she could find it in her heart to forgive him. 'She told me: "Men don't apologise to women,"' he remembers. 'It was such a crazy statement – basically she was saying that she had been raised to believe that men can do what they like to women.'

When we last met Sajid, the son of Abdul Ghani, he was working at his parents' shop, wiping the racist graffiti from the storefront. During the summer after college and before starting university, Sajid got a holiday job at Commercial Union in Bristol, where he sat next to a girl called Laura. 'I would see her every day and it took me two weeks to pluck up the courage to ask her to have a sandwich with me,' he says. Laura agreed and a week or so later she invited him for dinner with some friends. 'She made a pizza, but it had bacon and pineapple,' he says, 'and I can't eat bacon and she felt gutted. She hadn't dated anyone who was Muslim and had never come across a Muslim before in any meaningful way, so it was a real eye opener.' By Christmas, Sajid felt confident enough in his relationship to consider telling his father. 'I told him it was quite serious,' he recalls. 'I said, "I can imagine marrying her one day."' His father's expression changed, and he abruptly ended the conversation. A few days later he asked to see Sajid. 'He said let's just be clear on one thing – you cannot marry her,' Sajid recalls. 'I told him I was just saying it was a possibility but he again said I could not marry her and so I asked him why not.' It was then that Sajid learnt he was already engaged. 'I said, "Hold on, what do you mean I'm engaged?" It turned out that my father had basically agreed with his sister that I was going to marry one of her daughters – my cousin – without me even knowing.' Sajid told his father that he was not going to go through with the engagement but it remained an issue throughout the early years of his relationship with Laura. By the time they left university, the couple had decided to marry but opted to wait so as to improve the chances of securing his parents' blessing. 'I played the long game,' Sajid says, 'and it was a deliberate decision. Had my parents been more supportive from the start, I would have got married earlier. In the end, I got married at twenty-seven because I deliberately decided that it was worth investing time and getting it right.'

In May 1995, the Pakistani cricket star Imran Khan married Jemima Goldsmith. I was obsessed with this relationship, which felt both inspiring and unfair. Why couldn't *I* marry a beautiful daughter of a billionaire? (Aside from the fact that I was not a beloved cricketing god with matinee-idol looks.) I would sometimes throw out the example of Imran Khan and my parents would counter with Benazir Bhutto – if the Prime Minister of Pakistan could agree to an arranged marriage, who was I to complain? I would sometimes wonder whether anything might have prompted my mother to be less hostile to my relationship.

My mother was an unlikely fan of Diana, Princess of Wales. In the aftermath of Diana's death in August 1997, she was in near-constant tears when she watched the news, and I took her to Kensington Gardens to pay her respects. In the same year that Imran Khan married Jemima Goldsmith, Diana had begun a relationship with a Pakistani heart surgeon. His name was Hasnat Khan – a cousin of Imran Khan – and the relationship lasted until a few months before Diana's death.* Diana referred to Hasnat as Mr Wonderful and wanted to marry him – she reportedly talked about how having mixed-race children could be good for society. Khan was less convinced that the fame that would come with making their relationship public was a price worth paying, and was worried about the impact it would have on his life and work. The relationship ended in 1997 and Diana went on to have another relationship with another Muslim – Dodi Fayed – before her death in Paris. Diana's death, and Hasnat's reservations, robbed us of an alternative universe in which she and Khan married and had children. What might have been the consequences of such a union – the most famous woman on earth, a member of the Royal Family, married to a British-Pakistani? It would surely have transformed the image and reputation of Muslims and Pakistanis around the world, and it might even have helped persuade my mother that marrying a White woman was not the end of the world. Sadly, that remained in the realm of fantasy and my mother continued to voice her strong opposition to my relationship.

The contrast with Bridget's parents could hardly have been starker. It was almost embarrassing. I would take the train up to Dumfries, to the tiny community where they lived, and they would do everything they could to make me feel

---

* The relationship between Diana and Hasnat Khan is the focus of a feature film, *Diana*, starring Naomi Watts. The film is dreadful.

comfortable. They were so empathetic about my family situation that I sometimes found their overwhelming decency frustrating. It reminded me that I could not offer Bridget the same warm welcome from my family and that made me feel ashamed. I worried that Bridget would decide I was not worth it. She would sometimes say, with some sadness, that the parents of her previous boyfriends had always loved her. If she was to leave me and find someone less problematic, could I really blame her? I had to have faith that she was happy to pay the price that came with being with me, but I was frustrated that it was my family who were setting that price.

I don't recall ever seriously considering ending our relationship. How can that be given that my mother was threatening to go on a hunger strike, the barrage of abuse I was facing and the threats that I would never be able to see my niece and nephew again if I continued seeing Bridget? I don't consider myself an especially brave person. I loathe confrontation and, on the whole, I would rather everyone just got along. I also knew, however, that my chances of meeting anyone as special as Bridget, regardless of race or religion, were infinitesimal. I made a decision that I was on to a good thing and I did not want to throw it away. My resolve was not only rooted in an awareness of my good fortune in having met Bridget. I had been raised in a traditional working-class Pakistani Muslim family, but I had left that community, and this gave me an invaluable sense of perspective. My family often made me feel as if I was insane to want what I desired but I *knew* that what I was asking was not freakishly bizarre.

It was not ridiculous to want to marry the woman I loved; it was ridiculous to *not* marry her. Would I have had this confidence in my judgement had I not moved away from home at eighteen and lived the best part of two decades surrounded by White people who reinforced my new thinking? Perhaps not.

In the winter of 2009, Bridget and I visited Rome[7] and one night, after a romantic meal at a rooftop restaurant that overlooked the glittering city, I proposed. She agreed and, on returning home, I told my family. I wanted them to attend the wedding, but I knew that, for my mother, a religious wedding was far more significant than a legal ceremony. I arranged to have an imam visit our flat in London in February 2010 to conduct the Islamic ceremony, known as a nikah. I invited my family but, despite my repeated best efforts, they declined to attend. The imam offered to call my mother to explain that theologically there was nothing against Islam in what I was doing – Muslim men are allowed to marry Christian or Jewish women – but despite claiming to be religious, my family were not willing to concede that what I was doing was permissible. The nikah took place in our flat in north London with just Bridget and me, plus my friend acting as the sole witness, and another friend who was an imam officiating. The imam read passages from the Qur'an, we signed a few documents and, after the ceremony, we all ate a keema aloo curry I had made, and a carrot cake Bridget had baked.

My family did not attend the Islamic wedding, but I remained hopeful they might wish to attend the official wedding on 21 August. It was a very strange time: planning what was to be the happiest day of our lives but unable to share my joy with my family, indeed aware that my joy was inciting deep sadness and anger for them. My diary entries from the weeks leading up to the wedding hint at what Bridget and I were going through:

12 August 2010
I have been feeling a little strange all day. My heartbeat was a little fast and I felt like my blood pressure may be going through the roof. I was feeling anxiety prompted by the pressure relating the wedding. I am feeling very sad. The grim reality of what it feels to have one's family try to cut you off; the icy chill that emanates from them, it is very hard to process. I tell myself it doesn't matter— that I am a good person but it is wearying. My head is filled with bleak sadness and it feels like it is leaking into my brain.

18 August 2010
For my family they are convinced that this is a terrible mistake that I am making. They think I am totally lost from my own culture and that by being with Bridget I am only going to reinforce just how estranged and alienated from the person that I was when I grew up in Luton.

It is revealing that I used the phrase 'lost from my own culture'; my family's objections to Bridget were not explicitly about religion. This is not entirely surprising since it is generally agreed among Muslim scholars that Muslim men can marry Christian or Jewish women because they are 'people of the book'. There are, needless to say, some Muslims who dispute this, arguing that 'one of the conditions of marriage to a *kitaabi* [a person of the book] woman is that she should be chaste, but there are very few chaste women to be found in those environments'.[8] This freedom is not, as we will see, generally believed to extend to Muslim women being able to marry non-Muslims. I did once try reminding my family that mainstream Islamic thought agrees that it was permissible to marry Bridget, but it did not go down terribly well. I knew that if Bridget agreed to convert to Islam there was a chance it might persuade my family to consider attending the wedding. This was not unusual in mixed relationships, but Bridget had always refused. She respected Islam too much to insult it with a tokenistic conversion. That was not the only reason: Bridget also wanted to demonstrate to my family that one could be a kind, decent and loving person without being a Muslim. It was a laudable aspiration but not a winning strategy. The family continued to make clear they had no interest in coming to the wedding. My brother and older sister both had children and I suspected that they did not want to give any sense of legitimacy to what I was doing in case this was interpreted as them supporting my life choices.

The wedding day approached, and I became more anxious. I would wake in the middle of night, jolted into consciousness by traumatising dreams. In one, my brother and sisters appeared as ghosts; I could see them but knew they were dead, and I was crying out to them saying, 'Please don't die! I don't want you to be dead.' In another, I was sharing a bed with my older brother, just as I had when I was a small boy, but this time we were adults. In the dream I howled with pain that the brother I had once worshipped was not willing to witness my wedding. I sat in the darkness, my heart pounding as Bridget slept silently at my side. These dreams spoke to a deep sadness that I carried with me during the run-up to the wedding: a sadness that a family that had started life together were now so far apart. I was struggling to reconcile myself to the price I was having to pay for falling in love with an 'unsuitable' woman.

I spent the day before the wedding leafing through old family photographs. I stared hard at the faces and wondered how the ties that had bound us together had unravelled. The phone vibrated. It was a text from my younger sister.

20 August 2010
It began with the usual – her explaining how tricky it was for her and Mum's anger at what I am doing. But then it changed and she began to talk about how she wanted to come to the wedding. I asked her why. She then told me that she had been really upset on the train to work. She had been listening to Tunnel of Love[9] and she had burst into tears. She started talking about how there was a time when we had been inseparable and how it was strange for her that she would not be there. It was very moving and I

felt it could not be easy for her to say what she did. I had
had a really bad nightmare and I told her about the dream
but as I spoke I just broke down. It was totally unexpected
and I had to put the phone down to gather my composure.
We kept talking and it became clear that she really wanted
to come. She also said that she would try to talk to the rest
of the family.

I put the phone down and began weeping. I woke on the
morning of my wedding still not knowing whether my family
would be there. My speech was still unwritten, as that would
be influenced by who was in the audience. My sister rang.
There had been a two-hour family conference the previous
night. It had been decided that both my brother and older
sister, and their respective families, would not be attending
– but she was coming.

I was standing outside Islington town hall, where the
civil ceremony would take place, when a taxi pulled up and
from it emerged my sister, but she was not alone. She had
brought my mother. Inside the domed central room of the
hall, I stood waiting for my bride. Jackie DeShannon's 'When
You Walk in the Room' struck up, and slowly Bridget walked
in dressed in an antique gold lace dress that made her look
like a fairy-tale princess. The registrar spoke words I had
written, Bridget and I made our vows and slid rings on to
each other's fingers and, to a soundtrack of The Beatles' 'All
You Need is Love', we signed the papers that made us man
and wife. At the evening reception in the Garden Museum,

the hall thrummed with warmth and affection. Fairy lights twinkled on the trees in the garden. Flowers arranged by Bridget's mother adorned the banqueting tables and, to my right, my mother tucked into the egg curry and chicken jalfrezi. Friends and Bridget's relatives flocked to tell Rasool Bibi Manzoor how happy they were to see her. My mother had said she and my sister would be leaving at the end of the meal. In fact, they were there to hear the speeches, so I could thank them publicly for turning up. They stayed until 1 a.m.: my sister danced to Lady Gaga, my mother talked in broken English to Bridget's parents, and in basic Urdu to Bridget. At times during the evening, I would stop and look on in wonder. It did not seem real: my White Scottish wife, my Pakistani Muslim mother, and me.

20 August 2010
I can't quite believe it. I can't quite believe I found the courage to do it. I can't quite believe that I am as sure of what I am doing as I am. So Bridget will be the new Mrs Manzoor. How fucking mental is that? It would be lovely to have my family's approval for what I am doing but it doesn't stop me feeling I am the luckiest person in the world.

Alongside my older brother and sister and their spouses and children, there was one other family member who was not at my wedding – my father. In the days leading up to my wedding, I felt enormously conflicted about the fact that my father had not lived to meet Bridget. There was one part of me that dearly wished, and still wishes, that he had met my wife. The fact that my children never got to know their grandfather is a source of deep, profound sadness. And yet when I try to relive those early days of my relationship with Bridget, there is no scenario in which I can imagine my father would have been supportive of our relationship. It seems much more likely that he would have viscerally opposed it, which would have made life even more challenging. I still believe I would have married Bridget, but I suspect the fact that I only had to battle one parent made things marginally easier, although that was not how it felt at the time.

The odds were stacked against our relationship, but Bridget and I have made it work and I increasingly believe that mixed-faith marriages like ours can offer some clues as to how to build bridges across divided communities. The first lesson is about the importance of faith – not the faiths we were raised in but our faith in each other. Despite the criticisms and the challenges, Bridget and I never lost faith that what we had was worth fighting for – we shared a sense of purpose. This is akin to different communities having a shared faith in their citizenship and a shared sense of belonging. Bridget and I were both willing to compromise. I do not drink but I don't insist that Bridget give up alcohol and we have plenty of wine in our home. I only eat meat that is halal and don't expect Bridget to do the same, but she voluntarily gave up bacon because she appreciated that to cook meat from a pig in our home would make me uncomfortable. Alongside the willingness to compromise,

Bridget and I also have things that we are not prepared to sacrifice. We call them our red lines. Bridget would not want our children to attend a Muslim faith school and she wanted our family to fully embrace Easter and Christmas. That has meant me accepting things like Christmas trees in our home, which I never had growing up.* The sight of a Christmas tree in the living room triggers mixed emotions. It reminds me of my otherness: no matter how many baubles I put on it, I cannot claim a Christmas tree as part of my culture, heritage or tradition, but this feels like a minor compromise to make for a happy marriage.

When I was young, my father would tell me that White people would never accept me. I knew he was wrong because my friends at school, who were all White, did accept me. The human story of friendship contradicted the story my father told me. Today we are told that Muslims and non-Muslims can't get along, but the story of couples like Bridget and me contradict this narrative. It makes both of us ambassadors for love and tolerance. Bridget's parents live in a small village near Dumfries. Bridget never had a Muslim boyfriend before me. Her parents are by nature open-minded and tolerant, so it would not be true to suggest that spending time with me removed lingering prejudices, but they have got a more authentic insight into what it is like to come from my background.

---

* Christmas trees are a far more common sight in British Muslim homes these days than during my childhood.

In listing the benefits to a mixed-faith marriage I am aware that this might simply be self-justification – me trying to suggest that I acted out of some noble desire to foster greater harmony between communities when I don't recall that being a huge motivating factor at the time. There are benefits to marrying outside of one's faith and community but there are also costs. It can feel lonely being the only Muslim in the family. There are certain rituals I recall from my childhood – going to mosque with my father on Eid is one – which I doubt I will do with my own children. I am saddened that my children cannot speak Urdu and so cannot converse with my mother. I suspect that, if I had married a Pakistani Muslim, there is a greater chance that any children we had would be more familiar with my mother tongue. It can frustrate my wife sometimes when she has to drink alone because I am teetotal. And so on. The reason I did not end up marrying a fellow Pakistani Muslim was in part simply because I never met the right person. The world in which I lived was very White, and the world in which my family lived was very small. I remember once going online and looking up female Pakistani journalists – perhaps there was someone in Lahore or Karachi who was also over-sharing in national newspapers and opining about culture on television. This was probably some time in my early thirties when the pressure from my family was particularly extreme. I went to a speed-dating event but I appear to have erased the precise details from my memory. I tried to find someone who ticked both my family's and my boxes – but I never did.

This was a common dilemma for young Muslims of my age. In the late nineties, Adeen Younis was studying at Leeds University. 'A lot of my university peers were looking for marriage and I was looking for marriage,' he recalls. 'There were a lot of forced marriages – kind of culturally arranged forced marriages that were happening. My first cousins were going on holiday to Pakistan and coming back married and very unhappy – it was just a mess. It was absolute anarchy.' Adeen felt there was a gap in the market to help young Muslims find a partner so set up a website called SingleMuslim.com. He started printing cards with the website address and distributing them anywhere large groups of Muslims were likely to be gathering. He remembers attending many anti-war marches, handing out slips of paper while chanting 'Make Love Not War'. The website attracted controversy from some hardline Muslims who believed it was un-Islamic. 'We got white powder that we feared was anthrax in the post,' he says. 'You'd open the post and find hate mail and white powder.' But the site proved hugely popular among single Muslims. It now has over three million members worldwide with around 250,000 British Muslims currently active. More than half of the Muslims in the UK who are of marriageable age have registered at some point.

When I met Bridget in 2008, online dating was still in its infancy. I am not sure I had even heard of SingleMuslim.com or whether I would have felt comfortable using it. My suspicion is that I would have felt I was not Muslim enough for such a site. In the years since, the landscape has transformed and SingleMuslim.com is now only one of a number of websites and apps catering to unmarried Muslims. 'Young people want to be more empowered, and they want to find their own partner on their own terms,' says Shahzad Younas, founder of the muzmatch dating app, which claims to be responsible for 100,000 weddings in Britain. 'The tricky part for them is how they can do that in a way that is still respectful to their parents and their faith.'

Muslim parents are increasingly accepting that the traditional arranged marriage method of finding partners is outdated. 'I would not personally recommend arranged marriages,' says Aziz in Blackburn. 'I'm not saying they don't work but I would wish my children to spend the rest of their lives with someone they have chosen.' The rise of online dating is a reflection not only of younger Muslims wishing to have greater control but also the weakening of family networks. 'Families aren't as connected as they were,' says Shahzad, 'and they're nowhere near as comfortable talking about this stuff as they were. Muslims don't drink so online seems the most obvious way to meet other Muslims.'*

Mustafa and Haroon both grew up in High Wycombe. They are British Pakistanis in their thirties; Mustafa's parents are first cousins and the same is the case for Haroon. They are more than ten years younger than me and this is evident when I ask them what they assumed about marriage growing

---

* Shahzad recently got engaged and, when I asked how he met his partner, he told me it was through mutual friends.

up. 'The capacity and the option to choose was there,' Mustafa says. 'The idea that I was taking ownership over my own life was there. I think there was an understanding that after all the things my parents had done – sending me to a good school, letting me go to university and get a career – how could they sit me down and say, "I've brought you this girl" with pigtails and some badass glasses like in the film *East in East*?' Haroon agrees: 'My dad's approach was pretty much: leave the kids to it; they can figure it out by themselves.'

Haroon was in his mid-twenties when he started feeling he ought to settle down. As part of his attempt to figure things out on his own, he spent six months attending Muslim speed-dating events without success. Why, I asked him, was it so important to marry someone who was Muslim? 'Because a lot of the things that are part of my day-to-day life are centred around the practices and the culture of Islam,' Haroon replies. 'If I married someone who didn't understand those things, it would create a cultural barrier between me and my partner and that would never really work. And, at the same time ... it was important that that person was also Pakistani, just to be culturally close to my parents and have the same background.' Haroon tells me the reason he could not imagine being with a non-Muslim was 'that there are almost dogmatic things that you do as a Muslim that you don't do in other faiths: halal and haram;*

---

* Halal means permissible or lawful in Islam. Haram means forbidden by Islamic law.

understanding fasting; understanding that Friday is a holy day above everything else. These little things shouldn't really matter but if you're with someone who doesn't do these things, it will begin to matter.' I have not yet mentioned what Haroon does: he works for a betting company. What does Islam say about gambling? I asked. 'It's a vice, obviously haram, and I understand that,' he says. 'It's tricky for me actually, because it's given me a very well-paid position, which has afforded me and my family a very nice lifestyle. And that's something I feel I haven't really come to terms with. I do feel a bit like a hypocrite.'

Mustafa was also looking for a Muslim bride. 'It was always my intention when I got married for my children to be raised as Muslims,' he says. 'The ability to cement that part of their identity in a clear way, and in an indisputable way, the ability to do that would have been challenged if each of us were of different faiths or if I believed that the faith of our children was less important to either of us.' Haroon and Mustafa both signed up with SingleMuslim.com. 'I wanted someone who was Muslim but hadn't been raised in this patriarchal household where women were subservient to male rule,' Haroon says. 'That's not how I saw my ideal partner. I wanted someone who was observant and culturally aware, but also someone who was outgoing and confident.' Haroon met one woman through the site and they exchanged a few messages and a phone call before meeting for coffee in August 2010. 'At first we were just trying to get to know each other,' Haroon says, 'but from the second and third meetings it was really quite serious. We were discussing where we might live if we got married and how many children we would have. Those are the conversations often left to two or three years in, but we were having those conversations quite early on.' Haroon and Nazia were married the following summer – they now have two children.

Mustafa also contacted a woman called Sadia on the website and exchanged messages and phone calls before meeting for a date, but they were joined by the woman's father. 'It was a chaperone date with my dad,' recalls Sadia, 'which was the most awkward experience of all of our lives.' Despite the awkwardness, the couple hit it off and they too would get married. What I found striking when talking to both Haroon and Mustafa was that their lives were a blend of what you might call modern and traditional. They led very integrated lives – living in overwhelmingly White neighbourhoods rather than segregated communities like those visited in the previous chapter – but they held on to certain religious values, which meant it was important to them that they found Muslim spouses. That desire for a partner who shares their faith and culture could be seen as a nod to tradition but the way they found their wives is deeply modern. 'It's almost universal now,' Haroon told me, referring to the popularity of matrimonial sites. 'All of the Muslim friends I have tend to do it this way. I have a younger sibling and she also met her husband through SingleMuslim.com. My wife has two brothers. One of them also found his partner through SingleMuslim.com.'

The world Haroon and Mustafa grew up in and their resulting worldviews feel very different to mine. I assumed I would have an arranged marriage and they assumed they would not. 'There was such family pressure to keep couples together,' recalls Haroon of his parents' generation. 'They only stayed together because there was so much family pressure for them not to break up. These days, disappointing your parents is a secondary consideration to personal happiness. Your primary motivation back then wasn't to make yourself happy. It was to be a good son or daughter, be a good Muslim and your own happiness and everything else was secondary.'

Younger Muslims are more likely to have the chance to find their own partners, but just because they are in the driving seat does not mean that all destinations are equally welcomed. For my generation, marrying a non-Muslim was just about the worst thing you could do to a parent. It was unthinkable for most. 'It just wasn't going to happen,' Nazir says. 'You would somehow lose your family, or your family would want to express their displeasure in some way, and do you want to lose your family? That was the choice.' In Blackburn, Aziz was even more blunt. 'Marrying a non-Muslim?' he says. 'I am not doing that because would you get out of the house alive?'

Aziz's good friend Yaseen married his first cousin in 2000 and they have two children. 'I have told them I don't care who you marry – black, brown or yellow – so long as you're happy,' he says. Then adds, 'and so long as they're

Muslim.' Why is it so important that they are Muslim, I asked. 'Islam means everything to me,' he says, 'and I would not want them to walk away from their religion.'

In Bradford I met a man who told me that his children could marry anyone they wanted. So, no restrictions at all? 'I would forbid them marrying a Hindu,' he clarified, 'because now we are crossing a red line – and that's not because I dislike Hindus as human beings.' While I was processing what he had just said, he added, 'and the same goes for Sikhs.' It was not particularly surprising to me to hear these attitudes from parents, but I was more surprised to learn from the founders of SingleMuslim.com and muzmatch that those attitudes have not hugely changed among younger Muslims. 'Young people are less fussed about finding someone else along ethnic lines,' Shahzad from muzmatch told me. 'Pakistanis are happy to marry an Indian, whereas ten years ago it would have to be Pakistani and have to be from a particular village or Punjabi at the very least. But they still have to be Muslim.' 'It's the only thing that matters,' adds Adeem from SingleMuslim.com. 'People want to settle down with someone of the same faith. I think race, origin and background matter less, but faith matters a lot. In every community you lose some and win some, but on the whole Muslims want to marry other Muslims.'

While I am focusing on the British Muslim experience, it is important to note that interfaith marriages are not only an issue for Muslims. I am reminded of Rudi, a rabbi I met in Bradford. 'I know orthodox families where children have married out of the faith and those children have been expelled from the family,' he told me. 'Sometimes in a most grotesque way.' Rudi has four children and they all married outside the Jewish faith. 'It is disappointing,' he admitted. 'I'm sorry about it but there is nothing I can do.' I asked him whether his grandchildren were being raised as Jewish. 'They are nothing,' he told me sadly.

In 2016, fifty-five people were arrested after entering a Sikh temple in Leamington Spa, protesting against a marriage between a Sikh and a non-Sikh. The group issued a statement saying the protest was in objection to an interfaith marriage that was to be carried out as a Sikh wedding at Leamington Gurdwara.[10] One year earlier, a London wedding between a British Sikh bride and Polish Christian groom was interrupted when twenty men stormed in and demanded that the priests end the ceremony. The following weekend, an interfaith wedding in Birmingham nearly turned into a brawl after protesters tried to stop it, and a week later a Coventry wedding only managed to go ahead after negotiations with the disrupters. In each case, the match was between a Sikh and a non-Sikh.[11] These stories were reported in the press at the time but, as the journalist and commentator Sunny Hundal has noted, 'Sikh radicalism is rarely debated in the media. British Sikhs – who number about 400,000 – are largely seen as a model minority who aren't embroiled in controversies or plagued by extremists as Muslims are.'[12] Interfaith marriages are a source of controversy for many faiths, but the accusation of intolerance tends to cling only to Islam.

When I wrote about my wedding for the *Guardian*[13] I was inundated with emails from readers sharing their stories. The most common sentiment was that of regret from readers, saying they wish they had had the strength to fight for their relationship. One Muslim man told me about a White girl he had been in a relationship with. His parents found out, insisted that he break it off and marry someone more 'appropriate'. He had done so but was deeply miserable. The saddest part of the email was when he said that once a year on the anniversary of when he first met her, he would stand outside her home and wonder how different his life might have been had he had the courage to follow his heart. Sadly, I have continued to receive messages on social media and emails from young Muslims in secret relationships pleading for advice.

Ajaz contacted me via social media for advice and I ended up talking to him and his girlfriend. He is twenty-two and has, to my ears, the sort of posh accent that betrays his expensive public school education. He met Mary at university in Edinburgh. His parents are Pakistani Muslims and even though I am more than twice his age, Ajaz told me that reading about my relationship with Bridget reminded him of what he was going through. 'The similarities are that you were also nervous about introducing your girlfriend to your family,' he says. 'You knew that due to her background, the colour of her skin and everything, she was not going to be automatically accepted.' Ajaz tried to hide his relationship from his parents, 'It was clear from the beginning that the goal was to not allow his parents to know I existed,' Mary tells me. When he did eventually break the news to his parents, the reaction was entirely predictable. 'There was a solid month of not talking to me,' says Ajaz. 'There were a lot of tears and complete and utter non-acceptance. They asked me how I could have done this to the family and that I am tearing it apart. I am not saying they will disown me, but they have threatened it.' I was not surprised by this reaction – it sounded very similar to what I faced from my own family.

I noted earlier how Islam permits Muslim men to marry non-Muslim women, so what is Ajaz's family's problem? Is it simply racism against White people? 'It is not *intended* racism,' says Ajaz. 'I feel they wouldn't openly be racist, but it's more ingrained in their mentality.' What are they so scared of, I ask. 'They have said that I would dilute your bloodline,' replies Mary. 'They believe whatever offspring are going to be created from the two cultures merging are not acceptable,' says Ajaz. 'They say if I have a kid he is not going to want to go to the mosque.' Ajaz is still dating Mary and visiting his family, but his parents completely ignore the fact that he is in a relationship, presumably hoping that their son will see sense one day soon. It was so sad to talk to Ajaz and Mary; they seemed like two perfectly nice young people who were being punished simply for having fallen in love. The only advice I could give them was to accept that sometimes in life the things one most wants come at a price, and the question is whether one is prepared to pay it.

A wedding day should be one of the happiest days of one's life, but in my case it was bittersweet. I was sad that my father was not alive to see me married, and deeply disappointed that my brother and sister did not feel they could attend. However, when I start feeling sad, I am always lifted when I recall my mother's journey. A woman born fourteen years before Partition, who can barely speak English, who has not had any meaningful friendships with anyone White in her eight decades on this planet and who must have always imagined that her son would marry a good Pakistani woman who she could welcome as a new daughter. Her ideas about White people were entirely abstract. I have no doubt that, by marrying Bridget, I disappointed my mother, but her love overcame her doubts and fears, which is why she came to see me become the first person in her family to marry someone who is not a Pakistani Muslim. I cannot comprehend her journey from a tiny village outside Lahore to a wedding reception in London, but I know that there are few people whom I admire more or who better embody the possibility of change than Rasool Bibi Manzoor. My mother, who once refused to even meet Bridget, now embraces her whenever we visit Luton. Where before she saw Bridget as an unwanted threat to the family, now she's a daughter-in-law; where once she saw someone unacceptably different, now she sees another mother – the second Mrs Manzoor. If hope has a face, it is the face of my mother.

I am a fan of Hollywood romantic comedies and there was a part of me that was still hoping that, just as Bridget and I were about to say our vows, my entire family would rush in and take their seats. The fact they did not still hurts. The sadness and, yes, the anger were like a black sun I dared not stare at directly for fear of the damage that might be done. If I try to confront it up close, if I try to face what it truly means, it is overwhelming. I tried, instead, to deny their absence mattered. In time I have come to understand that this was just a form of trying to block out the pain. I tell myself there is no point in being angry and I try instead to focus on remembering that people generally think they are doing the right thing. I also take solace in the fact that relations have improved immeasurably since those dark days. The fact that some of my siblings did not attend my wedding was not because they actively wanted to hurt me but because they disagreed with what I was doing. I try to have empathy for my brother and sister even if I disagree with them. I have tried to put myself in their shoes – to try to understand what led them to make the choice they did. The answer always returns to fear – of the other and of a loss of cultural identity. It must be unsettling to find that *they* are now part of your family.

It is encouraging to me that today's Muslim parents are not binding their children as tightly to the old expectations around arranged marriage as in the past. This acceptance may be about a grudging rather than full-throated acceptance that times have changed – they fear that if they ask too much of their children they will lose them. Young Muslims now have more freedom and more opportunities to find their own partners than my generation, but these freedoms are not equally distributed. Muslim women, as we will see in the following chapter, have not always enjoyed the liberties and opportunities in choosing their partners as Muslim men. For most Muslim parents, the prospect of their child, son or daughter, marrying a non-Muslim remains deeply challenging. I asked Ajaz what he believed needed to change. 'Acceptance – accept that you've moved here for a better life,' he says. 'You can't expect someone who has been born and brought up in the UK to act like they were brought up in Pakistan. The mentality needs to change that people not brought up in this culture are bad people or won't be able to sustain a life with someone from our culture.' That such truths even need to be stated feels to me like a damning indictment of how stuck many British Muslims are in the prejudices of the past. 'For most families their children marrying a non-Muslim is still a big deal,' Haroon says. 'The sense of community shame overrides everything. I don't know anyone who hasn't gone down that route and hasn't paid a price.'

I paid a price. Things changed permanently with my family following my marriage – most dramatically with my older sister, with whom I have barely exchanged two sentences in the ten years since. My children would not recognise her or their four cousins were they to pass them on the street. My daughter Laila refers to my older sister as her 'mysterious auntie' because she has never met her, and has asked more than once: 'Why does my auntie hate me?'

I tell Laila her auntie doesn't hate her, but that she doesn't agree with my marrying Bridget.

31 December 2020 (from Laila's diary, aged nine)
I was thinking about family. There are gaps in my family tree and there are gaps in my head. I know virtually nothing about my grandfather, nothing about my aunt and four cousins. My auntie was cross because Daddy married Mummy. She wanted him to marry someone Muslim. Why? Why does skin colour matter? I watched Daddy's film* and more than ever the gaps in my family tree matter.

When Laila read that diary entry to me, I was reminded of a line I had written months earlier in the prologue to this book: 'It is not easy to feel rooted when one is drowning in a sea of unknowns.' The road was not easy, but in the end I did get to where I wanted to go, and it was a destination that had felt unreachable for most of my life. My hope is that young Muslims growing up today and in the future will no longer feel that in wishing to marry the person they love they are betraying their faith and their family.

---

* My wife and I had not allowed her to watch the film because we were nervous about her reaction to the racism but we relented and let her watch it as a Christmas Day 2020 treat.

THREE

THEY . . . DON'T TREAT MEN AND WOMEN AS EQUALS

'If you tell me that the burka is oppressive, then I am with you . . . it is absolutely ridiculous that people should choose to go around looking like letter boxes.'
Boris Johnson, *Daily Telegraph*, 5 August 2018

'Muslim girls regarded lying to parents as a normal survival technique.'
R. Sharif, *Interviews with Young Muslim Women of Pakistani Origin*[1]

In early 2011, Bridget and I had been married for six months, she was two months pregnant and the English Defence League (EDL) were marching through the streets of Luton. It is estimated that 3,000 supporters of the far-right anti-Muslim group, founded in Luton by Stephen Yaxley Lennon, aka Tommy Robinson, marched along the streets of my hometown. The *Guardian* reported that 'more than 2,000 police officers from forces across the south of England escorted the EDL march from the station into the centre of Luton. Fireworks and bottles were thrown, shops and businesses in the town were closed and petrol stations had been boarded up in what one resident compared to a "war zone".'[2]

When I was young, my parents would warn me to not go into town on Saturday afternoons when Luton Town were playing at home. The football fans would chant as they swaggered and staggered through Bury Park, smashing windows and chanting racist insults at the shopkeepers. The news of the EDL march brought back those memories. I had intended to visit my family in Luton but the prospect of having to fight my way past the demonstrators was not appealing. I wondered how the EDL supporters would have reacted were I to be coming to Luton with Bridget. The EDL march took place on 5 February, which, by some curious coincidence, meant that on the same day that Tommy Robinson launched what newspapers described as 'a broad attack on Islam and the UK's Muslim communities', the Prime Minister gave a speech in Munich. In his speech David Cameron said that 'under the doctrine of state multiculturalism, we have encouraged different cultures to live separate lives, apart from each other and apart from the mainstream. We've failed to provide a vision of society to which they feel they want to belong. We've even tolerated these segregated communities behaving in ways that run completely counter to our values. The failure, for instance, of some to confront the horrors of forced marriage, the practice where some young girls are bullied and sometimes taken abroad to marry someone when they don't want to, is a case in point.'[3] The status of Muslim women was a subject Cameron returned to in 2016, when he called for an end to the 'passive tolerance' of separate communities, which left many Muslim women facing discrimination and social isolation and declared he would not avoid telling the 'hard truths' required to confront the minority of Muslim men whose 'backward attitudes' led them to exert 'damaging control' over the women in their families.[4]

When I read his comments, my initial instinct was to recoil from what felt like bullying and blaming some of the most vulnerable members of society at a time when the far right were stoking up hatred. It felt cynical and dangerous, but the awkward truth was that his words hit home because they reminded me of my experiences growing up. I was raised in a household where my mother occupied a role that was deferential to my father. It was also a household where the opportunities my older brother and I were given were significantly greater than those granted to my sisters for no reason other than gender. I want to confront some of these 'hard truths' – to ask how much Islam should be held responsible for the 'backward attitudes' that some claim have held Muslims back. I want to explore how much progress has been made and what work remains. In *Greetings from Bury Park*, I wrote that 'I owe my life to two strokes of incredible luck: I was not born female and I was not the oldest son.' I was acknowledging my privileges then and it feels important to acknowledge them again now. I cannot know how it felt or feels to be a Muslim woman and I certainly cannot speak for Muslim women, but I can listen and share their stories.

My father was the decision-maker in the family; he dealt with the outside world while my mother's domain was entirely domestic. The power dynamic remained imbalanced even after my father was made redundant. He would leave the house in the morning in his suit and spend the day out – at the job centre, in the library, meeting friends for whom he would do unpaid work helping with paperwork on mortgages or visa applications. It was my mother and my older sister who would be working on the sewing machine earning money. The women in the house were the breadwinners but it was my father who wielded the power. It was just the way it was. Whenever anyone visited our home – and the only people who visited were other Pakistanis – the men would sit together at one end of the living room and the women would meet at the other end. My sisters were expected to fetch water or make tea, but my brother and I were not. The underlying assumption was that to be a girl meant one was fated to follow a different path – one defined by deference and domesticity. I benefitted from this and, growing up, I spent very little time reflecting on the undeserved privileges I enjoyed simply by an accident of birth. My father never explained his decisions explicitly but I don't think he was exceptionally backward or especially intent on holding my mother back; he was a man of his time and place.

At the same time my mother arrived in Luton in the early seventies, Mohammad Anwar was researching the Pakistani community in Rochdale. 'The majority of Muslims do not allow their wives and daughters to work or have contact with the outside world,' he found. 'They do not normally go out of the house without their husbands unless it is absolutely essential. In some cases, they do not leave their house at all except in the company of their husbands. My respondents felt that according to their religion women's place was in the home. Women also find it difficult to participate in literacy and language courses, because they are not allowed to leave their homes and to participate in any kind of social life ... The men feared that these English ladies might teach their women about liberty and other permissive ideas in Western society which could threaten men's authority over women.'[5] The notion of men fearing what freedom for women might do to their authority over them is a theme in this story.

Prior to 1962, migrants from the Indian subcontinent were overwhelmingly male. The 1961 census revealed that in Bradford, for example, there were only eighty-one Asian women compared to 3,376 men, mostly young and unmarried. 'However, as immigration controls put a brake on primary migration of men from 1962 onwards,' Humayun Ansari writes in *The Infidel Within*, 'migration was no longer seen as temporary. Much bigger numbers of fiancées, wives and daughters arrived as the process of family reunion accelerated.'[6] Between 1962 and 1967, 13,600 women and 29,800 children arrived into Britain from Pakistan alone.

In February 1965, the United States deployed combat troops to South Vietnam, Malcolm X was assassinated and The Righteous Brothers were topping the charts with 'You've Lost That Loving Feeling'. Shugra was living in a village near Rawalpindi in Pakistan when she learnt that a friend of a relative of her father was visiting from England. 'My mum cooked food and she asked me to come into the room and put chapattis on the table, and that was when he saw me,' she recalls. 'He saw me and said: "I like this girl and I want to marry her."' The man was Nasir Hussein, he was twenty-three and Shugra was not yet sixteen. Having selected Shugra, a wedding date was swiftly set. 'I was so little, just a little kid and I was really scared about the wedding,' she says. 'I remember crying, saying I wanted to stay with my mummy.' Within a month Shugra was pregnant. She left her village, flew to Britain and moved into a seven-bedroom house in Slough. She was the only young girl in a house occupied by Pakistani men. 'For many Muslim women, coming to Britain was the first encounter with urban life and with another culture,' writes Ansari. 'The instability and insecurity of a new physical and social environment, combined with the vastly different climate and living conditions ... and lack of social and linguistic skills restricted interaction with the wider society and so increased their isolation.'[7] Nasir would depart in the morning for work, leaving his pregnant teenage wife at home all day. 'I had no friends, no family and could not speak English,' Shugra says. 'I would just sit by the window all day just staring outside.' There was a small black-and-white television in her room, which she would turn off whenever she changed clothes because 'I thought the people on the screen could see me,' she explains.

Four years after Shugra arrived, Rabia landed in Britain. She was sixteen and accompanying her thirty-year-old husband Khalil. The couple had married in July 1969 and three months later they were sharing a rented room in a large house in Willesden Green in London. Rabia had been in her first year of college in Pakistan when she had learnt she was getting married. 'My first reaction was sadness,' she tells me. 'I loved to study, and I was angry because I really wanted to complete my studies. I kept thinking why me?' She had never been on a train or a plane and so London was overwhelming. Rabia had married Khalil in the same month that Neil Armstrong had walked on the surface of the moon. Coming to Britain made Rabia feel that she had stepped on to another planet. 'It was a different world to anything I knew,' she recalls, 'I was in a state of shock – who are all these people wearing these strange clothes and why is it so cold?' Khalil would go to work early in the morning and Rabia would stay in her room. 'I would be in that room all day listening to pop music on Radio 1,' she says. Among the songs in the charts that month were 'Bad Moon Rising' from Credence Clearwater Revival, and 'In the Ghetto' by Elvis Presley. 'I was so angry, and I would plead with him to let me go to college, but he would say, "What will people say if they saw that after getting married I was enrolling you into college?" He said that rather than going to college I should go to the library and read books and write stories, so I would pass the time writing fictional short stories inspired by my reality.'

In the summer of 1971, Rabia gave birth to a baby boy and at the end of the year the family moved to Bury Park. Khalil got a job on the Vauxhall production line, where he became friends with my father, and Rabia and my mother also became close friends. Rabia's son and I became best friends in infant school, and remain friends to this day. When Rabia would talk to other Pakistani mothers at the school gate, they would complain that their husbands did not let them go out or give them any money. 'I didn't want anyone to control me,' says Rabia. 'I don't want anyone to rule me or tell me I have to do this. I was raised to believe that women had a voice, and they should be respected – the idea that women were obedient and docile – that was not my life.' But when she pushed her husband to allow her to go to college, he would dismiss it with a laugh. 'He would say you are already too clever,' she says. 'He would say, "If you go to college, you will not want to look after our kids or care about me or the kids." He was a little scared.'

'He was a little scared' – there's that fear again. What was the fear? I suspect it was a fear that his dominance would be threatened, that his authority would be challenged. I think back to my own father and wonder whether if perhaps the reason he did not encourage my mother to learn English or to leave the house was that he feared that it would arm her to one day demand greater freedom and independence.

There is no doubt that women like Shugra, Rabia and my mother did not enjoy the same life chances as their husbands, but how much is Islam responsible for holding them back? The women themselves deny its impact. 'Islam gives you more rights than any other religion,' responded Rabia. The men too are unlikely to have cited religion as an explanation for their behaviour – not that anyone ever asked. I don't recall my father ever discussing religion apart from in general terms when he was reminding me that we were Muslims and even then he was more likely to refer to us as Pakistani than Muslim. It was Pakistan, and the culture in which men like him had been raised, which they imported to Britain. 'The vast majority of Muslim migrants in Britain,' notes Ansari, 'especially the first generation, still held the orthodox view that there are fundamental differences between males and females, with deep implications for their attitudes and functions. Muslim male-dominated communities in Britain have sought to apply their interpretations of Islamic texts to perpetrate asymmetrical gender roles.'[8] This asymmetry affected how the men treated not only their wives but also their children.

The suggestion that women should have the same opportunities as men was utterly alien not only to my father but also to my mother. When my parents had children – two boys and two girls – those ideas affected how they raised us. This was especially true when it came to education and work. It was assumed that I would go to university but that was not expected of my sisters. It is probably too simplistic to draw a direct line between the fact that my mother ended her schooling when she was thirteen and the lack of interest she had in my sisters' education. I suspect that my mother was raised to believe certain things about men and women and their respective roles, and these attitudes, formed in childhood, were never challenged by anyone she met because she only met fellow Pakistanis. It was these attitudes, shared by her husband, which meant that, for example, I was not expected to learn how to cook, unlike my sisters, and my education was prioritised while theirs was not. I did not get a free pass from doing any chores – there were many evenings of washing dishes, vacuuming the house and so on – but I still remember a subtle but unmistakable sense that my sisters were expected to have a mastery of domestic affairs in a way that I was not. The opportunities that I was given were not fully deserved or earned and were I to have been born female with the same set of talents and abilities, there is no reason to believe my life would have progressed as it has. At the very least, I would have had to fight much harder for the same opportunities and they would have come at a cost.

The stories of Shugra, Rabia and my mother arguably confirm stereotypes many non-Muslims have about Muslim women, so it is important to remember that the experiences of Muslim women and girls varied. Ghulam Maniyar was one of the cohort of men who arrived in the early sixties. He arrived in London from Bombay on 27 June 1962 with a piece of paper that had the address of an uncle in Dewsbury. He would eventually marry and have five daughters and two sons.

'He was quite traditional in the upbringing of my older two sisters,' says his younger daughter Fazila. 'There were more parameters and limitations set, but by the time he got to his third daughter he relaxed a lot more and embraced everything around him.' When I talked to Ghulam, he told me: 'I loved my daughters and treated them equal. There are some families where they think boys are more important than girls but as far as I am concerned they were all my children.'

Contrast that with the experience of Zoora Shah, who arrived from Pakistan and settled in Bradford, not far from Ghulam. She married her first cousin in a typical arranged marriage. Zoora faced violence and abuse throughout her marriage and was forced to undergo several abortions to avoid giving birth to girls. When she gave birth to another daughter – Nasreen – Zoora's husband was so disappointed he refused to physically hold or touch his daughter for the first eleven months of her life. When she had managed to produce only one son, her husband threw Zoora and their three children out on to the streets. 'I was a girl, and he wanted a boy,' Nasreen says by way of explanation. 'It was cultural misogyny, and it was really, really nasty.'

The likes of Shugra, Rabia and Zoora had grown up in Pakistan and when they raised their daughters they tried, to varying degrees, to pass their learned values down. But there was a problem – their children were being brought up in Britain and those dangerous ideas of freedom that their fathers feared were maddeningly hard to resist. No longer would daughters automatically embrace with open arms the prospect of forgoing education and marrying while still in their teens.

Shugra and Nasir had four children, including a daughter they named Shaista. Their marriage eventually ended and Shaista and her siblings were raised by Shugra as a single mother. When she was around sixteen, Shaista made a decision. 'I wanted to cut my hair really short,' she says. 'I used to have a long plait and I went to the barbers and told them to chop off the plait. They cut it off and I went home with really short hair and I handed it to my mum. She did not talk to me for a few days.' What did cutting your hair represent to you, I asked. 'I didn't like being controlled by anybody,' Shaista says, 'and my mum saying I shouldn't cut hair made me think that if I wanted to cut my hair I should be able to do it. I felt controlled.'[9] Shaista went on to university, which made her unusual among the young women in her community. 'When I compare myself to my peer group, all of them got married,' recalls Shaista. 'They hit about seventeen and they were married to someone in Pakistan and their husbands were coming over.'

Nusrat was a teenager in Small Heath in Birmingham around the same time as Shaista in Northampton and Nasreen in Bradford. 'I wasn't allowed out of the house alone without a male companion,' she recalls. 'I was allowed to go to college, but my family was upset I was at a mixed gender college. I was told I was ruining it for my parents.' How was going to college ruining things for her parents, I wanted to know. 'My parents were warned giving me this extra freedom meant I would become "Westernised",' she says. 'I was warned I was ruining my parents reputation by not conforming. I think they were afraid; I remember the conversations that elders would come to my father and say, "If she goes, then what are we going to say to our own daughters when they want the same freedom?"'

'I think they were afraid' – that same fear that Rabia described: the male fear of power bleeding away if their wives and daughters gained an education. When I listened to Nusrat talk about her teenage memories, it made me reflect on how when I was growing up it was expected that I would go to university. My parents worried, perhaps rightly, that by sending me to university I would be changed but that never translated into trying to prevent me from going. The contrast between my experience and that of my sisters is brutal and shaming. Neither were encouraged to study and in the same way it was understood I would go to university it was understood they would not. The sad truth is that in the case of my older sister, I don't think she ever truly forgave my father for not giving her the opportunity to study, and I am not sure she ever truly forgave me for being the one who got to do so.

The prevailing attitude to girls' education among my parents' generation was what was the point since their daughters would soon be getting married and no husband wanted a wife who was more educated than him. Nusrat recalls cousins in cars approaching her as she made her way to college. 'I knew if I ever got into that car, my life would be over,' she says. 'They'd just try and threaten you. I wanted more than what was on offer, but it was very hard to have a long-term vision when people threatened to snuff you out the whole time. I suppose it's all about control – if you haven't controlled her by the time she's in her teens, by the time she becomes self-confident and independent, it's really hard. Because the endgame is then you're not going to have an arranged marriage and do what they expect you do to.'

Selina, who we last met grieving over the murder of her brother Ahmed, also grew up believing that her fate was to get married. When she was sixteen she had an arranged marriage – her parents told her that they had found a man who was eighteen years older than her and living in Bangladesh who they wanted her to marry. I asked her how that made her feel. 'Angry actually,' she says. 'I was upset because I was thinking I can't do anything my friends are going to be able to do. They'll be able to do their A levels. They're going to go to university. I won't be able to do this.' In her wedding photograph the newly married couple stare straight into the camera. Her husband is wearing large, horn-rimmed black glasses, has a regulation drooping moustache and his hands resting on his legs. Selina is dripping with jewellery – on her wrists and around her neck – and is staring intently ahead. He looks like a man and she, frankly, looks like a young girl.

Ruby was seventeen and living in Crewe around the same time that Selina was in Manchester. It was the winter of 1988, the same winter when my father had that conversation about the girl in the village he hoped I would marry. 'My life was expected to pan out like my mum's,' Ruby told me. 'A marriage would be set up for me, I would produce a lot of children, and I would be pious, and I would be obedient.' That was the expected future and in 1988 it took on a greater urgency when Ruby learnt that a boy from a village in Pakistan was being lined up to marry her. Her father had already prevented her from studying at sixth-form college because he did not want her to mix with boys. 'I had academic potential, but it was not realised because of him. The only freedom I had was at school, so anything that made me happy was being blocked from my life.' With the clock ticking, Ruby became increasingly desperate. On the morning of 11 February 1989, she woke up and got dressed as if she was about to go to work. Instead, she went to a friend's house where she had stored a large suitcase. She went to the train station, where she was met by a social worker with whom she had been in contact. They took a train to Bristol and she was taken to a women's refuge. Ruby, still only seventeen years old, had run away from home. I think back to when I was seventeen and how restricted I felt my life was, and how anxious that conversation about the girl in the village made me. I thought I had it bad, but compared to someone like Ruby I had it so very easy – and all because I was a boy and she was a girl.

Ruby's parents tried to find her – they hired a private detective who tracked her down and brought her back to Crewe but Ruby ran away again. She changed her name by deed poll and moved from city to city. The years passed but there was no contact with her family. She did not know if her parents were still alive or any news about her sister and two brothers. 'I missed my sister incredibly, there was a gap in my life,' she says. 'The boys had been very young when I left but I had this deep longing for my sister – what was her fate going to be?' Ruby had a Scottish friend who asked her to accompany her to a wedding in Edinburgh. 'I got on a flight and at the wedding Malcolm was the groomsman.' They started seeing each other and they got married in 2000. Ruby and Malcolm went on to have four children. She resigned herself to never hearing from her family again. It was not until a friend mentioned a new website that had started to become popular. The website was called Facebook. 'I was not on it but my friend was,' Ruby says. 'I looked up my sister on my friend's Facebook.' It had been twenty years and her sister had been a young girl the last time she had seen her. She noticed one profile that looked like it could be her sister but so much time had passed it was hard to know if the adult woman in the photograph was the little girl she had last seen all those years ago. She started to read the profile in case there were any clues that might let her know if this woman really was her sister. It was only when she came to the end that she saw these words: 'if you are out there reading this, I want you to know I still think about you every day.' Ruby sent a message to her sister, communication was re-established and eventually she was reunited with her parents.

The details of her story are extraordinary but the broad contours of Ruby's story – a girl forced to run away from home to avoid a forced marriage – were not especially uncommon. Freedom often came at a price. Zena grew up in Preston with her parents, who had an arranged marriage in Pakistan. 'My mum is really religious and controlling and I could not do what I wanted or be who I wanted to be,' Zena says. 'She would say I shouldn't make friends with boys even if it was just a friendship. She would drop me off wherever I went, there were really strict curfews so I could not really go out. I felt suffocated.' The difference in how she was treated compared to her brothers was stark. 'I used to skateboard, and when I wanted to buy a skateboard, my mum said, "No way. What is the Asian community going to say? You're not a boy." But my brother is younger and my dad would let him do anything.' There was a White boy in her politics class at college. 'We were friends for ages and then I said, "I like you." He said, "I like you too, but your parents will never accept me, so I don't know what we can do."' What they did was to start dating in secret. 'I would tell my mum I was going to the cinema with my friends,' Zena says. 'My mum would drop me off and I would meet a female friend, then she would leave, and my boyfriend would come.' They had been dating for almost ten months before her mother learnt the truth. 'She saw a hickey on my neck,' Zena tells me. 'I tried to pretend it was just an innocent mark, but she looked at me as if I had slapped her face and then she ran to her room and started crying and praying.' She confronted Zena and said she no longer considered her as her daughter. When her father learnt the news he said, '"I don't know what makes you think you can have a White boyfriend," and he called me a slut.' Zena was worried for her safety so she told teachers at her college. One rainy morning she left home with three bags of clothes and college books, and after a few weeks with her boyfriend's parents she was taken to a Muslim women's refuge.

There are strong parallels between Ruby and Zena's stories – both were discouraged from studying, both treated differently because they were female, and both ran away to women's refuges when they were just seventeen. But there is one key difference: Ruby ran away from her home in Crewe in February 1989, while Zena ran away from her home in Preston in October 2019. I have to be honest and say, as horrified as I was by Ruby's story, I was not surprised – those sorts of things happened back in the eighties. What did surprise me was talking to Zena and learning that they are still happening.

It is worth stressing, again, that not all Muslim fathers were or are misogynistic tyrants. Take Mohammed Khan, who grew up in Wolverhampton during the eighties. He had a love marriage to a Croatian Muslim woman with whom he had two daughters: Mariam and Saffiyah. He was determined he would treat them no differently than if they had been boys. Mohammed was into sports and outdoor pursuits and shared his enthusiasms with his daughters. 'Saffiyah started martial arts and self-defence when she was two,' he tells me. 'She was taught to rock climb and mountaineer when she was three, and I taught her to shoot a rifle and do all the stuff she'd need to do for survival when she was about seven.' There was no question that his girls would be encouraged to pursue education and follow their dreams wherever they led. 'Undermining and belittling girls and daughters is not an Islamic thing,' he says, 'it's a Pakistani thing. My girls were given to me. Allah could have picked any old spanner on the planet to be their dad, and He picked me.'

Zena and Ruby were not so fortunate. Their lives were unquestionably affected by the fact they were women but how much, I wanted to know, was this about religion? 'They would say we don't trust you because you might be hanging out with boys and that is haram,' says Zena. 'So I always assumed it was religion.' Is she right? The Qur'an does, after all, contain passages that do at first sight seem a touch problematic when it comes to gender:

> Sura 4:12: *Allah commands you concerning your children; a male shall have as much as the share of two females.*
> Sura 4:34: *If you fear highhandedness from your wives, remind them (of the teaching of Allah), then ignore them when you go to bed, then hit them.*
> Sura 4:35: *So virtuous women are obedient, and guard the secrets of their husbands with Allah's protection. And as for those on whose part you fear disobedience, admonish them and keep away from them in their beds and chastise them.*[10]

I have seen these passages and others similar quoted by those who claim they prove that Islam treats women as second-class citizens. It might seem, reading those quotes, that those who argue Islam is sexist have a point, but whenever I cited them to Muslim women, they responded by arguing that the original texts are open to varying interpretations. 'I think there has been sufficient research into unreading patriarchal interpretations to put those comments in a historical context,' says Fauzia Ahmad, an academic at Goldsmiths University who specialises in female Muslim religious identity. 'With each one of those really problematic verses that Islamophobes try to beat us with, you can explain it with more research. There is no need to take them literally just because we haven't thought about it in terms of context and how they were translated.'

This might sound like a rather arcane and academic debate, but it has real-world consequences, as illustrated by a powerful article posted on Amaliah.com – a website aimed at Muslim women. The piece is entitled '12 Things I Can't Reconcile About Islam as a Muslim Woman'.[11] The writer, who rather tellingly did not give her name, lays out a dozen instances where the religion appears to treat women as less than equal to men. These include: why can men marry a non-Muslim woman but a woman cannot do the same? Why can't women divorce their husbands? Why do women only get half the inheritance available to men? Why can't women travel without a male chaperone? And why are the only prophets mentioned men? These are all, it seems to me, entirely legitimate questions to ask and, following publication, a response was posted which tackled each question in turn. To the question of why Muslim women cannot marry non-Muslim men, the response was that that 'there is also often an underlying assumption that there should be absolute equality between men and women in all aspects of life. However, Islam recognises some biological differences between men and women and accommodates for these differences . . . due to the concept of justice being defined by God, the premise of "why can't women do x if men can" does not fit in with the Islamic concepts of men and women to begin with.' The other queries were met with the argument that 'men are charged with being the caretakers, providers and protectors of women, and women are not charged with this particular duty. This being the case, the expectations on women and men must be different.' Anyone feeling uncomfortable with any of this needs to remember, the response continues, that 'ultimately, this law came from the Qur'an and we put our trust in knowing that Allah, in His infinite wisdom, knew what was better for His creation, equal in His eyes.' I find this response less than reassuring – it seems to confirm the very thing it is trying to deny. The notion of 'Allah knows best' is not hugely convincing, because the task of interpreting the Qur'an rests with human beings, who are not famed for their infinite wisdom.

I heard a slightly more nuanced response from Dr Shuruq Naguib, who lectures in Islam and gender at Lancaster University. 'This is one of those controversial topics in contemporary thought because it has become a hostage to the cultural politics of identity,' she says. 'It has become a yardstick issue that they cannot move on. If we change, then we are Westernising and liberalising in a way that undermines religion.* The pre-modern concerns were shaped by pre-modern realities. The contemporary debate is also shaped by modern reality, but they are shaped more by cultural politics than the wellbeing of individual men and women and – in this case – women.' In other words, the more non-Muslims make a big deal about the question of Muslim women marrying non-Muslims, the greater the resistance from some in the Muslim community to budge on the issue.

Selina went through with her arranged marriage and she and her husband are still together. 'My husband was very adaptive and very supportive,' she says. 'In terms of our general outlook we were very similar, so it wasn't a problem.' The couple moved from Manchester to Keighley in Yorkshire and have three daughters. The daughters grew up knowing that while their parents valued education, the fact they were girls constrained their lives. 'We grew up living opposite a playing field and there were always boys playing football there,' says Shabnam, the oldest. 'I can't imagine we could have easily gone across the road and played football. I don't think that ever occurred to us to do because that was the public domain. That was the boys' domain ... we had our garden that we played in.' Sabreen, the middle daughter, remembers: 'We had to go through the twenty questions drill if we wanted to go anywhere: Who's going to be there? How late are you

---

* It is fascinating that Dr Naguib refers to British Muslims both as 'they' and 'we' in this response.

going to be? Who's going to bring you back? All of that. So socially it was a bit of a struggle.'

I heard versions of this story many times, but the reason this one is noteworthy is what happened next. Shabnam had always expected to go to university but her parents made it clear that it would have to be in Leeds so she could live at home. One day at school a teacher asked why she had not attended the meeting for students who were applying to Oxbridge. 'And I said, "Well, I'm not going to go. What's the point?"' recalls Shabnam. 'She was not having any of it obviously and I think she cornered my mum at a parents evening and said, "She has to apply."' The teacher's name was Mrs Todd. 'We were still living in the time of girls don't go away from home,' says Selina. 'If you want to go to university, you apply to those universities and you study from home. There was nobody in our circle who had done anything different. There was nobody that we could say: "They sent their daughter away to university and everything's OK." But then the option of Oxford came up which was like – well, you can't study from home if you want to go to Oxford.' Selina and her husband were faced with a choice: to insist their daughter live at home and commute to a local university or have faith and give Shabnam the opportunity to study at Oxford. They consulted and reached a decision. 'Oxford is one of the best universities in the world,' Selina says. 'How could we deny our child that opportunity?' And so they told Shabnam that if she got the grades she could study at Oxford but if she didn't she would have to stay at home. It was Oxford or nothing. 'I had my predicted grades, so in my head there was no question of me failing or not getting those grades,' says Shabnam. 'I was going to get them. I hadn't thought about what might happen if I didn't get them, I didn't even entertain it.' Her faith was justified. 'It was absolutely amazing,' says Selina, of the day her daughter learnt her grades. 'Nobody we knew had gone to Oxford and suddenly we had a child who was going – the first in all our families and in our community. It was really special.'

And so Shabnam went to study at Oxford, but that left her two sisters. Having allowed the oldest daughter to study away from home it was hard not to give the same opportunity to their other two, and so Selina presented them with the same offer they had given Shabnam. 'We kept it at Oxford because that was the criteria that Shabnam was allowed go on,' says Selina, 'and so we told the others if you go away from home it will be for Oxford and if it isn't Oxford, then you study at home.' And that was how three sisters born to a working-class Bangladeshi mother all ended up studying at Oxford.

I found the story of Selina and her daughters fascinating. It powerfully demonstrates the importance of having a champion and being given support and, critically in my view, it shows the power of the individual to nudge towards change. If Shabnam's teacher had not believed in her and, more importantly, if she had not championed her to Selina, Shabnam would never have thought about going to Oxford. 'She thought that it was something I should do, and I would benefit from,' says Shabnam. That faith and support from

Shabnam's teacher helped give Selina and her husband the courage to change their minds and that, I think, is the second important lesson from their story: that the future is not condemned to look like the past. Things can change, and for the better, if people are given support, encouragement and confidence. That confidence flows from the opportunity to gain an education but also to be financially independent.

One rainy Monday morning in early 2020, I joined a group of Muslim women in a brightly lit meeting room in Whalley Range in Blackburn. The women were taking part in a confidence cafe – a six-week programme set up to try to boost Muslim women's self-esteem and prepare them for the job market. The confidence cafe gained its funding after Blackburn was named as one of five areas selected for special help and resources to improve community relations. The sessions were led by a White British woman called Mandy and conducted in English, which meant that as well as improving their self-esteem, the Asian women were having an opportunity to improve and practice their English. When I attended, the women were being taught the importance of self-care as Mandy listed strategies – going for a walk, making a cup of tea, and more unusually, playing with a Rubik's cube – that might reduce their stress. Mandy then showed them how to make a heart using strips of cardboard – it was a few days before Valentine's Day – and asked them to think about what they most loved about themselves. The exercises seemed quite playful and the atmosphere in the room was genial, but the impact of the sessions has, according to the women I talked to, been dramatic. They said that they were not accustomed to thinking about themselves – their identities were so heavily rooted in the fact they are wives and mothers. This meant that they were wary of speaking up in early sessions, but gradually that changed. 'I never used to be this confident,' one woman told me, 'I need to rein it sometimes.' Another told me that since starting the course she had also become more assertive. 'I have started to put my foot down a bit,' she said, 'and told my husband that I am not standing for this.' I wondered if her husband had noticed any change. She smiled. 'He did say there was something different about me,' she said. 'He said I am bitchier now.' A third woman said her husband told her that she was becoming cleverer, but it was unclear if this was said admiringly or with some concern. The women were clear that the sessions could be useful for more Muslim women. 'I know one woman who really wants to come,' one attendee told me, 'but her husband expects food on the table, and she can't come here and do that.' The juggle of looking after their husbands and children while trying to better themselves was still a challenge. 'I just decided to put myself first a bit more,' one woman told me when I asked why she came to the sessions. 'I have two little children and I wouldn't want my kids to be the same as me.'

The confidence cafe is an example of how Muslim women can be supported to enter or re-enter the job market. The level of employment for British Muslim women is only 28 per cent, significantly lower than the approximately 51 per cent for the overall female population, and also lower than for British Hindus and Sikhs. And this is despite the fact that young Muslim women are gaining more degrees at British universities than Muslim men. A study published in 2016 found that 25 per cent of Muslim women aged 21–24 now have degrees, compared with 22 per cent of Muslim men. This is particularly impressive given that in 1990 and 1991 British Pakistani and Bangladeshi men admitted to higher education outnumbered their female peers by more than two to one and more than three to one respectively. The co-author of the study, Dr Nabil Khattab, suggested that the younger generation of Muslim women in Britain were making a distinct break with the past. 'It is possible that Muslim women who are British-born, unlike their mothers, have undergone a cultural transformation,' he said.[12]

According to research published in 2015, most young British-born Muslims rejected the view that married women should stay at home while their husbands work. The research from the think tank Demos found that more than half of British Muslim 16–24-year-olds disagreed with the statement: 'A husband's job is to earn money, a wife's job is to look after the home and family.' Fewer than 24 per cent agreed. In contrast, 50 per cent of those respondents aged 55 or older agreed with the statement, while less than 17 per cent disagreed.[13] Times, then, are changing, and this is not only indicated by the rising numbers of Muslim women going to university but also in shifting attitudes towards work.

I don't recall seeing any women wearing the face veil when I was growing up in the seventies and eighties. My mother only wore a thin dupatta or shawl over her head and neither of my sisters covered their hair. When younger British Muslim women started wearing the burqa, my reaction was one of puzzlement and frustration: why would someone choose to stand out in such a stark way? What message – if any – were they trying to send? I could only imagine what a native White British person might feel. 'I ask myself how I honestly feel about it and I feel very uncomfortable,' says Dilwar Hussain, chair of New Horizons in British Islam. 'You have the freedom to dress like that if you really want to, but, to quote Spider-Man, "With great freedoms come great responsibilities." All of us have the responsibility in that we have inadvertently become sort of standard-bearers of Islam. If you're that visible, you are constantly signalling a message about Islam as you're walking down the street and you need to ask yourself, what signal are you giving the people that are looking at you.' There is nothing Muslim about the niqab – it is an Arabic style of dress from the eighth century, and so I found it bizarre that young women largely born here whose ancestors came from the Indian subcontinent were trying to dress like Arabic women more than a thousand years ago. 'The idea of the niqab when it emerged in ancient times was anonymity,' says Dilwar Hussain, 'or in some places even class because a niqab was associated with free high-ranking elite women. You take that completely out of its context to modern-day Britain. You're not more anonymous but actually more blatant and obvious in society: you're standing out.'

If you are going to stand out, is it surprising if it provokes mockery and abuse? In a column for the *Daily Telegraph* published in August 2018, Boris Johnson, then a backbench MP, referred to Muslim women who wore the full face veil as 'letterboxes' and compared them to 'bank robbers'. According to Tell Mama, a national project that records and measures anti-Muslim incidents in Britain, there was a 375 per cent increase in anti-Muslim incidents in the week following Johnson's comments.[14] In the three weeks after the article was published, 42 per cent of offline Islamophobic incidents reported 'directly referenced Boris Johnson and/or the language used in his column', the monitoring group said. Online abuse reported also repeated the same words or incorporated them into pictures and memes. My own feelings about Johnson's comments were as conflicted as they had been about David Cameron's speech seven years earlier. I was appalled at Johnson's cynical exploitation of Muslim women as a political strategy. I found the actual comments both offensive and provocative, bordering on dangerous. And yet, the blunt truth was that I too was deeply apprehensive about the niqab. I resented the implication that women who wore the niqab were somehow more Muslim than my mother. It seemed obvious to me that anyone who wore the niqab was making a clear statement that they wanted to be seen as different and to stand out. It was also obvious, to me at least, that the niqab hindered social interaction,

When I read about Islamophobic attacks on Muslim women wearing the niqab, I would feel outrage and sympathy but would also wonder whether it might not be better for everyone if the women weren't wearing the niqab at all. My opinions on the niqab and the women who wore it were strong, but I couldn't recall having a meaningful conversation with a niqab-wearing Muslim woman, ever. None of the Muslim women I knew even wore a headscarf. I wanted to meet women who wore the niqab, but not only did I not know anyone who did so, no one I knew seemed to know anyone either. It was a somewhat bizarre situation to see women wearing the face veil everywhere I travelled researching this book but not be talking to any of them. I continued making enquiries and that was how I came to be sat in a coffee shop in Leicester one Saturday afternoon with four women.

All four women were wearing black full-face veils. I knew better than to shake their hands. This was the first time I had spoken to any women who wore the niqab. The first challenge was that, in a usual conversation, I would have identifying markers to help me make a judgement about the individual. I would know if they were smiling or annoyed. I would be able to guess how old they were.* This felt like doing an interview by phone but in the flesh. I was also aware that, in the initial

---

* I did not know when I met the women in Leicester that twelve months later, Britain, like most of the world, would be in the grip of the coronavirus pandemic and the rest of us would become used to coverings.

absence of visual distinguishers, I was falling into the trap of assuming all four women were somehow the same. But, as we talked, what was fascinating was how each woman's distinctness emerged, and while I never stopped noticing the niqab, it became less important in how I saw each of them.

I had my own preconceptions about women who wore the niqab, but I wanted to know what the women felt were the biggest misconceptions people had about them. 'That we've been forced,' says Zainab, a teacher at an Islamic school, 'that's the biggest thing.' 'That we accept what terrorists are doing is OK,' adds Amina. 'That we are uneducated,' offers Rohana. 'They assume we can't speak English – we get a lot of slow talking, very loudly.' 'And that we don't want to mix,' says Zainab. Is that true, I ask. 'It's not true,' says Zainab. 'At all,' adds Rohana.

Yusairah started to wear the niqab when she was fourteen. 'My sister wore it, and my mum wore it,' she says. 'I was always taught that this is something you do when you grow up.' I asked her how it felt to put it on for the first time. 'I was very wary of the way people perceived me,' she recalls. 'Very, very much so, because suddenly I was an adult in a lot of people's eyes, including Muslims and non-Muslims who were around me. So, if I was going to the shop, I was treated a hundred per cent differently.' I was meeting the women a few months after Boris Johnson's comments, and I wondered how they felt about the criticisms levelled at women like them. 'If you're gonna keep putting me down because of it, I'm gonna keep wearing it,' says Yusairah. 'When people say things to me, it never made me feel like I want to take it off. In fact, it made me stronger about wanting to keep wearing it.' One of the criticisms of women who wear the niqab is that they are failing to 'fit in' and that they are signalling a lack of affiliation or respect to Britain and its cultural norms. I wondered if there was anything they could do to show that these worries were unfounded. 'I think that's an unfair question, because many Muslims are living their lives being normal people, having their jobs, bringing their children up, being good to their neighbours,' says Amina. 'That's not being recognised enough or brought to attention enough. We're just being ourselves; we're not harming anyone.' 'We're always thought to be of a lower standard and then held to this higher standard,' says Yusariah. 'We have to apologise a lot more; we have to justify ourselves a lot more. If I get on a bus and I accidently brush past someone, I am overly apologetic with my veil on because I don't want them to continue to have this negativity about Muslims. No matter what we do, it's just not enough. So, we're always doing something wrong, we're always apologising when we're just trying to live our lives. We don't have the luxury and privilege of individualism.'

The luxury and privilege of individualism – that phrase stayed with me after I said goodbye to the four women. It illuminated the mistake that so many of those who have an issue with the niqab – including me – were making. I had always fixated on the fact that the niqab was not a south Asian form of clothing and that it is not mandatory for Muslim women to wear it. I also, perhaps unconsciously, projected an entire set of beliefs on to women who wear the niqab, but to do so was to deny each woman the luxury of individualism. I had, in other words, viewed those who wore the niqab as *they* and made all sorts of assumptions without having ever had a meaningful conversation with any of them. It only took an hour or two in the company of the women in Leicester to both educate me and change my mind about the entire issue. I was fortunate that I had the excuse of writing this book to prompt me to set up such a meeting, but most people, particularly non-Muslims, may have fewer opportunities to spend any length of time with a niqab-wearing woman. Perhaps if there was more interaction, there would be less temptation to fear the niqab and treat those who wear it as *they*. The women I met had differing reasons for wearing the niqab. 'I was actually a rebellious teenager,' says Yusariah, 'so part of wearing my niqab was, if you're going to put me down because of it, I'm going to wear it.' 'I wasn't rebelling,' Amina told me. 'I was wearing it because I thought as a Muslim woman this is what I should be doing. That's why I wear it, for God.' The niqab does make these women stand out but there are plenty of other people whose fashion choices make them visible, such as those who opt for multiple piercings or tattoos, but future Prime Ministers don't target them in newspapers. *

---

* The dangers of making blanket assumptions about niqab wearers was brought home to me in a story I heard about a tattoo parlour manager in Preston. One day a Muslim woman wearing a full niqab walked in asking for a tattoo. When the manager asked if she wanted a tattoo, the woman told him she wanted a rose tattoo around her anus. It took the manager and an assistant to fulfill the woman's request. She then left the parlour, with her friends and family presumably unaware of how she had spent the afternoon.

While meeting the women in Leicester changed my opinion on the niqab, that is not quite the full story. I would still rather women didn't wear full-face veils; I don't think Islam demands women dress in such a way and I still think it hinders social integration. But I also think that, frankly, none of those reasons justify the outsized criticism or attention Muslim women who choose to wear the niqab attract. The key word is 'choose': I support the right of Muslim women, or anyone else, to choose what they wear, just as I support their right to choose an education or their spouse. It also struck me that the reason some non-Muslims respond badly to Muslim women in niqabs is not dissimilar to why some Muslim parents respond badly to their daughters pursuing an education: fear.

Nusrat in Birmingham described her fear that she might be denied the chance to go to university and forced into an arranged marriage. 'I just didn't want to get married until I'd lived my life,' she says. 'I didn't want to be a commodity; I didn't want to be sold and purchased. I just wanted more than what was on offer.' Nusrat did go to university and then started working for a charity. In October 2000, she was at a Labour party conference event in Brighton campaigning for Breakthrough Breast Cancer when she bumped into a man called David in the lift. Nusrat and David, who was White, had a short conversation during which she gave him her card. He got in touch a few weeks later and they started dating. The relationship grew serious and eventually she broke the news to her parents. 'I knew that the news of my engagement to David was going to be incredibly hard for them to take and I was going to break their hearts and bring shame on the family,' she says. 'I felt awful telling them I was in love and my wedding was planned. There was a lot of emotion and my parents were incredibly distraught.' During one meeting, Nusrat's father said he wanted to kill David. 'I pointed out this would take some time as my father can't see,' says Nusrat, 'so my mother offered to stand up to take the hit as she couldn't show her face again anyway.' Nusrat told her parents that she understood if they wanted to disown her or not attend the wedding. 'When the news spread about my planned wedding, I was told that killing myself would save someone the job of stopping me dishonouring the family,' she says. 'Decades later, I still remember my horror and my mother's tears when a relative "gifted" me a funeral shroud and not the expected wedding gift of brightly coloured sari.' In time the shock and anger abated, eased by her family getting to know David and the fact he had converted to Islam. They were married three months later and Nusrat's immediate family attended the ceremony.

Nasreen was out on the street in Bradford with her mother. It was 1980. Homeless, destitute and isolated, Zoora met a man called Mohammed Azam, a drug dealer from the criminal underworld of Bradford. Azam was convicted of dealing heroin and sent to prison for ten years. After his release, Zoora started to fear he might have sexual intentions towards Nasreen. She obtained some arsenic, mixed it into a plate of samosas and served them to Azam. Zoora was charged with murder and attempted murder and a number of other offences. At her trial in 1993, she was found guilty on all counts and given a life sentence with a tariff of twenty years. Nasreen was eighteen years old.

While her mother was in prison, Nasreen campaigned for her release and Zoora was finally freed in 2006. 'I am very resilient,' Nasreen says. 'I'm just not a negative person. The thing that kept me going is that Mum had lost all her *izzat** for us. That kept us on the straight and narrow. That kept me away from drink, away from drugs, away from men. She had done so much for us, we owed it to her to give something back.' Nasreen became a mature student and got a job in social services, later becoming an advocate for people with disabilities. 'I have this knack, and it still applies today,' she says. 'I look at somebody doing a job and I think, "I could do a better job." And I remember looking at George Galloway and thinking: "I'd be a better MP than you."' In February 2015, Nasreen (otherwise known as Naz) was selected as the Labour candidate for Bradford West in the upcoming general election. The night before the election, Naz went to her brother's home where her sister was also waiting. They lit some candles and talked about their shared memories: seeing their mother beaten by their father, of sleeping on hard floors, living on Pot Noodles because they didn't own a cooker, of Naz being battered by her husband

---

* Honour, reputation, or prestige.

and her brother being beaten up by racists. 'It was the most overwhelming night of my political career,' she says. When the results came in that confirmed Naz Shah was the new MP, the first person she told was her mother. 'We just cried,' she recalls, 'it's making my eyes water even now.'

Zoora Shah's story is tragic, dramatic – and rare: most of the Muslim women who came to Britain in the late sixties and seventies did not have husbands who were drug dealers and pimps who they were driven to murder. I debated whether to include this story and how much prominence to give it because it is so extreme and does not reflect the lived reality of most Muslim women. I chose to include it not because of Zoora's story but because of the journey of her daughter. The fact that Naz Shah could come from the background she did and still rise to become a Member of Parliament is a story of hope and resilience. As she says, 'If I hadn't lived it, I wouldn't fucking believe half of it. It's like something from a movie.'

When I think of the journeys that Naz, Nusrat and Ruby have made, it reminds me of the phrase 'history is written by the victors'. In my desire for hopeful stories and an uplift at the end of each chapter there is a danger that inconvenient truths are overlooked. It is also the case that when seeking out people to talk to it is easier to speak to those who have transcended their upbringings and 'won'. I did not want, in my determination to find hope, to ignore harder truths.

I arranged to meet a group of Muslim mothers in Birmingham whose children attended Parkfield Primary

School in Alum Rock, a predominantly Muslim area. The women were dressed in traditional clothes but some had their hair showing, others had headscarves, while one woman wore a full-face veil. 'We were not allowed to go out,' recalled one mother about her teenage years. 'There was a park across the road and we used to sit at home thinking: "Why are we not allowed to go out? Why are our brothers allowed to go out?" Our parents were very strict. We weren't allowed to colour our hair, we weren't allowed to wear make-up.' I wanted to know how the lives of the Muslim women in Alum Rock were today. 'A lot of the women here have never been out in twenty-two years in England,' one woman told me. Another added: 'The Bengali and Pakistani ladies are isolated at home. They can't drive, they can't do nothing and have no social life.' One woman told me about her friend who had passed her driving test. 'She wants to buy a car, but her husband says it is embarrassing for him if she is in the driving seat and he is a passenger. Our religion can be so judgemental.' Another woman interrupted to deny it was religion. 'It's cultural,' she says. The stories I was hearing were second-hand – the women in the room were allowed to drive and work– so what was so different about them compared to the women whose lives were more constrained? 'My husband is very open-minded,' one woman, who had also had an arranged marriage, explained. 'I can wear what I want, I can dress how I want, and we can do and go where we want. And he's always encouraging me as well. He's always been my support. Maybe if he wasn't and was one of those husbands that . . . I think we need to educate the men.'

While I was in Birmingham, I also visited the offices of the Muslim Women's Network UK, a charity that works to improve social justice and equality for Muslim women and girls and operates a national helpline. The helpline has been running for more than six years and helps around 1,200 women and girls each year, ranging from girls as young as fourteen to women in their sixties. I visited one afternoon to ask the chair what the most common issues were that women rang about. 'Domestic abuse – whether it's violence, financial control, emotional abuse, verbal abuse,' she says. 'The other issues that we get are mental health and depression, a lot of self-harm . . . If you look at the suicide rate, it's two to three times higher than their White counterparts.' You might have noticed that I have not as yet named the chair of the Muslim Women Network: her name is Shaista, the daughter of Shugra, whose story we have been following throughout this chapter. Shaista was one of very few in the Pakistani community in Northampton to attend university. She later got married to a man of her choice and had three children. She remembers being at home around 2005. 'I was at home watching Sky News all the time while the kids were on the floor playing,' she recalls, 'and I found that the only people on TV that were being interviewed about Muslim issues were men. I'd wonder, where were the women's voices?' She started becoming interested in activism on women's issues and that led her to set up the

MWN. I told her that it shocked and saddened me to hear that such things were still going on today. 'These spouses from abroad are coming over and not really stepping outside of that bubble,' she says, 'so the same ideas are going round and no one is mixing.'

I heard more about the consequences of not stepping outside the bubble from Naz Kazmi, manager of the Keighley Association Women and Children's Centre in Yorkshire. She is in her early fifties and wearing a dark green headscarf draped over the top of her head and she gives the distinct impression of someone who has neither the time nor inclination to suffer fools gladly. 'We still have that 1960s perception that has even infiltrated into the second and third generation,' she says, 'the men are men. Women have to be very submissive, bowing to their family's patriarchal style of living. The second- and third-generation girls are drawn back – even if they're educated and independent – into that culture. They have dual lives. When they're outside, they're free to do what they want, but once they're home, they're restricted in their environment.' It was bracing, if dispiriting, to learn that some young Muslim women were still facing some of the same challenges around marriage and freedom I had heard from the likes of Nusrat about growing up in the eighties. 'There are stereotypical perceptions about the effect of Western society on their daughters,' Kazmi says. 'If we allow our daughters to be set free, they might go and marry an Englishman and bring him home.'

In the previous chapter I talked to the founders of Muslim matrimonial sites, who assured me that this was how all young Muslims were meeting their partners. 'Not in my world,' says Kazmi. 'The majority of the girls get taken back to Pakistan. They're trying to look for the more educated young men but some of them will just get them married to a first or second cousin.' The world Kazmi was describing was pretty grim and it prompted the inevitable question of how much any of this had to do with Islam. 'Religion doesn't stop you being who you want to be,' she responds '[the problem is] the mentality of the men. They can't let a woman lead. It's not in their understanding or their family's culture. This is about a clan mentality.' Her implication is that an imported village mentality is largely responsible, and the fact that the community is so segregated means that attitudes that have been abandoned elsewhere are still dominant.

Shigufta Khan is the CEO of the Wish Centre, which supports victims of domestic abuse in Blackburn. 'Most parents are now OK with their girls going to university, that is improving and increasing,' she says, 'but there are still restrictions in place on the roles that a woman can do or should do. There's still an expectation that a girl will get married at a certain age. When she starts getting over the age of twenty-five, she's going past her sell-by date, and there's an expectation that you will have children, so even if she is academic there's a ceiling there.' Shigufta highlighted another issue – young women from Pakistan who are pressurised into marrying men without knowing their full histories. 'We have had cases were somebody has a serious offending background, even a sex offending background,' she says, 'and the girl marrying them is not aware of any of this.' The women arrive from the subcontinent alone and vulnerable and some families exploit this, Shigufta told me, to use them essentially as domestic slaves. 'We are helping someone who is being used as a domestic slave,' she says. 'The expectation is that she's going to do all cooking and cleaning, serving everyone hot food all the time whenever they want it. The sister-in-laws are dumping their washing on her and asking her to do work for them as well. They are just using her as a servant because they've brought her from abroad and they feel like she should owe them gratitude for coming here.'

The women Naz and Shigufta were hearing from lived in working-class northern towns and hearing their stories was a useful reminder that there is no single narrative when it comes to British Muslim women. Any conclusion that declares things have emphatically improved, or worsened, over the decades is hopelessly simplistic. It would be more accurate to say that some Muslim women have been able to take advantage of gaining an education and have secured more freedom and opportunities but there are pockets of Britain where Muslim women have not had those same opportunities. 'There is a class divide and there is a north and south divide,' says academic Fauzia Ahmad, who has researched the challenges facing professionally educated Muslim women. Women, and again it is worth stressing that this should not be taken to suggest all women, in Blackburn and Keighley, for example, may be struggling in exploitative marriages. The women who Ahmad has studied are struggling to find suitable husbands. 'One of the reasons Muslim women are keen to be educated is a belief that getting a degree will secure a better quality husband,' she says. 'They have high expectations and they're finding that a lot of men aren't meeting those. Women are becoming the men they want to marry.'

Shaista, Shigufta and Fauzia are all inspiring Muslim women and talking to them I was reminded of the question I had begun this chapter with: to what extent should Islam be held responsible for holding Muslim women back? 'When I used to hear about Islamic things – what girls can do and what they can't do, there was something in the back of my mind saying, "Did God say that or is it men saying it?"' recalls Shaista. 'It made me think that I must take time to read the Qur'an myself. I must take time to look into things myself. I got twelve copies of the Qur'an because, depending on the English translation you get, the wording is slightly different, and that's when I started thinking this is all about interpretation.' I had heard the interpretation defence repeatedly, and initially dismissed it as slippery excuse and a way of avoiding the hard question of whether misogyny was baked into the religion. But perhaps I was asking the wrong question – rather than asking if Islam treated women differently, maybe I should have been looking at how the interpretation of the faith has evolved over the decades.

I wanted to end this chapter by hearing from some of today's young Muslim women. We heard from Zena earlier, who had run away from home and was living in a refuge. I asked her how typical her parents' attitude was. 'I think it's quite typical,' she says. 'A lot of people try to make out that it's become better in recent years, but it really hasn't. My Asian friends are dealing with these issues now. It's not been any better for us than it was in the past.'

In Telford I talked to Henna, a university student in her late teens. 'There are still some things that I know a hundred per cent my brother would be able to get away with when he's my age that I wouldn't be able to get away with,' she says. 'People aren't comfortable with the idea of a powerful woman. They can see the potential in their daughters, and they worry about their daughters achieving their full potential. It's almost like a control thing – if they give their daughter too much freedom or they let their daughters act in the same way as their sons, as a family, they no longer have that control over their children any more.'

Given these limitations, often justified by culture and religion, it would be tempting to reject the culture and religion entirely, which is why I was so fascinated talking to Amanni. She is in her early twenties, raised in Bradford by lawyer parents and educated at a private girls' school. We met in Manchester, where she is studying medicine. 'I think it's hard being in Britain and being a Muslim,' she says. 'I'm trying to find a happy balance.' She recalls being seventeen and visiting her grandmother, who had a book about women in Islam that stated men were allowed to beat their wives. 'I remember thinking, "I'm done being a Muslim",' she recalls, 'but the point is you don't have to stick to all of the religion. If I was to really stick to all of the religion there'd be some crazy things going on.' Amanni was arguing for was the right to interpret the religion as she sees fit rather than letting others, particularly men, interpret it for her. Amanni interprets it to believe she can wear short skirts. 'If I want to wear a skirt, why does that make me a bad person? I like clothes, I've never felt like I have to hide all of me. I've tried staying away from the religion completely because I didn't think I could call myself Muslim if I was wearing shorts, and that didn't make me happy. I tried sticking to all of the rules and being as Muslim as I could manage, and that didn't make me happy either. I'm happy now because I've just thought: "You know what, sod it all. I'm going to follow the bits that make me feel good, follow the bits that I believe in." I'd rather follow fifty per cent than none of it.' I asked her what she would say to those who claim Islam holds women back and use passages from the Qur'an to support their claim. 'People are always going to find some quote from the Qur'an to support whatever they're feeling,' she replied.

'Texts have an essential role in shaping cultures,' says Dr Shuruq Naguib, 'but in contemporary times – as throughout history – if there are social and economic circumstances, they impact on how the text is received and how the culture is shaped. There isn't one way that the culture is static and the text is either progressive or conservative, or shaped by a culture that is limiting it. It is a much more complex scenario – the Qur'an and the ability to clarify are entwined. God wants to inspire and invite your interpretative agency to have that dialogue. It's the text that invites that conversation. There isn't one way of receiving the text.' The process of interpretation is, she told me, as old as the religion, and women have been at its heart. It was the Prophet Muhammad's wife Khadija who interpreted the first revelation the Prophet received and talked him through his experience. 'A woman is the one who frames to the Prophet how to understand his own experience,' Dr Naguib told me. 'Women were the midwives of the Qur'anic texts.' When exploring the question of whether Islam holds women back, the most common response I heard is that the text is not sexist but some of those who have interpreted it have been. I assumed that there was a literalist and a relativist approach one could take to Islamic texts, but talking to Dr Naguib I wondered whether I had been wrong all along.

It is 11 August 2011. Bridget and I are in the maternity ward of Homerton Hospital in Hackney. My wife has been in labour for more than thirty hours. I am holding her hand, doing what I can do to help with her breathing and offering what encouragement I can. Bridget is somewhere else; she is exhausted, dripping sweat. She breathes and pushes. Later she would tell me that the thought she clung to was that she wanted me to see our baby.

11 August 2011
And then suddenly there was progress. There was a head
and then the body. It was an animal-like thing, pale

skin, soft, vulnerable. They gave it to Bridget and then I
cut the cord. I looked between its legs and said to Bridget
'It's a girl!'

16 August 2011
So what does she look like? Tiny, like a little chimp the
way she clings to her mum. She makes watery moves with
her hands — as if still in amniotic fluid. She has dark blue
eyes, long fingernails on big hands. She sometimes looks up
at us with big eyes gazing up open and I wish I knew what
she was thinking. I just keep looking at her and she looks
at me, both of us as bewildered and confused as each other.

Our little girl had gorgeous long dark hair and that was
one of the reasons we would come to name her Laila, which
means 'dark-haired beauty'. I feel profoundly grateful she is
growing up in the third decade of the twenty-first century
and not in Pakistan in the 1960s or Britain in the 70s and
80s. Had she been born in the same village as Shugra she
too might have been fated to marry while still only fifteen or
sixteen. If she had grown up in the seventies and eighties,
with different parents, she too might have lived a life under
constraints. She might have been told education was not for
the likes of her, and that the most she could expect from life
was to get married to a boy from 'back home' and be a good
wife and mother.

In 2009, forty years after first arriving in Britain, Rabia,
who came to Britain at sixteen and constantly fought to be

allowed to go to college, enrolled in evening classes to study Mathematics, English and Islamic Studies. 'Do you feel angry that you were stopped?' I asked her. 'No,' she said, 'because I found a way.' It is only due to the efforts of women like Rabia that my daughter and young Muslim girls like her are able to dream bigger. 'I think it is through the children,' Amanni told me, when I had asked her how to push towards progress. 'We have to show the kids where they can end up and who they can be, and how happy they could be being themselves. You are not going to convince parents to just magically let go of their kids but you can convince the kids that there's a big, wide world out there.'

I went back to Ruby, who had been forced to run away from home when still a teenager and spent decades on the run from her parents. 'In my personal opinion, Islam *is* heavily biased towards men,' she says, 'but I would be mindful of not giving Islam a bashing about inequality as it's not just Islam. In Islam, like other religions, Catholicism for example, men are regarded as being superior to women, but it is not only religion. The world and society in general, broadly speaking, is sexist, isn't it? Nothing is handed to women on plate. We have to work hard or fight for these advances and in some cases women give their lives, or more accurately have their lives extinguished, for trying to challenge patriarchy even in the smallest ways.'

In the early months of 2017, the English Defence League marched through the streets of Birmingham. The demonstration attracted only around one hundred people, including then EDL leader Ian Crossland. According to reports, Crossland and twenty other EDL supporters surrounded a hijab-wearing woman after she called them racists. The woman looked scared but the minutes ticked by and the police did not intervene. It was then that an eighteen-year-old woman, who had been watching what had been going on, decided to act. The woman confronted Crossland. He was short, dressed in a black football T-shirt and baseball cap, while she was taller, wearing a denim jacket over a black hoodie. A photograph captured the confrontation. In the photograph the young woman looks calm and composed. She is smiling with her hands in her pockets. She has an expression that suggests power, fearlessness and amusement. Crossland by contrast looks twitchy and tense. He looks like the past and she embodies the future. The photograph went viral, and the young woman would be hailed as an inspiration for young Muslims everywhere. The woman's name was Saffiyah, and she is the daughter of Mohammed who told me: 'undermining and belittling girls and daughters is not an Islamic thing, it's a Pakistani thing.' When I saw that photograph, it instantly felt like an iconic image,* not only for what it depicted but for it what represented. The Saffiyah Khan in that photograph is someone who does not feel she has to apologise for any part of who she is. She

---

* Saffiyah Khan would, in the aftermath of that photograph, go on to perform on stage with The Specials and sign with the Elite modelling agency.

is someone so secure in her skin she can smile in the face of ugly bigotry and reveal the supporters of the EDL as the mirthless clowns they are. There was no fear in her eyes, and that gave me hope.

THEY . . . FOLLOW A VIOLENT RELIGION

'We are at war and I am a soldier. Now you too will taste the reality of this situation.'

Mohammed Siddique Khan, Yorkshire, 2005

Islam For Dummies
The book bought by Mohammed Ahmed and Yusuf
Sarwar while preparing to travel to Syria, 2014

Sajda was running. It was an early morning in July 2005, and she was on her way to Turnpike Lane underground station in north London. She was working in recruitment in financial services. 'I was just your average twenty-two-year-old girl,' she recalls. 'I was getting my monthly salary, spending it on shoes, make-up and bags, with not a care in the world.' She raced into Turnpike Lane station, ran down the escalator to reach the platform. The train arrived and Sajda boarded. It was around 8.30 a.m. and her carriage was full of rush-hour commuters. The train trundled along the Piccadilly Line and reached King's Cross. It was around ten seconds into the tunnel after leaving King's Cross when Sajda heard the loudest bang she had ever heard. The train shook as if someone had lifted it up and shaken it. The lights went out. 'I went into a state of shock,' she says. 'I could see black smoke starting to fill up the carriage. People started to scream, people started to bang on the doors, people started to bang on the windows.' Sajda saw a pregnant woman being helped. Water bottles were brought out of people's bags. People were panicking and screaming. 'I remember I was wearing a suit and I took my blazer off and that's the only time I moved. I took my blazer off to cover my face because I was choking.' The minutes ticked by, ten minutes, twenty minutes, thirty, forty, fifty . . . 'It felt as if someone had taken a rope,' she recalls, 'and tightened it around my heart and I couldn't breathe.' It was then that Sajda heard a male voice saying, 'It's police. We're coming to get you', and it was only then that Sajda began to believe that maybe today was not the day she would die.

The emergency services escorted the passengers through the carriages and along the tracks to King's Cross. The station was empty even though it was rush hour and Sajda staggered into a nearby McDonald's. She walked into the toilets and stared at herself in the mirror. She looked at the smoke stains on her face and broke down. After cleaning herself up, she bought a cup of tea. There was a television reporting that there had been a derailment. She tried to call her mother, but the phone lines were down. There were no buses and no taxis, so the only way to get home was to walk. It was only when she reached home that she learnt that it was not a derailment but a bomb that had almost left her dead. A bomb detonated, she would later learn, by four men who shared her Muslim faith. 'It wouldn't sink in,' she says. 'It was incomprehensible to think this terror attack had been carried out by four Muslims. That just shocked me.' I asked her if she could recall what had gone through her mind in the time leading up to her rescue. 'I was thinking that I hadn't said bye to my mum. I haven't got married, I haven't had kids, I haven't seen the world. I was thinking that today – 7 July 2005 – will be the day that I die.'

How much is Islam responsible for inciting terrorist acts such as the one committed in London on 7/7? Why have so many young British Muslims chosen to embrace a radical and violent strain of Islam, and what can be done to prevent other young Muslims from being lured into extremism? Sajda did not die that day but the date has been etched alongside 11 September 2001 as dates forever connected to acts of murderous terror committed in the name of Islam. Each time such an attack took place it would prompt questions about how much Islam was culpable. These were questions aired in the media, but they were the same questions I was myself asking. 7/7 affected me more profoundly than 9/11 because it hit closer to home. The attacks were committed in London – the city where I live, the bombers set off from Luton – my hometown, and three of them came from British-Pakistani families.

I felt a mixture of shock and bewilderment on learning that the men who committed these crimes were like me, and yet nothing like me. 7/7 was the first time British Muslims became directly implicated in acts of terror at home, followed by Glasgow Airport in 2007, the murder of Lee Rigby in 2013, the Westminster Bridge, London Bridge attacks and Manchester Arena and Parsons Green bombings in 2017, the Manchester Victoria stabbing in 2018 and the Streatham stabbing in 2020.[1] In the winter of 2020, the UK's terrorism threat level was upgraded from 'substantial' 'to 'severe', meaning security chiefs believed that an attack was highly likely, but there was no specific intelligence of an imminent incident. The move followed a shooting in Vienna in which four people died, a knife attack in Nice that killed three and the murder of a teacher in Paris. I have become wearily accustomed the sequence of events – the news breaking on social media followed by 'Allahu Akbar' trending on Twitter as it is revealed that the attackers are Muslim. As a journalist in the days and months following 7/7, I was repeatedly asked by newspapers to explain what might prompt a young British Muslim to carry out such an attack. I accepted the writing commissions, offered my views and banked the fees, but inside I felt like a fraud. The truth was that I had absolutely no idea how and why anyone would do what the 7/7 bombers did nor how significant a factor religion played in their actions. It is these questions to which I now want to return.

Alyas was running. It was early 1989 and Alyas, who had grown up in Bradford and then Tooting, was at university in

Glasgow. 'You can reinvent yourself when you get away from home,' he says. 'I was running away from being Muslim and Pakistani. I was running away from all of that.' In Glasgow Alyas started calling himself Ali. He gained a reputation as the heart and soul of the party, running club nights and organising parties. His social circle was mostly White. When the Ayatollah in Iran issued a fatwa against Salman Rushdie following the publication of *The Satanic Verses*, Ali felt, not unreasonably, that it had nothing to do with him. His friends felt differently. 'They would say to me, "Why have you put the fatwa on Rushdie? Do you support this?"' he recalls. 'I didn't have a clue about any of these things. To me it wasn't about the fatwa. Why are you guys – who I have been at university with for four years – asking me to pass this loyalty test? People's racism became evident.' It was around then that Ali met some men at a mosque who invited him to an event. 'It wasn't my scene at all,' he recalls, 'but then I met these guys, and they were sexy, man. They were fine, they were standing up, they were saying: "Fuck you". They weren't holding back; they were proud and when you met them it was like a solid brotherhood. They were strong. It was a real powerful pull. It was attractive. I'd never seen this before. What they were saying was very simple. We were going to turn back to Islam, we were going to bring justice, help the oppressed and change the world.' Ali became Alyas again and, as he now puts it, went 'from being part of a liberal hedonistic group to a militant fundamentalist Islamic group'.

In summer 1990, Alyas stopped partying, swapping club nights for study circles and meetings where he tried to recruit others into the group. 'They were a family,' he says, 'they were really tight. I had never experienced such camaraderie and brotherhood and spirit and unity, and it was wonderful.' The acceptance that he had felt was missing from his White friends was present from his new Muslim associates. 'The group I belonged to gave me a clear identity,' he says. 'It gave belonging and acceptance. It gave enlightenment. You felt a spiritual cleansing. But actually, the number-one factor, it wasn't the spirituality or the theology: the number-one factor was the belonging.'

Six years passed. In 1996 two events took place that are important to this story. The first is that Nicola Benyahia, a White British Muslim convert living in Wales with her Algerian husband, gave birth to a baby boy named Rasheed. 'He was very energetic right from when he was a little baby,' Nicola recalls. 'As a toddler he just really easy going, always taking the mick out of his sisters and being mischievous in a little boy kind of way.'

A few months after Rasheed was born, Hadiya Masieh started university in London. She was a boarding-school-educated daughter of middle-class Mauritian and Ugandan parents and had been raised as a Hindu, but even before leaving to study in London she had begun to question her faith. In the months before she left home, Hadiya began to read and learn about Islam, and the more she studied it, the more certain she became that Islam was the path she wanted to follow. Within months of arriving at Brunel University, she converted to Islam and began searching for fellow Muslims. 'I went looking for people who were religious,' she says, 'and they were the most prominent ones.' 'They' were the members of Hizb ut-Tahrir (HT), the radical Islamist organisation that rejects democracy and campaigns for a single Islamic caliphate. 'They would be in the prayer rooms and they seemed very religious,' Hadiya says. 'I was a clean slate, and I was impressed by how well they spoke. I prided myself on being someone who was really literate and interested in history, and when you meet these guys they start speaking about politics, which was an area of interest to me, talking about society and change and how to change society. What they said seemed to make sense to me.'

Just as Alyas in Glasgow was vulnerable because of his estranged relationship with his family, so Hadiya's decision to become a Muslim made her vulnerable. 'My vulnerability was that I converted to Islam and knew nothing about the whole religion,' she says. 'I felt excluded from my Hindu family and felt alone and, because I had no prior knowledge of anything, I relied on people to educate me and give me that knowledge. And they (HT) looked Muslim, they're acting Muslim, they seem Muslim – so I went there.' The radical Muslims with whom she was spending ever more time became her substitute family. 'We would talk, and it wasn't just religion that we were discussing – it was about building a perfect world and establishing an Islamic state. My studies were secondary to what I was doing. I felt I was doing God's work.' They told Hadiya that the entire Western world was out to destroy Islam and that the West feared the rise of Islamist ideology. 'I was interested in trying to understand the world and they were able to offer a solution: they would say that because of Western foreign policy children are being killed and women are being raped in the Middle East and you need to be a soldier and fight them. Because I was so ignorant and naive, what they said seemed persuasive,' she says, 'and it appealed to my political side. So before long I was spending every night with members of HT, getting more and more brainwashed.' Like Alyas, Hadiya found a sense of belonging in her new group. 'They seemed fun, nice people talking about issues that were relevant to me and offering support and help at a time when it was exactly what I needed.'

I had read more recent reports from women who had travelled to Syria to join IS and how their roles often felt limited to the domestic sphere and I wondered if Hadiya felt that as a woman she wasn't treated as equal to the men in the group. 'I didn't see it like it was not equal,' she says. 'When you're in it, you're like, "Oh, we have different roles to play as women." So, a man does this – it doesn't make him superior, it's just different roles. So, I'm happy to make my role nurturing my children and the house, but even then it's not always got to be the case because we would talk about female warriors and women who fought in different battles and women scholars.' Looking back, what she most remembers is the friendliness. 'I had just converted, and my family was none too pleased,' she says. 'These people are kind of like your new-found friends and your new-found family.' Hadiya spent the following few years immersed in her new-found family and she recalls their collective reaction to 9/11 as one of vindication. 'It was confirming that I was doing the right thing,' she recalls. 'There was all this stuff going on in the Middle East. There was a lot of meddling and injustices happening and the Western powers feel like they can get away with this. And this is now a reminder of the repercussions of your meddling because this has finally come to bite you in the ass.' I asked her what the people she was spending time with – the people she describes as fun and nice – felt about 9/11. 'I remember people were saying "Serves you right",' she says. 'You go and bomb all those places and carpet-bomb and kill civilians all the time and you think you can get away with it. When it happens on your turf, it should be a wake-up call for you.'

This suggestion that the politically motivated, violent actions of the West justify a response in kind from the Muslim world predates 9/11 and stretches back from 2001 to 1979 and the fall of the American-supported Shah of Iran and return of Ayatollah Khomeini, to the Western manipulation of the Middle East around oil during the seventies, to the creation of the state of Israel in 1948, to the colonial era and even further back to the Crusades. The times might change but the central argument remains the same: *they* are trying to undermine us, hurt us and exploit us and now *we* have to fight back. 'If you look at Bin Laden's message and the message from the 7/7 bombers, it was the same,' says

Dilwar Hussain, chair of New Horizons in British Islam. 'They say, "We have been hurting and now it's time for you to feel the pain. We have been dying and hurting for centuries. Now you feel what we have for the past five six or seven hundred years."' This grievance narrative implies a religious response to a political action – the foreign policy of the West is shaped by geopolitics but the response is clothed in religion. One explanation is that this is a reflection of the continuing potency of religion in the Islamic world – and by extension among Muslim communities in the West. 'Religion has lost its power as a means for convincing others in the West,' says Dilwar Hussain, 'but in the Muslim world religion is actively used for social control in countries like Iran, Saudi Arabia and Pakistan.'

Nicola and her family were in Yemen in the autumn of 2001 because her husband was teaching there. Rasheed was five years old and attending kindergarten. 'We had a tiny television and I remember watching the news about 9/11 on this tiny little screen,' she recalls. 'I was shocked but also quite distant from it because we were in Yemen, we were so detached and remote from it. I don't think it would have had the same impact if I'd been in the UK.'

Alyas was in Glasgow, and the attacks in New York and Washington were beginning to confirm doubts he was having. 'I had started seeing the hypocrisy and the manipulation and the control,' he says, 'and it leaves you in a bit of a free fall as you are essentially spending your life trying to find a place where you belong.' 9/11 was a defining moment in his journey as he began to believe that the group had 'ultimately nothing to do with faith – it was just about power, manipulation and control and exploitation.' In the same way that he had not felt like he was truly accepted by his family or his Glasgow liberal circles, he found it hard to reconcile the reality of who he was with what the group demanded. 'The number-one loyalty was towards Islam,' he recalls. 'They were trying to put the primacy of our Islamic identity above all of our other identities, so it has a nihilistic effect in that regard in that it annihilated lots of other things and so I found myself in another double life.' Alyas was part of an extremist Islamist terrorist organisation while holding down a job as a sex therapist for men with HIV. 'Obviously, I couldn't tell them this,' he adds.

It was fascinating hearing about Alyas' journey, but he was talking about experiences that took place in the nineties and I wanted to ask whether what he had to say was relevant to young Muslims of the next generation – those who bombed London on 7/7 and went to fight in Syria. 'The appearance has slightly changed but it's the same thing,' he replies, adding that, if he was that age now, 'I would probably have gone to Syria. It's the same thing. It's the same human factors. People searching for belonging, searching for attachment, searching for significance.'

This is not how the terrorists themselves see things – they routinely cite Western foreign policy as a factor in their actions and often employ martial language that suggests they believe Islam is at war with the non-Muslim world.

'Your democratically elected governments continually per-petrate atrocities against my people all over the world,' says 7/7 ringleader Mohammed Siddique Khan in a video that emerged after the attack. 'Your support makes you directly responsible. Until we feel security, you will be our target. Until you stop the bombing, gassing, imprisonment and torture of my people, we will not stop this fight. We are at war and I am a soldier. Now you too will taste the reality of this situation.'

'I knew two of the 7/7 bombers,' Alyas says. 'I had a lot of insider knowledge, so I became recognised as an expert in the area and started working to develop psychological profiles of people convicted under the Terrorism Act.' Since leaving the extremist group, he has gone on to advise the government on anti-radicalisation strategies. 'I've been an expert witness in around ten terrorism trials,' he says, 'of those terrorism trials, six of them have got life sentences – they were planning bombing attacks. I don't see them as terrorists at all . . . most of them are oblivious of the ideology. They're not religious people.'

A 2016 analysis of thousands of leaked Islamic State documents revealed that 70 per cent of recruits were listed as having just 'basic' knowledge of Islam with just 5 per cent considered advanced students of Islam.[2] The trial of Mohammed Ahmed and Yusuf Sarwar revealed the twenty-two-year-olds had ordered *The Koran For Dummies* and *Islam For Dummies* in preparation for joining extremists in Syria. They were arrested on their return to Britain and convicted of terrorism offenses in 2014. 'These are not spiritual people,' says Alyas. 'They're apolitical. They're extremely damaged people – in most cases there is experience of exclusion, racism, domestic violence, social exclusion and emotional trauma. There are so many issues.'

Those who are sceptical about Islam being a religion of peace argue that the Qur'an condones violence. When you read a quote from the Prophet Muhammad such as 'I did not come to bring peace, but a sword', or Allah's instruction to 'utterly destroy all that they have, and do not spare them ... kill man and woman, infant and nursing child, ox and sheep, camel and donkey', it feels hard to dispute that the Qur'an does seem rather bloodthirsty. The only minor issue with this conclusion is that it was not Muhammad who said those words but Jesus (Matthew 10:34), and it was not Allah ordering the killing but the Christian God (Book 1 of Samuel). This is not to suggest that the Qur'an does not contain violent passages – it does. 'Slay the idolaters wherever ye find them, arrest them, besiege them, and lie in ambush everywhere for them', Allah instructs Muhammad (Qur'an, 9:5). He continues: 'Prophet! Make war on the unbelievers and the hypocrites! ... Hell shall be their home, an evil fate.' When the religious historian Philip Jenkins compared the Qur'an and the Bible, he concluded that 'by the standards of the time, which is the seventh century A.D., the laws of war that are laid down by the Qur'an are actually reasonably humane. Then we turn to the Bible, and we actually find something that is for many people a real surprise. There is a specific kind of warfare laid down in the Bible, which we can only call genocide.'[3]

The point is that it can be somewhat disingenuous to cherry-pick phrases without any context. In the passage that begins 'slay the idolaters wherever ye find them', 'the '"them" are those terrorists who persecuted people for their faith, exiled them from their homes and then pursued to kill innocent people in their new homes', notes author and human rights activist Qasim Rashid. 'In other words, "them" is close to a modern-day Isis. The Qur'an permits killing terrorists in self-defence because they have waged pre-emptive war against you, or against Christians, Jews, or people of any faith. Yet, even then, if terrorists desist, the Qur'an forbids aggression against them.'[4] What unites Muslim extremists and Islam haters is that both prefer to overlook nuance and context so they can believe that the religion endorses holy war.

In spring 2014, Nicola and her husband were having marital issues. The tensions at home seemed to particularly affect their son Rasheed, who had just turned eighteen. After taking his GCSEs he had started an electrical engineering apprenticeship in Birmingham, where the family lived. 'It was subtle,' she says, 'he became more conservative in his dress sense. He'd been quite a funky kid. He was very much into free running. He stopped doing all that, stopped wearing his hoodies. He stopped being engaged when we had a birthday or anything like that.' He left his local mosque and starting spending time with a new, younger group. He asked

Nicola if she would shorten his trousers – often a sign of growing religious observance. 'There was something going on,' says Nicola, 'but with him being the only boy it was really sometimes very difficult because you don't always know what they're doing at that age or what they're thinking and how they're feeling. So, I would brush it off as maybe it was just being a teenage boy and because it wasn't anything signif- icant at that point. It was a gradual thing.' Rasheed talked about attending late-night Islamic study circles far from home. He talked about attending stalls in Birmingham city centre where Muslims hand out leaflets to passers-by – some stalls are used to select those impressionable to extremist causes. 'They get an idea of what that person's character is and what their vulnerability is or what ignites them and that is what they home in on,' says Nicola. 'With my son he wanted to make a difference and that was what they ignited in him.' Rasheed was deeply interested in events in Syria. For three years the news had been full of Syrian unrest and the subsequent civil war. The focus of the story that summer became an austere-looking man in black, addressing the masses: Abu Bakr al-Baghdadi – the self-proclaimed leader, or caliph, of the self-styled Islamic State. 'What they were getting sold about the Islamic State was that it going to be fair and just, and everyone was living in harmony,' Nicola says. 'I think there was a part of Rasheed that wanted to live in that Islamic setting, in a Muslim country.'

On Friday, 29 May 2015, Rasheed dashed out the door as normal. He was not expected back before 10 p.m. It was only when her husband said he could not contact Rasheed that Nicola started to worry. She checked with friends, she tried to call him, and rang local hospitals. Nothing. The weekend passed in a flurry of fear and uncertainty. 'We didn't get hold of him for three days,' she says. 'It was Monday morning and I had been constantly trying to text him and phone him. I got a text message from him saying he was in good hands and he was fine. He said he would be without a phone for thirty days. He talked about paradise. He said, "I wouldn't do this if I didn't know the reward for it." He warned me not to go to the police or the media because they would make my life hell.' Nicola had been going through hell for the past three days, not eating or sleeping and with her phone constantly by her side.

Nicola wasn't completely convinced the text really was from Rasheed, so she asked him a question that she knew only he would know the answer. She asked him what he always said to her when he kissed her goodnight. 'I put a lot of cream on my face and things like that – I have very dry skin – so every time he'd come to my bedroom to kiss me and forget that he'd get a mouthful of moisturiser in his face. And that's why I asked, "What do you say to me?"' It took a few minutes before she got a response. The text read: 'I always moan about your cream.' 'It was then I realised,' says Nicola, 'that I really was talking to Rasheed.'

Her son had travelled from Birmingham to Turkey, where he had crossed the border – almost certainly with the help of IS-supporting smugglers – and was most likely heading to an IS camp for military training and indoctrination. 'It was literally like you get this brick in your stomach,' says Nicola. 'I'm just panic-stricken because I think, "What do I do? Where do I go now with this?"' For the next six months Rasheed and Nicola would exchange occasional text messages and phone calls. 'I would long for them but at the same time I would dread them,' she says. 'I felt really guilt-ridden, because I thought, "This is my son. How can I dread the phone calls?" You look back on the whole history and you unpick everything because it's almost like you're trying to make sense of it all and that's why I was feeling incredibly disorientated and detached at times, because it was the only way to survive.' During those early months, Rasheed would not explicitly say where he was, but Nicola has now learnt that he was in an IS training camp. New arrivals would usually spend thirty days in the camp, but Rasheed spent sixty-four days there. 'I later heard from some good contacts that they remember him,' she says. 'A mutual friend asked why he was in so long and they said, "We remember him and he looked ever so young and so little and he was a really difficult one to break."' Rasheed would not talk about what his daily life was like, so even though Nicola was watching news reports about the atrocities committed by Islamic State, she couldn't talk to her son about them. The months passed and Nicola sensed a slight change in Rasheed and started to feel hopeful that she could persuade him to return home.

'I saw a bit of a shift in him – instead of being so rigid and kind of how he had been for the first few months there was almost a softening up. He made a comment to his sister, saying something like, "If I'm wrong about what I've done or about this decision I've made, I'll ask Allah to guide me away from this." For me this was a shift and an opening.' Throughout the time that Rasheed was in Syria, Nicola also had to live with the very real possibility that he would not return home alive. She had heard of other mothers who had only learnt of their sons' deaths via Facebook. 'I spoke to Rasheed about that,' she says, 'and I said, "Please don't ever do something like that to me because it's bad enough that I've got to deal with losing you." He actually promised me. He said, "I will let somebody know." So he kept our number in his trousers with him at all times.'

The phone call came at noon on Friday, 20 November. Nicola was at work, so her husband answered and heard someone speaking first in broken English, then Arabic, who said, 'I am sorry to tell you that Rasheed has been killed by a drone.' Rasheed was killed near Sinjar, a key IS position over the border in Iraq – he had been hit by shrapnel in a coalition drone strike. Nicola was not due home until 5 p.m., so her husband held on to the news for five hours. It was not until she walked through the front door that he approached her, pulled her close and held her tight as he quietly told her, 'I've had a call. Rasheed's gone.'

'It's changed all of us,' says Nicola. 'You go through something like that, or you lose a child in any circumstances, it changes you for ever. You're never the same person again.' Nicola feels that she failed her only son. 'It comes in waves,' she says. 'I still struggle . . . and I don't think that'll ever go away. I do go into that pit where I think I didn't protect him. I didn't do enough.' Rasheed died a terrorist, but to his mother he was a sensitive, impressionable young man whose vulnerability was exploited. 'We call what happened to Rasheed radicalisation, but it is very similar to grooming,' she says. 'His softer nature and that vulnerability was manipulated.'

I noticed parallels in the process Nicola was describing and what I heard when exploring child sex grooming – in both cases it involved identifying the vulnerability of a potential victim. 'If you can find out what ignites someone's emotions, you can make them react and respond in ways we cannot conceive,' says Nicola. 'They are no longer thinking logically.' Hadiya tells me: 'They put out their feelers everywhere, they cast a net and if someone is showing some curiosity they reel you in. The narrative is sophisticated and tailored to each individual – they will do a psychological assessment of each person and find what is missing for that person and then manipulate them – is this person lacking friendship? Has this person got mental health problems? How can I manipulate that and use it?'

Following her son's death, Nicola started a charity – Families for Life – that offers support and advice to the families of children who have been radicalised. I asked her if there were any common threads in the stories she heard. 'It's often been that something has happened, particularly when it comes to emotional stuff,' she says. 'They've been tipped, or there's been an imbalance and they've been grappling with something. It can be a lot of other things, maybe marital breakdown or grief, learning difficulties, which a lot of us go through and come out the other end, but it just depends on the responses and who is there at that time and what happens. A lot of the families I've spoken to, it's not been about the religious thing. It's always been about other things that were going on, whether it's an absent father or a relationship breakdown. There were different things where this person was feeling slightly vulnerable or lost.' I was reminded of what Alyas told me about how estranged he felt from his violent father and later his middle-class White friends and how vulnerable Hadiya had been when she had converted to Islam and found herself far from home. It feels so neat to blame Islam, or a version of Islam, for the actions of those who kill in its name but what I kept hearing was that religion was a convenient peg rather than a convincing explanation.

Tariq (not his real name) is currently in prison after returning from Syria, where he travelled to join Islamic State. 'There was a video that he had done where he was talking about what life was like over here [in Syria] and people should come over,' a friend of his told me. 'But he became disillusioned and tried to come back [to Britain] and he was on his way back when he got arrested.' The friend told me that Tariq – who comes from a British-Pakistani family – was a politically active person who had been watching the news from Syria and wanted to help fellow Muslims. This concept of wanting to help fellow Muslims – in Syria for Tariq and Rasheed, or in Palestine, or for an earlier generation in

Kosovo – has always somewhat baffled me. I understand the concept of the ummah – the global Muslim community – but I have never really understood why a young British Muslim should care so deeply about events in Palestine or Syria when they don't directly affect them. Why not care as much for the plight of Muslims in Kashmir, or Keighley, for that matter?

I asked a prominent Muslim lawyer who has represented British Muslim terror suspects who have travelled to Syria. He turned the question around. '9/11 didn't happen to the UK,' he says. 'It happened to America. America is a terrorist state, according to the UK tradition, in that they fought against King George III and they went off on their own and somebody attacked them for their own reasons. But why did the UK and Europe care so much about 9/11? It's the same answer, really, it's because there's a similarity, a common identity with people, partly because of where they come from but also because of how they look and the religion they have is part of their identity. And it was perceived that an attack on them is an attack on the greater commonality between the Americans and the UK and Europe generally.'

Religion might have been how Tariq explained his decision to travel to Syria but, as with Rasheed, Alyas and Hadiya, his decision to embrace extremism can be more convincingly explained by examining his family situation. 'The main reason Tariq went is because he went through a very bad personal phase in his life,' his friend told me. Tariq had recently emerged from a painful divorce and a traumatic custody battle. 'That screwed him up big time and he was just looking for a sense of empowerment and a sense of worth,' his friend told me. 'He just wanted to escape from it all and then someone else told him why don't you go to Syria where you can remake yourself – it wasn't religious, it was just an escape.'

The prospect of escape and reinvention appear to be common pull factors tempting young Muslims towards extremism and it seems, based on the stories I was hearing, that religion and politics were often harnessed by recruiters who exploited young people's interest in politics and foreign policy, and their ignorance of Islam. The broad concepts of escape and reinvention could mean different things to different people and it sometimes depended on gender. For Tariq the appeal of going to Syria was tied up with the feelings of emasculation he experienced following his divorce and losing custody of his child. 'One of the main things [why men like Tariq wanted to go to Syria] was that it had to do with wanting to be a man,' his friend says. 'It was almost like wanting to be a celebrity – being someone of worth, basically.' Following this logic, joining the likes of Islamic State afforded 'zeroes' the chance to become 'heroes' – they could wave goodbye to their humdrum lives and reinvent themselves with new Arabic names, wave big guns around while driving military vehicles and indulge in sex and violence and tell themselves that it was all for the greater glory of Allah. 'ISIS put false hope and ideas to vulnerable people,' says Tariq's friend, 'and there can be very different facets of vulnerability and they could be for different reasons.'

And what about the girls? In the reporting of young Muslim women who left to join IS – such as the Tower Hamlet schoolgirls filmed trying to enter Turkey – there was particular confusion and consternation as to why young British Muslim girls who it was presumed enjoyed freedom and equality in this country would willingly travel to Syria to join a society that manifestly appeared to treat women as second-class citizens? 'The girls are going for the same reason the boys are going,' says Alyas. 'They're going because they want to kick ass. They want to change the world. They want to be part of something big. They're also running away and they're vulnerable.' Hadiya adds, 'You've got girls who want the attention and it's just way more glam than working in Morrisons on a Sunday morning. So the ability to become recognised is definitely appealing.' It wasn't only dull supermarket jobs that women were escaping. 'If you look at a lot of women who went out there, they were actually escaping personal issues with husbands and family members, and they couldn't get out of their particular situation,' says a lawyer who has represented many terror suspects, including Shamima Begum. 'We can talk about freedoms and opportunities,' he says, 'but when you look at their personal specific scenario they don't have opportunities: they've got nowhere to go really.' Nowhere to go but into the arms of manipulative recruiters offering the chance of escape and reinvention and the promise of Paradise. 'I'm aware of several women [who joined IS] who'd run away from their husbands, gone into shelter and been forced back in to the relationships,' he says. 'And then ISIS tell them: "We'll give you a house, we'll give you benefits and we'll even pay for your tickets." In the end it's all about the feeling that people have that they can determine their own futures. Some of these women didn't feel that they had that opportunity, they felt trapped and they saw ISIS as a way out. There were young girls who left who thought maybe my future is marrying my cousin from back home and I have no agency over that, and they wanted some agency, so they went over to a place where they can pick their own spouses.'

I found it fascinating how some of the themes of earlier chapters, especially the difficulties that young Muslims still face around questions of love and marriage and the particular challenges Muslim women face, were resurfacing when I started looking at the factors leading some young Muslims towards extremism. I found these explanations plausible and, in truth, not hugely surprising. I could see the vague contours of a journey that began with a young Muslim woman yearning for freedom she felt was denied to her in this country, who is then contacted by a recruiter who feeds her a handful of tempting lies to lead her towards the Islamic State. It feels sad but plausible. What I could never have predicted was Alyas telling me that when he interviewed Muslim men who had joined IS there was an over-representation of men who were also gay. When he told me – and I heard this from others that I talked to – I was stunned. Why on earth would anyone who was gay join a group who specialised in throwing gay men off the roofs of buildings? Alyas reminded me of the story of three Muslim men who travelled to Syria from Cardiff. 'One of them was called Reyaad Khan,' he says. 'I went and did some interviews afterwards in his college. He wasn't on the radar. And then someone said to me: "Reyaad was gay. He was seeking redemption." I have heard of a number of men who were gay who joined IS for the simple reason that they were seeking redemption.' I wondered what redemption meant in this context. 'That God will forgive them,' Alyas says. 'I have had cases where men who were gay and were having sex with men said that the only way I can escape from this lifestyle is by going to Syria. People want to believe what they want to believe, everyone has a back-story, has a vulnerability, has an experience and that is the key to understanding what this is all about.'

So how do we make things better? It would firstly be useful to put the problem of Muslim extremism and terrorism into perspective. A 2016 survey revealed that Britons hugely overestimate the number of Muslims in this country. The average guess was that Muslims made up 15 per cent of the population – while the true figure was less than 5 per cent.[5] There is a similar overestimation, I suspect, in how Muslim extremism is perceived, and I am as guilty as anyone. When I was working on the chapter on segregation, one question I asked myself was why it should matter more if Muslims live in bubbles than any other community. My answer was that other communities aren't going around blowing anyone up – and that is why segregation in a Muslim community in Bradford matters more than a Jewish community in London. I was surprised to learn, then, that less than 0.1 per cent of British Muslims have been involved in terrorist-related activity and that after 9/11 only 0.5 per cent of all terrorist deaths have occurred in Western countries. We are more likely to die in our bathtubs or from being stung by bees than in a terrorist attack.[6] This is not meant to imply that we should not take extremism seriously, but it is important to note that in the West we are more likely to be killed at the hands of a terrorist with a far-right, nationalist or supremacist ideology than someone killing in the name of Islam. In 2020 the number of White terrorism suspects arrested in Britain outstripped those of Asian appearance for the third year in a row.[7] Add to that the fact that the domestic terrorists who stormed the Capitol in Washington, DC, on 6 January 2021, some with the apparent intent to assassinate US politicians, were neither Brown nor Muslim, and it feels reasonable to wonder how legitimate it is to only associate Muslims with acts of violent extremism.

It is worth contrasting, for example, the attention given to the horrific murder of Lee Rigby on 22 May 2013 by Michael Adebolajo and Michael Adebowale, two Britons of Nigerian descent who were raised as Christians and converted to Islam, and the fatal stabbing of Mohammed Saleem, an eighty-two-year-old man, in Small Heath by Pavlo Lapshyn less than a month earlier. Saleem had been attending prayers at a mosque and was yards away from his home when he was stabbed. Later, Lapshyn planted three bombs near three mosques in the West Midlands. When asked why he targeted the mosques he replied, 'because they are not White – and I am White.' Saleem's daughter Shazia Khan said: 'He did not do anything to deserve this – other than be a Muslim.'[8] Lapshyn was sentenced to forty years for Saleem's murder and the bombings, and charged under terrorism laws. 'Yet, to this day, the media, the police and the government have not treated Pavlo as they would if the terrorist was a Muslim,' Saleem's daughter Maz noted at the time. 'When Lee Rigby was murdered – three weeks after my dad – his murder received global news coverage and cries of protest. But my father's brutal murder on the street, in a similar attack, received comparatively little attention. Instead of loud and heartfelt condemnation from politicians and the police, instead of hashtags and long discussions about the danger of neo-Nazi beliefs in our society, there was deafening silence. A Muslim terrorist, on the other hand, would certainly have led to conversations about the dangers of radical Islamism.'[9]

I have to admit that I remember the killing of Lee Rigby, but had forgotten – or perhaps never even learnt – about the murder of Mohammed Saleem. If I had read about it I would in all likelihood have labelled it as a crime committed by a 'lone wolf' murderer, someone with severe mental health issues rather than the actions of an extremist or a terrorist. It is bracing to be made aware of how deeply these unconscious biases that suggest only Muslims can be extremists and terrorists penetrate inside us.

One question I have often asked when I have read reports of young Muslims convicted of terrorism is what the responsibility of the wider Muslim community is – could it really be true that nobody knew? And if they did know, does that mean the Muslim community is turning a collective blind eye to the actions of a tiny but dangerous minority? 'A lot of people who go down these routes don't involve their parents or families,' says Hadiya. 'I kept a lot from mine.' Nicola told me that part of the radicalisation process is building an emotional bond with the vulnerable person and then directing them away from their friends and family. 'Some of it is face to face but a lot is online and it is very hard for parents to monitor that, especially when you are dealing with young adults who you are trying to help find their independence and identity.'

It is tempting to claim that surely a parent must know if their son or daughter is on the brink of travelling to Syria, but perhaps that is another instance of Muslims being expected to conform to higher standards than we expect of others. 'How much does a parent actually know about their teenager?' asks Dilwar Hussain. 'If you have a troublesome teen stuck in their bedroom, that's a normal part of growing up. That's normal tension between one generation and another. Let's say a young man is getting groomed online. They're not going to talk to their parents or their local imam. They probably would see their parents as on the other side of that – one of the bad guys – so they'll keep it hidden. And how are the neighbours or wider community expected to know if even the parents don't?'

Muslim extremists, despite their protestations, seem to know very little about Islam. There are numerous examples of irreligious behaviour among these allegedly devout killers: the 9/11 hijackers are reputed to have visited strip clubs in Las Vegas and Florida in the weeks before the attacks;[10] Omar Mateen, who killed forty-nine people in a mass shooting at the Pulse nightclub in Florida in 2016, was said to have been a regular at the venue, where he would sit and drink on his own before trying to chat men up;[11] Mohamed Lahouaiej Bouhlel, who killed eighty-five people by ploughing a truck into a Bastille Day crowd in Nice, was said by neighbours to have had little apparent interest in religion. 'He didn't pray, he didn't fast,' his father told reporters, 'he drank alcohol and even used drugs.'[12] His father also did not mention that his thirty-one-year-old son had a string of male and female lovers, including a seventy-three-year-old male pensioner.[13]

In August 2008, British government research concluded that 'a large number of those involved in terrorism do not practice their faith regularly and many engage in behaviour such as drug taking, drinking alcohol and visiting prostitutes . . . many who become involved in violent extremism lack religious literacy and could be regarded as religious novices. Indeed there is some evidence that a well-established religious identity may actually serve as a protective factor against violent radicalisation.'[14] I find this fascinating because it suggests that rather than fearing a stronger Muslim identity, it might be the very thing that helps protect young Muslims from being radicalised.

I kept hearing that religion was mostly a useful veneer to mask other factors. Those factors included issues facing the Muslim community such as reluctance to discuss mental health. 'As Muslims we just don't talk about it – it is such a taboo,' says Nicola. 'We would rather say they are possessed than say they are depressed.' This reluctance to discuss mental health is not limited to the Muslim community. 'When an individual claiming to be Muslim commits a horrible act, many on the right will tell us Islam is the problem,' noted Shaun King in *The Intercept*, whereas 'white men who resort to mass violence are consistently characterised primarily as isolated "lone wolves".' If there had been greater investment in mental health resources and if there had been a place where he could have talked freely about his feelings, it is possible, his friend told me, that Tariq might not have ended up in Syria. 'He would have been a prime case for one of these interventions,' he told me. 'Tariq would have benefitted from some form of mentoring – a space where he could have talked openly.'

I asked Nicola if, looking back, she thinks she could have done anything that might have meant her son did not end up dying in Syria. 'There were opportunities missed just because I wasn't alive to how serious this could be,' she says, 'so if I had spoken to somebody about my little niggles or tiny gut things about what was going on, and somebody would have said that this is what I need to look at, I feel like I could have taken it more seriously, but the support was not there.' At Families Together Nicola helps other mothers going through the same experience. 'I get referrals from the police and local authorities and I support families to counsel them through psychological trauma and distress,' she says.

In May 2017, Naveed Yasin was at home in south Manchester. When he was eleven, Naveed had become ill and was admitted to hospital where he noticed that the vast majority of the doctors were Asian. 'They were treated with respect and looked up to,' he recalls. 'There were White kids on the ward and if I had bumped into them on the street, they would have hurled racist abuse at me but when the doctors came round, they would treat them with respect.' Naveed noticed that it was possible to be Asian and treated with respect if you were a doctor and it was then and there he decided he would have a career in medicine. He went to school and college in Keighley before studying medicine in Cardiff and eventually ending up working in Manchester.

It was very early in the morning, 5 a.m., when Naveed got a phone call and learnt there had been an incident. The first thing Naveed thought was: 'Please let this not be a terrorist incident,' and the second was: 'Please let it not be a Muslim.' Naveed went to work at Salford Royal Hospital. At 7 a.m. he learnt that somebody had detonated a bomb at the Manchester Arena during a concert by American pop star Ariana Grande. This affected Naveed particularly deeply because he had a young daughter who had asked if she could go to the concert. 'She said she wanted to go to the concert,' he says, 'but my wife said it was a school night so she could not go. It was a very blasé decision of my wife and if she'd said yes, and given in, my daughter would have been there.'

It was Naveed's job to assess the injuries of the victims from the bombing as they arrived at the hospital. 'I saw people with nuts and bolts embedded in their bodies,' he recalls. 'There were people with limb injuries and spinal injuries – you question the humanity of whoever did this.' Naveed spent the next twelve hours treating the bomb victims. The next morning, before returning to work, he had a conversation with his daughter about the attack. 'I told her that we think it might have been a terrorist attack,' he says, 'and people are going to say, "Is this what your religion tells you?" I told her the person who did this was not a Muslim. He's got his own reasons for doing this, this is not what our religion tells us: this is not the right thing to do. I told her we are not the same as him. We're different and we're better than that, so don't let anyone else make you think that you are in any way related to that.'

Later that morning, Naveed was driving in to work for a meeting. He was close to the hospital when he pulled up outside a junction. He noticed a van pulling up alongside his car. The man driving the van was White, balding and in his forties. 'He pulled the window down and that's when he started hurling abuse. He started yelling, "Go back to your own country – we don't need terrorists like you", and there were a lot of profanities thrown in.' The tirade continued, with Naveed in too much of a state of shock to respond. 'I wished I had a sign that said: "I'm not one of them, I'm a good guy",' he says. 'I wanted to say, "What have you done to help those people? You've done nothing to help them, but you are accusing me of all sorts of things."'

I was at the Hay Festival when I learnt about the Manchester Arena attack. I remember following the news, and a familiar sensation of sadness, anger and confusion. The attack had taken place in Manchester, a city where I spent my university and post-university years, and at a venue where I had seen countless concerts, and so I felt a personal connection to the bombing. And then there was the sad fact that the bomber claimed to be a Muslim. British Muslims had been fighting in Syria with Islamic State, but this was an attack on home soil. It was easy to see how it could be exploited by those who hated Muslims. The more I read about what had happened, the more I despaired. It was around then that I learnt about Naveed and he seemed to represent a counter to the terrorist who detonated the bomb. Here was someone who was also a Muslim but whose reading of his religion had led him to be a healer. There was a powerful symbolism to how the person in charge of helping the victims of an Islamist terror attack was himself a Muslim. Naveed was a rebuke to the idea that 'they are all the same', so how galling and depressing to help the victims of such a horrifying attack and then to be attacked yourself by someone who assumes you have sympathy with the perpetrator. 'The one thing I feel my profession teaches me is that you have to treat people with empathy,' Naveed told me. 'So when someone blows someone up I can understand how they've arrived at such an absurd and wrong conclusion. It's because their perceptions of reality are made up of very different things. They align themselves with individuals who give them those very extreme views,' he says. 'If you think everybody's out to get to, you pick up the newspaper, you will only read articles that show everyone's out to get you. So, they then read things and they then identify themselves as the victims because one thing they can't do is understand someone else's point of view.' He was talking about the bomber but also, I think, about the van driver who abused him.

I was struck by Naveed's use of the word 'victim'. It is an entirely appropriate word for those who died in the bombings but what of those who had carried out the attacks? I felt conflicted – to suggest they were groomed and exploited would be to underplay their personal responsibility. 'If you scratch deep enough with anybody who's a wrong 'un you'll find some underlying factors there that have led them to that position,' says senior Prevent* official and extremist expert William Baldét. 'The challenge is at what point do you say, "OK, the victim's now become the perpetrator?" If we're going to do that with Shamima Begum [who left Tower Hamlets and joined Islamic State while still a schoolgirl], do we then apply that to child sexual exploitation where people who've been victims of it throughout their childhood have now become perpetrators of it? We don't look at them and say, "Yes, but they're just victims." We look at them and say, "Bang them up and throw away the key."' It is a knotty question with no simple answer, but my suspicion is that

---

* Prevent is part of the Government's counter-terrorism strategy and aims to stop people being drawn into or supporting terrorism.

if we want to try and prevent more young Muslims from turning to violent extremism, we need to be honest about the intersecting factors that might lead them down that dangerous road. 'They are victims,' says Alyas Karmani. 'It's not popular for us to say that, but they are victims. They're people who have fallen through the net for want of a better description. They are people who have been let down.'

The Manchester Arena attack was the bloodiest terror attack in Britain since 7/7. But let's go back to 7 July 2005. On the same July afternoon that Sajda was recovering from being in the train carriage where the bomb was detonated, Hadiya was pregnant and in the hospital waiting room where she saw the news of the attack on the London transport network. 'I was sat there thinking, "What the hell was that?"' she recalls. Hadiya was still involved in the extremist group HT, but had started having doubts. '7/7 was a massive contrast to how I thought about 9/11 because I hadn't realised, at that point, how I was contributing to the negative perception of Islam,' she says. 'Then I realised that all those things that we're doing, marching and talking about it, seem to be making the situation worse. And it hadn't dawned on me before that. I just thought I was doing the right thing.' The synchronicity of being about to give birth at a time when so many had died at the hands of Islamist terrorists felt like a wake-up call.

Hadiya gave birth two weeks later, on the same day as the foiled second attack. Having a baby made her confront the journey she had been on. 'I was still involved,' she says, 'still talking about injustices and trying to recruit people to join Islamic state, or our version of it – that utopia state where we could take charge of our own destiny, the Islamic world could take charge of its own destiny. I was still doing that, but I was just looking at personalities [in the group]. I had thought these guys were faultless. I almost believed that they were almost perfect human beings. But I started to see that things are not quite how they're trying to make out. They want this perfection but they're completely faulty. And then I just thought, actually, they're a bunch of arseholes.' She laughs.

Hadiya's journey towards anti-radicalisation began on 7/7. While she was having her baby scan, Sajda was at home recovering from having been caught up in the terror attack on the Piccadilly Line. Hadiya left the group and went on to set up the Groundswell Project, an organisation dedicated to bringing communities together. 'The whole recruitment tactic is to ensure that you find the vulnerability and you work on that,' she says. 'So most people who are recruited definitely do have a vulnerability. I've seen almost one hundred people and I've had a hundred per cent success with trying to lead them away from these groups – and what I've seen is you can reverse whatever mindset they're in by using their vulnerabilities and offer an alternative way of helping them. All of the issues they have about foreign policy or Israel or Palestine, it's important not to shut them down. My finding has been that the young people have all had those questions in their lives and they've gone to the wrong people for the answers. If you offer them that alternative answer to the question they have, you manage to win them over.'

'That day changed me,' Sajda says. 'I knew this was not the Islam I was brought up with. This is not what Islam is about and it spurred me even further to want to do something.' Sajda joined the JAN trust, a charity her mother had started that works with Asian women. Since 7/7, Sajda has travelled across Britain. 'I've worked with all sorts of mothers,' she says, 'and what I've tended to hear from them when we've had these discussions is the sense of belonging, the isolation that they feel here within the UK and the racism that they have been facing.' Part of her work is to support mothers so they can recognise if their children are being radicalised. 'I sometimes hear them saying they didn't see any signs that their son was being radicalised,' she says. 'Well, I'm sorry, how can you not? Maybe if you were more involved in his life you might have been able to see a sign because nine times out ten there is at least one sign in the home. Your son coming home with extreme views or talking about having a new set of friends that he is disappearing with. There is always a sign.' And so Sajda has, like Alyas, Nicola and Hadiya, committed to doing what she can to prevent other young Muslims becoming radicalised and turning to violence at home and abroad.

Inevitably there are no straightforward answers to such complex challenges, but if we want to combat radicalisation it means directly challenging the supposed religious justifications that are cited to support the extremist ideology and offering a more hopeful and positive narrative of faith and belonging. It is also important for Muslims to acknowledge and discuss mental health in the community and for non-Muslims to put Islamic extremism into perspective and not criminalise an entire faith based on the actions of a tiny minority. Perhaps it is too much to view that tiny minority who are drawn to extremism as victims, but it is not, I hope, too much to hope that they can be seen as other young people who are groomed and exploited by unscrupulous and amoral outsiders. We need to focus on the psychological and social vulnerabilities that lead young people towards extremism, encourage parents to have more open and honest relationships with their children, and support those, like Hadiya and Sajda, doing the hard and necessary work on the ground. 'These four guys [the 7/7 bombers] were from within the community,' Sajda says, 'so that's why then I came on board to this charity, working at changing hearts and minds. I have engaged with thousands of mothers across the country and I can put hand on my heart and say I've made a difference and that's why I am able to sleep at night.'

FIVE

THEY . . . FOLLOW A RELIGION THAT HATES JEWS

'The leader of Britain's largest Muslim charity has quit after putting anti-Semitic posts on social media. Heshmat Khalifa said Jews are "grandchildren of monkeys and pigs".'[1]

Daily Mail, July 2020

'Anti-Semitic beliefs plummet . . . amongst Muslims whose friendship groups act as a bridge between themselves and non-Muslims – suggesting integration may offer the solution.'

Dr Rakib Ehsan, 'Muslim Anti-Semitism in contemporary Great Britain', August 2020[2]

Mohammed Sajid Khan's dating profile declared he was looking for a wife 'in this life and the next'. He was born in Pakistan and grew up in Bradford, where he ran a car valet service, but he was unemployed in July 2010 when he registered with the matrimonial website SingleMuslim.com. Among those who noticed Mohammed's profile was Shasta Khan, the daughter of a Pakistani migrant who arrived in Britain in 1963 and settled in Oldham. Shasta had had two failed marriages and was hoping it would be third time lucky. Mohammed and Shasta met in July and he proposed three days later. 'He seemed a decent enough person,' recalls Shasta's brother. 'The only thing I was upset about was, "Hang on, have you done your due diligence? Have you gone through the background checks? Do you know enough about this person?" That's what I was recommending to her, but she was adamant that she wanted to marry him, and we were happy with that.'

The couple were married in August 2010 and marriage appeared to change both Mohammed and Shasta. He started wearing long white robes and grew a beard, while she put on a burqa. They started watching extremist Islamist propaganda videos online and reading Al-Qaeda-inspired media. One day the couple were driving through north Manchester when Mohammed saw Jewish worshippers leaving a synagogue. He looked at them and turned to his wife to say, 'We must kill them all.'

In spring 2011, the couple downloaded a manual called 'Make a Bomb in the Kitchen of your Mom' from the internet and, following its instructions, began gathering material for a homemade device. They also started visiting possible targets, including synagogues in two strictly orthodox neighbourhoods. Between March and July 2011, they made nine visits to areas with strong links to the Jewish community. It was only when the police were called to the couple's home following a domestic dispute that their activities were discovered. Shasta's brother told the police that he believed his brother-in-law was a 'home-grown terrorist' and this led to Shasta revealing details of her husband's activities to the police. She told them he regularly made anti-Semitic comments and had made her drive him around Manchester to look at possible targets within Jewish communities. Her allegations led to an investigation and, when officers searched their home, they found a number of items suggesting the couple were preparing to commit a terrorist act. Their plan had been to build a DIY bomb using chapatti flour, hairdressing chemicals and a set of Christmas tree lights to attack Jewish communities in Manchester. Shasta Khan was found guilty of preparing for acts of terrorism and possessing information likely to be useful in an act of terrorism. Mohammed Sajid Khan pleaded guilty to engaging in conduct in preparation for acts of terrorism. After their trial the head of the North West Counter-Terrorism Unit said 'the evidence suggests they were in the attack-planning stage of a terrorist act motivated by anti-Semitic beliefs'.

'Disgust and dismay' is how Shasta's brother summed up his reaction at the time. 'It's very concerning, especially when your sister has been embroiled in all this. We were actually disgusted that she had met someone and turned out like that.' I wanted to know what impact the terror conviction had on Shasta's family. Her brother told me that his parents were furious because they believed he should have done more to warn and protect his younger sister. 'It broke them,' he says. 'Terrorism is not like a theft or a fraud charge where it goes [away] after a few years. Terrorism is something that will stay with you and your family for the rest of your lives. Every time you travel, you are going to be flagged up. Every time you decide to apply for a job, buy a house, rent a house. You are effectively an enemy of the state and that is a very, very serious charge.'

The overwhelming majority of Muslims are not like Shasta and Mohammed; most do not download guides to building bombs or spend their time on reconnaissance missions to synagogues they dream of destroying. Anti-Semitic attitudes, however, are sadly common among Muslims. In 'Anti-Semitic Attitudes among Muslims in Europe', Günther Jikeli notes that: 'since the early twenty-first century, Muslims have emerged as a new group of anti-Semitic perpetrators in Western Europe. Perpetrators of the most extreme cases of violence against European Jews in recent years were Muslims, and they partly justified their actions by their interpretation of Islam.'[3]

A 2015 opinion poll of British Muslims showed that 30–40 per cent subscribed to anti-Semitic beliefs, such as Jews having too much power over government, media, business or global affairs.[4] In a survey of 5,466 British adults published in 2017, the prevalence of anti-Semitic views among Muslim respondents was two to four times higher than in any other segment of the population. Twenty-eight per cent of Muslims agreed with the assertion that 'Jews think they are better than other people', compared to 13 per cent of the general population. Among Muslims, 14 per cent said the Holocaust was exaggerated compared to 4 per cent of the general population and 8 per cent said the Holocaust was a myth. Whereas nearly 80 per cent of Christians agreed with the statement 'a British Jew is just as British as any other British person', only 61 per cent of Muslims, and 59 per cent of the Muslims who described themselves as religious, concurred.[5]

Another study, published in 2018 by the Institute for Jewish Policy Research and the Community Security Trust, revealed that anti-Jewish and anti-Israel attitudes were two to four times higher among Muslims than the population in general. Dr Jonathan Boyd, director of the JPR, was quoted at the time as saying that: 'there does seem to be some relationship between levels of religiosity in the Muslim population and anti-Semitism.'[6] 'It pains me to have to admit this, but anti-Semitism isn't just tolerated in some sections of the British Muslim community,' suggests commentator and broadcaster Mehdi Hasan, 'it's routine and commonplace . . . It's our dirty little secret. You could call it the banality of Muslim anti-Semitism. I can't keep count of the number of Muslims I have come across – from close friends and relatives to perfect strangers – for whom weird and wacky anti-Semitic conspiracy theories are the default explanation for a range of national and international events.'[7] A 2016 survey, which revealed that only 4 per cent of British

Muslims could correctly identify who was responsible for the 9/11 attack on the World Trade Center, could be interpreted as confirmation of Hasan's claims.

There were no Jewish children in my school or perhaps it might be more accurate to say I did not know anyone who was Jewish when I was growing up. My father held stereotypical attitudes towards Jews but his was a positive prejudice – he thought Jews had a lot to teach Muslims about hard work, faith in the power of education and business acumen. Whenever he referred to Pakistanis, my father was withering and dismissive and he always compared them unfavourably to Jews. I realise Pakistanis are defined by nation and Jews by religion, but growing up my father talked much more about us as Pakistanis than Muslims. I grew up obsessed by politics and current affairs, but the knotted agonies of the Middle East never held much fascination for me. There was a period in my later adult life when I would question whether I was really Muslim because I could not summon enough rage about 'what Israel was doing to the Palestinians'. It was not that I was indifferent but rather that I did not understand why I, a British-Pakistani living in Luton and later Manchester and London, should be overly concerned about Palestine rather than injustices in Kashmir, Tibet or Luton, Manchester and London. I also could not understand why having views about what a particular politician or government was doing in Israel should affect how I felt about everybody who identified with that faith.

I drew a distinction between religion, culture and politics. It seems self-evident to me that Muslim and Jews have more in common than what divides them. They are both descended from the Prophet Abraham – I had not realised until researching this book that the Prophet Muhammad was also a descendant of the Prophet Abraham through Abraham's second wife Hagar, and Abraham's first-born son by Hagar, Ishmael. Both pray facing their holy cities – Jerusalem for Jews and Mecca for Muslims. Both are commanded to make religious pilgrimages, sacrifice animals, donate a portion of their income to charity and fast at certain times. They both have foods that are permissible and impermissible; swine is forbidden and only meat from animals that have been religiously blessed while slaughtered is permissible. They command that boys are circumcised and advise that on death the body is buried as soon as possible, ideally the next day.[8] Muslim anti-Semitism was particularly baffling to me because, alongside these ritualistic religious parallels, the cultural diet I most enjoyed was often the product of Jewish artists. The list was nearly endless but included Bob Dylan, Leonard Cohen, Steven Spielberg, Philip Roth, Woody Allen* and Larry David. I owed a massive debt to artists, mostly American, with Jewish heritage,

---

* I know that admitting an appreciation for the works of Woody Allen and Philip Roth could be seen as controversial, but Allen's films, particularly *Annie Hall*, and Roth's novels, particularly *American Pastoral*, have amused, entertained and inspired me for decades.

and that made the anti-Semitism that some associate with Muslims feel completely bizarre.

Naz Shah had been MP for Bradford West for eleven months when, on 26 April 2016, the political blog Guido Fawkes published a screenshot of three Facebook posts she shared in 2014. One argued for Israel's population to be 'transported' from the Middle East to America. She also appeared to liken Israeli policies to those of Hitler. Shah was a member of the House of Commons home affairs select committee, which was conducting an inquiry into the rise of anti-Semitism, as well as parliamentary private secretary to shadow chancellor John McDonnell. Shah stepped down as PPS and issued an apology. In a statement to the House of Commons she said: 'I accept and understand that the words I used caused upset and hurt to the Jewish community and I deeply regret that. Anti-Semitism is racism, full stop.' Shah was suspended from the Labour Party but later reinstated, given a formal warning for bringing the party into disrepute, and told to apologise. 'When it all kicked off on that morning the question I asked myself was a really simple one,' Shah says. '"Do I have a hatred of Jews?" And I don't. I could absolutely, with conviction, say, "No, I don't hate Jews." I had a hatred of what was happening to Palestinians, but I didn't have a hatred of Jews. I understood anti-Semitism just to be the hatred of Jews.'

One week after the revelation of her Facebook posts, three Muslim Labour councillors were suspended after it emerged they too had used social media to promote views that appeared anti-Semitic. The former mayor of Blackburn,

Salim Mulla, had shared social media posts that appeared to draw a link between Zionism and Islamic State. Nottingham city councillor Ilyas Aziz shared the same post that had resulted in Shah being suspended – the one that suggested Israel should be relocated to the US. A third man, Burnley councillor Shah Hussain, was suspended after it emerged that he had told an Israeli footballer on Twitter in 2014, 'you and your country are "doing exactly the same thing" that Hitler did', in reference to the violence against Palestinians.[9] In 2018, Mohammed Pappu, a newly elected councillor in the London borough of Tower Hamlets, was revealed to have shared Facebook posts claiming that Israel staged 9/11, the London bombings and the Paris terrorist attacks.[10] Pappu later told *The Times:* 'I apologise unreservedly for having shared these posts. I regret having done so and they absolutely do not reflect my views. They were posts which I shared at a time when I was developing my political ideas and I accept they paint a picture of conspiracies and political perspectives that do not belong in mainstream politics.' This may have been genuine remorse, but it did seem to suggest that anti-Semitism was nothing but a rite of passage for young politicians finding their ideological feet. It barely needs stating that anti-Semitism is not limited to Muslims, but when I look at the instances of Muslim anti-Semitism it is striking how much of it is related to the political situation in the Middle East. It is almost as if the historic tensions in Israel and Palestine blind Muslims, and perhaps Jews, to how much they have in common.

In the autumn of 2014, Sajid Mohammed was in Nottingham running a Muslim social justice group. When Sajid was a young boy, the only book in his house was the telephone directory, but his mother would take him to the local library and urged him to study hard. He went on to get a degree in management and technology at the University of Bradford, followed by a Master degree in information systems. He found work in IT but became tired of the corporate world and decided to focus on empowering his local community. His work with the social justice group brought him into contact with Nottingham's local Jewish community. Late 2014 was a particularly fraught time in the Israeli-Palestine conflict. 'There was the Gaza incursion and there were lots of local protests,' he recalls. 'I was having a meeting at the synagogue and the rabbi said she was really worried that the events in the Middle East would have a lasting effect on the Jewish and Muslim community in Nottingham.' Sajid told the rabbi that what was needed was a way of getting regular folks of both communities to meet so that the caricatures they might hold were challenged. 'I said, "Let's do it over food." We were looking to set up a hot meals project, I said, "Why doesn't the synagogue partner with us and we can do a joint community soup kitchen that demonstrates our shared values of compassion, dignity, justice and service? And that way members of our communities can meet each other and build friendships."' They secured funding from a government-backed scheme called 'near neighbours'.

The Salaam Shalom Kitchen was officially launched in February 2015.* The kitchen operates every Wednesday evening from a community centre in a church. Muslims and Jews, inspired by the cuisines of those two cultural traditions, prepare the food, which is free for anyone in need of a hot meal. 'I think whether we like it or not, every human being, through their own lived experience, parenting, schooling has some kind of bias and baggage,' Sajid tells me. 'The only real way to deal with it is sharing human to human interaction.' He set up a steering group whose members are Jewish and Muslim, which meets each month in one of the members' houses. 'We go to each other's houses and that's when you realise that they are exactly like us,' he says. 'The same fears, the same hopes, wanting to keep a bit of your culture, wanting your kids to be doctors and business people.'

The last time we met Zulfi Karim he was seventeen and being urged to marry his first cousin in Bradford. Zulfi went on to leave school and started work in the cultural sector in Bradford, rising to board director of the Yorkshire Board. His career was progressing, but he felt unfulfilled. 'I felt I had done it all and got the T-shirt,' he says, 'but something was missing in my life.' When he turned forty he went on pilgrimage to Mecca. 'Seeing all those people

---

* It was later revealed that Meghan Markle had secretly donated £10,000 to the charity, which had been used to stock the food bank and provide funds for the Salaam Shalom Kitchen.

together in one place and being peaceful,' he recalls, 'I didn't see any aggression or hate or violence. I just saw peace. I thought, why can't the rest of the world see what I see? I came back and religion took hold of me,' he says. 'I had a kind of calling to look at my faith and to ask: why do so many people hate Muslims? I wanted to really get out there and show people that Isis is not all of us. People like me aren't like that. I wanted to raise the exposure of non-radical Islam.' It was that desire to show the true face of Islam that drew him towards interfaith work. He started attending mosque events and at one such evening an old man introduced himself. His name was Rudi and he was from the local Jewish community.

Rudi was born in 1926 and travelled to Britain in 1937 with his parents and sister. There has been a Jewish presence in Bradford since the 1850s and Rudi was a regular worshipper at the Reform Synagogue in the heart of Manningham. The synagogue – a Grade-II-listed Moorish building – dates back to 1880 but had fallen into disrepair: there was serious damage to the eastern wall, where the ark held the Torah scrolls, and the roof was leaking. The Jewish community in Bradford had shrunk over the decades and couldn't fund the repairs, meaning that Rudi, the synagogue's chairman, was facing the prospect of selling the building. That was why he had come to the mosque: to try to persuade the local Muslim community to help repair the synagogue. 'When we have Friday collections, it is usually for the mosque,' Zulfi told me, 'or it's because something's happened in Palestine or Pakistan. So, this was a bit of a new one on me: to have a whip round at Friday prayers for a synagogue?' Zulfi arranged to meet Rudi at the synagogue the following day. 'I went inside, and I've never been so mesmerised in a space,' he recalls. 'It had tall ceilings, it was almost Islamic and for me it became so tranquil. It was a holy place, a peaceful place. And there's this old, frail man.' Rudi tried to turn the lights on and showed him four buckets into which were falling drops of water from the leaking roof. Rudi told him that most of the congregation had moved away so there were few local Jewish people who could help. Zulfi asked how much it would cost to repair the roof and Rudi handed him a typed estimate that Zulfi took with him when he returned to work. 'I went into the boardroom and I had a cup of tea and I sat there,' he recalls, 'and then I realised I had to do something.' Zulfi wanted to help but he wasn't sure whether financially aiding a synagogue was acceptable from an Islamic point of view. 'I needed that to be sorted out,' he says, 'because what I didn't want to do was to be stoned to death at Friday prayers at the mosque next week.' He consulted an imam.

It probably will not come as a huge surprise that the question of what the Qur'an says about Jews is open to interpretation. Those who argue that the Qur'an is anti-Semitic quote passages such as 'do not take the Jews and the Christians as allies' and 'thou wilt surely find the most hostile of men to the believers are the Jews and the idolaters', which appear to substantiate this. Those who argue that Islam is a tolerant faith point to passages that warn against belittling other faiths, such as 'O you who have believed, let not a people ridicule [another] people; perhaps they may be better than them.' They cite a passage such as 'those who believe, and those who are Jewish, and the Christians . . . any who believe in God and the Last Day, and act righteously – will have their reward with their Lord; they have nothing to fear, nor will they grieve' and argue that this and the fact that synagogues and churches, along with mosques, are praised in the Qur'an demonstrates that there is nothing hostile to Jews in Islam. What this demonstrates, I think, is the danger of cherry-picking and the importance of reading the whole Qur'an in context. 'In all faiths, more exclusivist or militant verses are taken out of context by some,' John L. Esposito, author of *Unholy War: Terror in the Name of Islam*, told *The New York Times*, 'and amplified in popular culture.'[11] This amplification can drown out quieter voices, which point to the times and places in history when Muslims, Jews and indeed Christians lived in relative peace and harmony.

The imam Zulfi consulted was aware of this shared history and told him he had no concerns about Zulfi helping Rudi repair the synagogue. 'I looked at the amount that was needed to repair the roof and I thought this isn't a massive figure,' Zulfi says. 'I thought business is doing all right. Really, why don't I and a few of my friends dip into our pockets and just underwrite the costs?' Zulfi approached the owner of Drummond Mill, where his office was based. A Jewish descendant of Joseph Strauss had run Drummond Mill, where Zulfi's father had worked after emigrating from

Pakistan in the 1960s, and was the rabbi who founded the synagogue in 1880. Zulfi and the mill owner decided they would split the cost of repairs. 'I rang Rudi back and I said, "Just get on with the works and I will underwrite it. Just tell them tomorrow and give them my contact details and I'll arrange a payment." And that's exactly what happened.'

This payment was only the start of the relationship between the Muslim and Jewish communities in Bradford. 'The Israeli Ambassador in London got to hear of it,' says Zulfi. 'He visited Bradford. We had all the Jewish communities up and down the country suddenly interested in Bradford like never before. They weren't interested in the synagogue. They were interested in the interfaith relationships with this Muslim community.' Since then, the Muslim and Jewish communities collaborate and interact on issues of mutual interest. 'Literally, we're on speed dial,' says Zulfi. 'We deal with issues that concern our two religions – political issues, race issues, definitions of Islamophobia and anti-Semitism. We work together and we share a lot of intelligence.'

Rudi recalls the funeral of one of the Jewish elders of the synagogue around ten years ago. The funeral was held at the synagogue and at one point the hearse got stuck between cars on the road. The hearse was surrounded by local Muslims, who started throwing insults and rocking the vehicle. My concern about the co-operation described by Zulfi was that it didn't fully reach down into the community and the masses. 'It is definitely getting out to the masses,' claims Zulfi. 'People have seen me and Rudi walk down the streets, they'll say hello to us both now and they won't scream insults at him because he's a friend.'

Rudi and Zulfi now get on so well that when Rudi goes on holiday he gives the synagogue keys to Zulfi, as well as the alarm code. The Jewish community invites local Muslims and Christians to Friday night dinner, Muslims return the invitation for a Ramadan feast and Christians share the harvest festival. Rudi and Zulfi consider each other friends, yet growing up neither knew anyone from the other community. 'There was no interaction at all,' says Rudi. 'They were there and we were here, and we lived separate lives. The opportunity to meet Muslim people and for us to become friends was minimal.' Now the synagogue has a Muslim on the governing board. 'As far as we know it's never happened before, or since.' Zulfi is convinced such initiatives will help build tolerance. 'You look at those who killed Lee Rigby, supposedly in the name of Islam. The question is: what makes these young men so radicalised, so angry, so intolerant? I strongly feel that the way forward is interfaith.'

Sadiq Patel is based in Blackburn and also involved in interfaith work. Since 2003 he has been helping Renee Black, a Jewish woman born two years before Rudi in 1924. 'She lives alone, never married,' he told me. 'She lives a very lonely life so three days a week I go visit her and we go shopping.' In May 2017, Sadiq was planning on taking Renee to Manchester. 'We were planning to go shopping in Manchester because there's no Jewish shops in Blackburn,' he says, 'so we always go shopping in Manchester, go and get meat, bread, all the groceries and everything else that she needs. We'll go to the Jewish cafe and have a Jewish lunch.' Sadiq and Renee travelled to Manchester and decided to lay some flowers at Albert Square. It was only days after an Islamist suicide bomber had killed twenty-two people at an Ariana Grande concert and the city and country were in a state of shock and grief. 'I said let's go and lay some flowers and carry on with the shopping,' he recalls. Sadiq and Renee went to the vigil, they each said a prayer and added their bouquet of purple flowers to the sea of floral tributes. Sadiq also left a handwritten card that read: 'Words can't describe what happened or how we are feeling. One thing is for sure: we are in this together. We feel the same grief as you do.' The plan was to be there for ten minutes but soon the couple began to notice that people were looking at them. The sight of an Asian Muslim man, in a black hat and robes, gently comforting an older Jewish woman attracted photographers and the images were used worldwide. In the immediate aftermath of a horrific act of terror committed in the name of Islam, the image of Sadiq and Renee offered a glimpse of a more hopeful iteration of Islam. 'We never expected those pictures to go round the world,' says Sadiq, 'but I really hope people looked at them and saw that two people from different faiths can come together in harmony and stand united.'* I saw the photograph and it led me to contact Sadiq. What interested me was not the powerful

---

* Renee Black died in May 2020, aged ninety-six.

symbolism in the photograph or the tragic timing of when it was taken. It was the fact that, had there not been an appalling terror attack which brought them to Albert Square, most of us would never learnt about Sadiq and Renee's friendship. The dominant narrative is of Muslims not getting along and counter-narratives that challenge this find it hard to attract attention – unless a Muslim kills young music fans. 'Ours is just one example of the thousands of friendships and acts of kindness we don't see,' says Sadiq.

The contrast between my childhood and that of my children could hardly be starker. My daughter has Jewish friends and she has a greater understanding of what that means in lived reality than I did when I was her age. When I see Laila playing with her friend Talia, what strikes me is not their different cultural heritages but the ways they are similar – in their temperaments and interests. If I were to tell Laila that there are Muslims who have prejudicial attitudes towards Talia and her family simply on account of their religion, she would think that is absolutely ridiculous and makes no sense, because it doesn't. I am lucky that we live in a part of the country that is truly diverse and my children do not go to faith schools where they are surrounded only by other Muslims. If the area we lived was monoculturally Muslim, how would my children have the opportunity to interact with Jewish children?

Tahira Parveen was the head of religious education at a Muslim faith school for girls in Manchester. In late 2012 she was worrying about the girls she was teaching. 'Working in an

Islamic girls' school, the biggest issue is the perception that Muslim girls are segregated,' she told me. 'I understand why that criticism comes about, I think it is valid and not just for Muslim schools – they're valid for any faith school. I wanted that criticism to have no weight with our girls.' Tahira's school had around 240 students and the overwhelming majority would have absolutely no interaction with anyone Jewish. Tahira felt it was important that her pupils had some understanding of and interaction with the local Jewish community, so she contacted King David, a Jewish faith school, and talked to Rabbi Benjamin Rickman, her counterpart at the school. He suggested that she bring some of her students to the school. 'I told her to bring your Muslim girls with their hijabs into our school,' he recalls, 'and let my kids hear about what Muslim girls experience, wearing distinctively religious garb in the street, and we can have that conversation.' When Tahira brought the girls to the school, the first thing they noticed was a huge Israeli flag in the foyer – at their school there was a map on the wall, but Israel had been rubbed out. 'It was incredible,' says Benjamin. 'We had a hundred Jewish kids listening to ten Muslim girls and then they broke into smaller groups. You had these Muslim girls with their hijabs teaching our Jewish kids in their classroom. Very quickly the ice melts. You start off differently and, within minutes, you're discovering, "Oh, I like that music. I watch that show. I do this." It was such a powerful event.'

In later encounters, which would take place in both schools, the Muslim and Jewish children would discuss the stereotypes each had of the other. One Muslim girl wanted to know what was it with Jews and money. 'I explained to her that in history Jews were barred from certain professions, but money lending or collecting the debts from the non-Jewish overlords in a village were jobs they were allowed to do,' says Benjamin. 'I wish I could have filmed her face. "Oh, so it comes from anti-Semitism? It's not really about being Jewish. You were forced into this role." It was amazing because she was able to learn – until that point, she was blinkered and couldn't understand.' The Jewish pupils wanted to know if the girls were bald under their hijabs and what was it with terrorism and Islam. 'It was a big eye opener for the girls because most of them thought Jewish people don't like Muslims,' says Tahira, 'so it was an eye opener to learn that that's not the case.' On Holocaust Memorial Day, Benjamin invited the Muslim girls to tell the story of the Holocaust to the Jewish students and the Jewish pupils told them about the Muslims who rescued Jews in the Holocaust. Later, the Muslim girls were invited on a tour of the orthodox neighbourhood. 'The reaction that we had was incredible,' recalls Benjamin. 'A builder who saw us was so overwhelmed by what he saw that he took out forty pounds and offered to buy us all cakes because he just couldn't believe what he was seeing.' What makes this story particularly powerful is when you compare these young Muslim girls touring this Jewish part of Manchester to Shasta and Mohammed making a similar tour but with very different intentions.

The central revelation that emerged from the interactions – that young Muslims and Jews have much in common – is almost comically banal and yet the fact is that most British Muslims and Jews do not get the opportunity to learn about each other and discover this obvious truth. In that context something as outwardly simple as two groups of students spending time together carries potential. There were similarities, but talking to Tahira and Benjamin, it was revealing how both were careful to stress that there were limits on what they want in terms of the extent of the interaction. 'We don't talk about Israel,' says Benjamin. 'We're talking about being Jewish or Muslim in a British context only.' Tahira recalls seeing the Israeli flag at Benjamin's school and being told that the school raised funds for Israel. 'I remember he said, "We have to fundraise for our own people." The students are all politically oriented, but we didn't bring politics and it makes you think maybe we can have dialogue with the Jewish community without bringing the conflict up every time.' The young people could connect over the things they had in common instead. 'When they met the Jewish students, the girls discovered that, yes, we will have differences, we may look different, we may wear different attire, celebrate different festivals,' says Tahira, 'but we have similar interests in music, we enjoy very similar food, we have similar issues with religion where our parents are saying one thing or our school is saying one thing and then we're having to pick and choose.'

I listed earlier the numerous ways in which Islam and Judaism are similar but there is one difference which particularly fascinates me, and it has to do with the relation-ship between religious identity and belief. A 2013 US survey illustrates the point well. The survey found that 22 per cent of American Jews said they were atheist, agnostic or simply did not follow any particular religion – similar to the pro-portion of the general public without religious affiliation.[12] 'They are not connected to Jewish life the way their parents or grandparents were,' commented Rabbi B. Elka Abrahamson, president of the Wexner Foundation, a Jewish philanthropy group. 'I don't think this means we count them out.' The term often used for such Jews is a 'cultural' or 'secular' Jew and I have long been fascinated by the question of why there is less acceptance of a cultural or secular Muslim than their Jewish counterpart. My experience of Islam is that if one tries to claim a Muslim identity without being strictly observant, there are plenty who will say you are not really a Muslim. Muslims who go further and declare they are atheists are often accused of apostasy and some Muslims believe that the punishment for apostasy is death. I have often been asked if I really am a Muslim. The implication is that, aside from not drinking and not eating halal meat, there is not much in my outward behaviour that suggests I am Muslim. I don't fast, I don't pray, and it has been years since I have stepped inside a mosque for Eid prayers. So why, given all this, am I so reluctant to relinquish my Muslim identity? My brother likes to joke that the only time I am a Muslim is when I am paid to write about being a Muslim and, as wounding as that jibe is, it contains a grain of truth. The wider context is that growing up I did not have a religious education. I did not attend mosque and my perception of Islam was as a set of rules and restrictions. I missed out on this education during the years I was living at home in Luton and by the time I left it was too late. This has had inevitable consequences and left large holes in my Muslim identity. It is somewhat shameful to admit that I know far more about American history than Islamic history, can quote more song lyrics than I can quote verses from the Qur'an. Working on this book, then, has literally been an education and it has confirmed to me why it is important to know more about the religion I claim to follow. It has also helped me understand that there are different ways to be Muslim. Am I a liar in claiming to be a Muslim? I don't think so and this is where I think Jews have something to teach Muslims – just as there are cultural Jews, I would like a greater acceptance of cultural Muslims.

The writer Saif Rahman, founder of the Humanist & Cultural Muslim Association and author of *The Islamist Delusion – From Islamist to Cultural Muslim Humanist*, defines cultural Muslims as 'secular, religiously unobservant or irreligious individuals who still identify with Muslim culture due to family background, personal experiences or the social and cultural environment in which they grew up. Subconsciously, many question the traditional interpretations of the Islamic faith; yet remain proud of their religion's architectural, literary and poetic heritage. They embrace the positive aspects of its culture – its camaraderie, charitability, hospitality and respect for elders – and still enjoy its cuisine, clothing and music.'[13] That sounds like me, and it sounds like many British Muslims I know, but there is, I think, a lack of widespread acceptance among other Muslims of a cultural or secular Muslim identity.

The emergence of cultural Muslims is not just a Western phenomenon. According to a 2012 poll that looked at religion in Saudi Arabia – which, as the birthplace of Islam, claims to be the holiest of the Arab countries – found that 19 per cent of the population said they were not religious and 5 per cent described themselves as convinced atheists.[14] 'Increasingly we will have Muslims who don't want to believe in Islam and that's absolutely fine,' says Dilwar Hussain, chair of New Horizons in British Islam. 'The Qur'an says, "Will you force them to have belief?" We need a space where if somebody decides not to believe, they shouldn't be ostracised or criminalised. They should be embraced and wherever that journey takes them that's up to them.' He suggests the phrase 'belonging without believing' and that seems to capture the essence of a secular or cultural religious identity.

When I think of my Jewish heroes – Philip Roth in particular – so many belonged despite not believing. The American Jewish artists I most admire – from Jerry Siegel and Joe Shuster, who created Superman, to Steven Spielberg to Leonard Cohen – were able to mine the specificity of their culture to create art with universal appeal. In this Muslims can once again learn from Jews: how to create art from pain. It saddens me that, given how much the two communities have in common, and how often they are both attacked by the same hate groups, anti-Semitism is so prevalent among Muslims. Benjamin told me that he has become used to being abused by strangers. 'I've been yelled at,' he tells me. 'Students have been yelled at by groups of Asian youths or boys saying things or making comments. Anti-Semitism is rife. It's part of the Jewish experience of living in the UK. I've experienced it plenty of times myself. The most recent one was an Asian and I wanted to say to him we ought to be together. We shouldn't be attacking each other.'

Jews and Muslims both have experience of abuse. Asma, who grew up in London to Libyan parents, recalls being on a bus on her way to see her family in Wembley. It was 2011 and she was pregnant with her daughter when a White man in his fifties started to swear at her, pulling at her hijab. 'I said to him to just be respectful,' she tells me. 'I said, "Don't call me these things and don't swear."' The swearing continued and then just as the man was about to get off the bus, he turned towards Asma and spat at her. Eight years later, Asma was travelling on the London Underground, feeling tired and distracted, when she saw a man start to hurl anti-Semitic abuse at a Jewish man traveling with two young boys. The man started to read anti-Jewish passages from the Bible. 'I was in a state of shock,' she says. 'I thought, "Is this still happening?" He was really loud and then he started getting aggressive and threated the other guy.' When another passenger intervened, the man threatened to 'Smack you right in the nose, man ... I'm not no Christian pastor,' adding, 'back the fuck off from me.' The man seemed volatile and the situation could have turned violent. Asma could easily have ignored what was going on and got off at the next stop. She didn't. She watched as the man started to talk to the Jewish man's children. 'I saw him talking to the little children and I could see the fear,' she told me. 'Being a mother you can see the fear in a child's eyes. The child was going from one person to another. He couldn't understand. He started looking around – looking at his dad, looking at his brothers – what's going on? I just automatically saw my kids there and, as a Muslim, when you see injustice, you have to talk.' Asma made a decision: calmly and slowly, she confronted the man, remaining calm and distracting him so that the attention was no longer on the Jewish father. The man eventually got off the tube and peace was restored to the carriage.

It was an incident, like Sadiq and Renee laying flowers in Manchester, that offers an example of positive interaction between Muslims and Jews but no one would ever have known about it were it not for the fact that someone filmed the encounter on their phone and shared it on social media. The clip went viral and Asma was hailed as a heroine for having the courage to defend the Jewish father. The symbolism of a hijab-wearing Muslim woman coming to the aid of a Jewish man was not lost on anyone. What struck me watching the footage was how Asma had managed to remain so calm. 'I was reading a passage from the Qur'an that day on my way to London,' Asma told me, 'and it said, you have to be patient. You always get rewarded for patience.

In situations like this, if you're going to get angry and if you are going to start shouting, he would have hit me. The calmness and the patience, it just came from the passage I read in the Qur'an.' After the incident went viral, Asma was reunited with the Jewish father at his home in Manchester. 'He brought a big, massive bouquet of flowers,' she told me. 'We sat down and spoke about the experience and he said to me, "If you didn't step in that day, I don't know what the situation would have become."' It is chilling to think that the man lived in the same part of Manchester that Shasta and Mohammed were planning their terror attack. So why did Asma help a Jewish man when Shasta wanted to kill them? I suspect there are a number of reasons, but two key ones seem to be that Asma was intimately familiar with the religion and attended a school where the other students were predominantly Jewish. 'We have a stereotype that says Muslim people don't like Jews,' she told me. 'I don't know where they get that from but it's not right. We don't have to dislike Jewish people because of their religion. That's not right.'

The more I talked to people for this chapter, the more hopeful I became that the stereotype often perpetrated that Muslims and Jews have to be in conflict is overblown and inaccurate. I assumed that co-operation would be between those Muslims and Jews who were not hugely religious, but repeatedly I came across Muslims whose favourable attitude towards Jews was rooted in their familiarity with their faith. 'Benjamin is an Orthodox Jew,' said Tahira, 'and he would tell us that from a religious point of view Jews have to do this and do that and women have to dress like this, and the girls in my school noticed that there was a similarity between Orthodox Judaism and Islam.'

Nasim Ashraf grew up, like Tahira, in Oldham and set up his own phone dealership in the late nineties, which made him very financially successful. 'My mentality was all about making money, nothing else really mattered,' he recalls. 'Success equalled money but then I started getting interested in religion. I always believed that God existed, but I did not know what he wanted from me. Why I was born?' Nasim began to study Islam. 'I started reading the Qur'an in a language that I understood,' he says. 'That's when it sort of connected and I found that Muslim is a verb, it's not a noun. It's a doing word.' This realisation inspired him to co-found the UK Education and Faith Foundation in 2009 to address 'the concerns and issues in society but from an Islamic ethos'. The charity runs the largest food bank in Oldham and serves anyone, regardless of their faith. 'In my eyes there is no such thing as "faiths",' he says, 'you either have faith or you don't have faith.' Nasim grew up believing that 'so long as I never touched alcohol and as long as my chicken is halal, I am Muslim'. It was not until he began studying other religions that he started to go deeper into Islam, and to see how much it shared with Judaism. 'Contrary to popular belief, Islam has love and compassion for people of all beliefs,' he says. 'Islam tells you that they are human beings first before anything else. I would go further with that with the Jewish community – they are literally our cousins. Their beliefs and what we believe are actually closer than anything else – we are both parts of the Abrahamic clan.' Nasim acknowledged that the lived reality did not always match this aspiration. 'Anti-Semitism is not specifically something that we [Muslims] have a monopoly over,' he says. 'It's across the world [but with Muslims] maybe it's because of sibling rivalry, where you are always fighting with your sibling.'

I wanted to share Nasim's story and his thoughts on how much Muslims and Jews have in common not only because it demonstrates the compassionate and tolerant face of Islam. It is also because of the stark contrast in how he sees the relationship between Islam and Judaism compared to his sister – Shasta Khan, the woman arrested and convicted of preparing a terrorist act motivated by her anti-Semitic beliefs. How was it possible that two siblings raised in the same home, only a few years apart, could diverge so dramatically in their attitudes towards Jews? I asked Nasim how he explained the actions of his sister and her husband. 'The fact of the matter is that God Almighty guides whom He wills and lets go whomever He wills,' he says. 'Maybe he had some insecurities growing up or self-confidence issues, insecurity issues growing up that led him to believe that Jews are bad people. I don't know. Maybe it was his life experiences. God only knows what his reasoning was behind it.' When I asked about his sister, Nasim was naturally protective and claimed she was 'definitely an innocent accessory. The relationship became very, very sour six to eight months into the relationship – he [Mohammed] became very controlling, he became manipulative and because she'd had those marriage break-ups, she was desperately trying to hold on to that marriage. I just wish my sister had spoken to me in the early years of the marriage where the first signs started to become clear – his narrative on Islam and his interpretation of certain verses.' It was evident talking to Nasim that he believes his sister was manipulated. He also had faith that Islam was not responsible for Shasta and Mohammed Khan's actions. 'All I can say is that, whatever his reasoning was, it was wrong,' he says, 'and it was against the tenets of Islam.' Shasta Khan was released from prison, having completed her sentence. I asked Nasim how she was. 'God Almighty says in the Qur'an, "The best of my servants are those who return back to me", so as a Muslim I am hopeful that people come back,' he says. 'She has returned to quite a big degree; she has done a big U-turn. She's much better. She gets on and she does help out with charitable events.'

The conviction that Muslims and Jews have more in common than what divides them was what drew Shahnaz towards interfaith work. She is the middle daughter of Selina, who grew up in Manchester before moving to Bradford. In earlier chapters we learnt about the murder of Shahnaz's uncle Ahmed Ullah and how she and her two sisters all ended up studying at Oxford University. While she was at Oxford, Shahnaz joined the university interfaith society. 'My dad had been involved in interfaith work after 9/11,' she says.

'That was my first experience of interfaith: let's go to each other's places of worship and eat food together. I always thought it was a really good thing and my parents were very open to it. I had a lot of Hindu friends growing up. I went to a Catholic school. So when I got to university, it was at fresher's fair and somebody invited me to join this special Muslim-Jewish interfaith group, and I was like, "Yeah, great, don't know much about them, I'll join."' She was manning the stall when a young man approached. 'I was just really looking for people to sign up and he was at the same college as me,' Shahnaz recalls. 'As soon as I found that out, I was like, "Just put your name on the list, I need people to sign up." So, yes, that's why I remember, and also he had massive hair. So, I just remember this guy with this massive crop of hair.' The young man was called Avi and he was Jewish.

'I was conscious from a young age about the connections between the Abrahamic faiths,' says Shahnaz, 'but if there were any Jews in Keighley I never knew about them and never met them. That only happened at university.' Shahnaz and Avi became friendly through the interfaith group but rarely actively spent time together. Shahnaz graduated from Oxford before returning to Keighley to study a master's at Bradford University. She then moved to London after securing a job working with a national Muslim-Jewish interfaith group and it was there that she attended a class reunion. It was November 2013 and Shahnaz was with a group of friends when she noticed Avi. 'I thought he looked really good,' she recalls, 'and we had had a really nice conversation.' It had always been expected that Shahnaz would marry a Muslim. 'I don't really know how that messaging happened, I don't remember being lectured that this is what we would do but we were just aware that this was what the expectation was,' she says. 'I always knew that there would be a little bit of wiggle room on the ethnicity. My parents would have preferred someone Bangladeshi but if I'd ended up meeting and really wanting to marry someone who was of a different background but still Muslim, I think I knew that would be all right in the end.' Despite this, Shahnaz and Avi began dating, but the fact that Shahnaz was due to go to graduate school in the United States seemed to offer a natural end to the relationship. Except that it did not. 'I went abroad but we stayed in touch,' she says, 'and that seemed to be the time actually where we got really close because we weren't even in the same country any more and yet we still wanted to talk all the time and were still emailing and making time for each other in our days.'

The closer they got, the more it became important for Shahnaz and Avi to have a serious conversation about faith. They both strongly believed in the principle of interfaith co-operation but neither had imagined that it would have affected their personal lives. 'We had always known each other in the context of our faiths,' says Shahnaz. 'It's always been an intrinsic part of how we see each other and that made the conversations easier actually. I knew that, with Avi, him being Jewish wasn't just a footnote, and it wasn't just part of an identity checkbox thing either. I knew that he prayed twice a day, or three times a day. I knew that he observed, would do the Friday night prayers and blessings, and that kind of thing. So, I knew the extent to which it mattered to him, and I think similarly for me, like I fast during Ramadan. And I think us being able to understand each other's levels of observance meant that we're able to respect that in each other and understand it.' Shahnaz returned from the United States in late summer 2015 and told her family about Avi. 'I remember my dad saying, "If you've chosen him, I'm sure he must be really nice, but we can't get behind that",' she recalls. 'He was into the idea of interfaith but no one ever thinks that it'll end up in getting married.' Her mother was equally sceptical. 'Our expectation was that our kids would marry Muslims – that was almost like a non-negotiable given,' Selina says. 'That's what you do. We don't mind you finding somebody yourself but somebody we can say yes to and, at that point, we didn't feel like we could say yes. There was a degree of anger as well: "How could she do this? How could she be so stupid?" There was also a sense of disappointment and betrayal. It did feel almost like, "Well, we've given you all this sort of freedom and this is what you do to us as a result."' Shahnaz had empathy for her parents and appreciated that she was putting them in a difficult position, but there was something in her, and in her feelings for Avi, that meant she did not want to give him up. 'I believe in God, I believe everything happens for a reason and that we met for a reason,' she says. 'I just really strongly felt that this was my life partner and so, in a way,

I was informing my parents but I wasn't really asking for permission. It was a case of I really want to do this with your blessing but if it doesn't happen it is still something that I want to do.'

Time passed but her parents refusing to countenance meeting Avi. Then, around a year later, her father turned to her mother and said, 'This can't go on for ever. We need to do something. Let's meet him.' Avi duly came over to Keighley, staying in a hotel. 'We went for walks and had tea and stuff, and everyone was very polite,' recalls Avi, 'and then suddenly there'd be like a section where we'd have a conversation about children and inter-communal relations.' Shahaz's father was immediately won over by Avi and so, eventually, was her mother. 'He's a chilled-out kind of guy, very mellow,' says Selina, 'and just seeing how he was with her. He's caring, considerate. All the qualities you'd want in somebody.' Avi proposed to Shahnaz in early March 2017, and they were married in August that year. There was no off-the-shelf version of a Jewish-Muslim wedding so Shahnaz and Avi set about creating their own. 'If you had just walked into the room you would have thought it was a big Asian wedding,' says Shahnaz. 'We both wore Asian clothes: Avi wore a shirani and I wore red, very traditional. I wore my mum's wedding jewellery, which was really nice.' They walked out to Sam Cooke's 'What a Wonderful World'. Both families attended the wedding, and their parents have become firm friends. 'They've got a shared WhatsApp group and they ring each other when they've been travelling,' says Shahnaz. 'I always grew up thinking it was quite an Asian thing, like so-and-sos going away on holiday, or they're going back to Bangladesh for six months, I need to call them before they go. Our parents do that with each other.' 'They're very similar to us in terms of background and expectations,' says Selina. 'There's a lot more in common in terms of socially, mentally, educationally – all of that – and so it's much easier to get on with them. So, yeah, we do meet up regularly. We've done Passover with them. They've done Eid with us.'

I had always assumed that the only way a marriage between a Muslim and Jew could succeed was if they were both, essentially, Jewish and Muslim in name only. The most eye-opening revelation in talking to Shahnaz and Avi was that what was more important was that they shared the same degree of religiosity. For Shahnaz the biggest realisation was that one didn't need to lose anything when marrying outside one's faith. 'There's a temptation to believe that if you want to get married to someone of a different religion, then you can no longer be your religion, or you have to leave your family behind,' she says. 'We have been blessed to have the families that we've had and have the community that we've had, and I think I guess the biggest lesson has just been that you don't have to give everything up in order to be able to do this.'

It was inspiring to meet Shahnaz and Avi and it provided me with the hope I was searching for. This hope is, however, tinged with an awareness that the reason I was focusing on this particular story was precisely because it was so unusual.

What is more common is two faith communities barely interacting in any meaningful fashion and allowing events thousands of miles away to sour their perceptions of each other. Anti-Semitism, it barely needs saying, is not limited to Muslims, but what the likes of Sajid, Shahnaz and others in this chapter have shown is that interaction can help alleviate fears and misconceptions and remind both Muslims and Jews of all that they have in common.

SIX

THEY ... BELIEVE HOMOSEXUALITY IS A SIN

'We don't believe in homosexuality.'
Leaflet distributed at a school by Muslim parents,
Birmingham, 2019

*'Todoshecho, nada dicho.' (Everything is done, nothing
is said.)*
Spanish saying quoted in 'Islamic
Homosexualities: Culture, History and Literature'

There had never been any doubt who Shazad would marry. The youngest child of Matloob and Jamelia, who ran an Indian restaurant in Bradford, he grew up knowing he was promised to his cousin. The vow was made when Shazad was only two years old, and his parents even arranged a mock wedding ceremony when Shazad and his cousin were children, where the couple exchanged toy wedding rings. Matloob was a contradictory character who preferred drinking to visiting the mosque and had numerous affairs with White women but still acted as an old-fashioned authoritarian father to his children. He forbid his daughters from wearing Western clothes and did not want his children to go to university because he feared it would spoil them. Jamelia did not share her husband's fears and prejudices. 'My hope was that my children would be well educated,' she told me in Urdu, 'that their every wish would be granted. I wanted my children to see the world.' When it came time to apply for university, Shazad applied to study in London. He won a place, and was set to leave home and head south. His father had other plans. 'I had my bags packed but my dad physically tried to stop me from leaving the house.' It was then that Jamelia came to his rescue. 'My mum was always my partner in crime,' Shazad explains. 'Whenever there was a difficult conversation to have with my dad, we would hatch a plan on how to tackle him.' With Matloob ranting that there was no way his son was leaving, Jamelia stepped in. 'I remember Mum told me to leave through the side door,' Shazad says. 'She said, "Just go and let me deal with your dad." So I literally ran away to London.' In London Shazad was able to enjoy the freedoms that came with being hundreds of miles from family. But the promise made in boyhood still hung over him. Shazad wanted to be a good son, he wanted to fulfil his parents' expectations and didn't have the confidence to let down his parents. There was only one problem, and his name was Mohsin.

Shazad was living with Mohsin, a friend from Yorkshire whom his family knew. His parents knew the two were best friends and that was, in part, what had reassured Matloob about his son leaving home. What his parents did not know was that when Shazad and Mohsin were fifteen they had become more than just friends. Shazad recalls one time when the couple had enjoyed a hug. 'The hug became a very long hug, and then each day the hug became a kiss,' recalls Shazad, 'and the kiss carried on to sex.' Shazad and Mohsin did not consider themselves gay and the day after having sex they would see two men holding hands and say, 'Look at those poofs.' 'We didn't use the label of "gay",' Shazad says. 'We would sometimes hang out with other mates and then the others would leave, and we would get drunk and have a dilly-dally.'

In college, Shazad and Mohsin would go to daytime night-club parties held while unsuspecting parents assumed their children were in class.[1] In their MC Hammer baggy trousers, dancing to bhangra music, they would somehow find a time and a place to kiss but 'the next day we would just carry on and not acknowledge that anything had happened'. Shazad and Mohsin continued seeing each other through college, but while they might have been behaving like a gay couple, neither was able to admit this to themselves or each other. One day Mohsin told Shazad that he now had a girlfriend. 'He was denying his sexuality,' says Shazad. 'The idea of us being able to live together as lovers and be accepted was unimaginable, so he took the easy road.' Shazad later ended up helping find his former lover a wife. 'He had grown up in a very traditional and religious family and his dad was chairman of the local mosque,' Shazad says. 'When he started looking for a wife, he asked me and my mum to help introduce him to people.' Since getting married Mohsin has become very religious and ultra conservative. 'I sent him a happy birthday message just a couple of months ago,' Shazad says. 'He replied that he didn't celebrate birthdays as it was not acceptable in Islam. I think he's doing that to compensate for some kind of guilt.'

Shazad returned to Yorkshire after graduating and started to feel the pressure to meet his duty to his parents. 'I wanted Shazad to get married,' says Jamelia, 'and he said OK.' Shazad agreed to get engaged, but the closer it came to the wedding day, the more his doubts grew. He did not have the courage to reveal the whole truth to his family, but a close friend noticed his anguish and confronted his parents. 'He told them, "Shazad does not want to get married",' Shazad says. 'He said, "He is not happy, but he wants to make you happy."' Jamelia stood up for her son and persuaded her husband to ease up on Shazad. In 2000, Shazad moved to Birmingham to take up a new job. 'I rented a house and with no shackles and no acquaintances that was when I explored my sexuality,' he recalls.

It is very possible that on one of his nights out in Birmingham's gay bars and clubs Shazad might have run into Naz Mahmood. Naz was, like Shazad, a young British-Pakistani hiding his sexuality from his family. He was twenty-one and a medical student whose family lived in

Birmingham. In November 2001, Naz was in a gay nightclub called Subway City. He saw a young White man whose name was Matthew. 'Excuse me, may I sit there?' said Naz. The two men started talking. They were busy in conversation when Naz suddenly said: 'I'm Muslim, is that going to be a problem?' It was not a problem for Matthew but for Naz it meant that when he and Matthew started seeing each other they had to ensure that Naz's family did not suspect anything. When they bought a house the following year it had two bedrooms so that his family could assume that they were just housemates. 'We used to have to keep the blinds in our front room closed so no one would see us,' recalls Matthew. 'When we walked down the street, we made sure there was some distance between us just in case a family member of his spotted us together.'

Naz and Matthew grew tired of looking over their shoulders, so when Naz was offered a job at a London hospital in 2004, they seized the opportunity. They would be far from their families, in a city where they could fashion a new life together. 'In London we felt free,' Matthew says. 'We didn't have to worry about bumping into our parents.' They made friends and created a social world that reflected the people they were. Out of necessity, this new life was founded on sadness and deceptions. Naz didn't like to talk about his family. He had left Birmingham and felt that to talk about pain or sadness or guilt would have infected their new life in London – he was resigned to playing the dutiful Muslim boy to his family in Birmingham when, in fact, he was a happily gay man in London. His family had barely met Matthew and thought he was an investor in their son's flat.

Shazad was also leading a double life – the dutiful son to his parents while leading a secret gay life away from home. By 2004, Shazad had moved to Leeds to study for a Masters. He had spent the last few years exploring the gay scene in Birmingham, but was not in a relationship. 'I had convinced myself that if I had not found someone to settle down with in the gay world by the time I was thirty, I would do what my family wanted,' he tells me. 'I didn't want to lose my culture and my family if my expectations were not met.' On 20 September 2004, Shazad met a New Zealander named Craig in a bar called Oporto. Shazad was twenty-nine and half. They started dating and by the end of the year they had moved in together. Shazad and Naz: two British-Pakistani Muslims both living with partners whom they loved and who loved them, but both unable to tell the truth about their love to their parents.

When Bridget and I first started dating, I would worry about how I was going to break the news to my family. This was a genuine and heartfelt concern but, when the worries became overwhelming, Bridget would sometimes joke that there was one guaranteed strategy to ensure my family accepted our relationship: I could start by declaring I was actually gay and while they were reeling in shock I could quickly reassure them that this was not true and to prove it I had a girlfriend. My family's relief at my heterosexuality would, the theory went, mean that the fact Bridget was a

White non-Muslim would suddenly subside as an issue. The advice was given in jest, but rooted in fact: homosexuality and Islam make awkward bedfellows.

Almost all of the ten countries that allow the death penalty for same-sex sexual relations are Muslim-majority nations.[2] A 2009 Gallup poll of 500 British Muslims found that *none* of them believed that homosexual acts were morally accept-able. A later survey released in 2016 revealed that 52 per cent of British Muslims said they thought homosexuality should be illegal – compared with 5 per cent for the public at large.[3] In early 2011, stickers were found around London's East End declaring it a 'gay free zone'. The messages, posted on buildings and lampposts close to Shoreditch gay nightspots George & Dragon and the Joiners Inn, read: 'Arise and warn. Gay free zone. Verily Allah is severe in punishment.'[4] Two years later, again in London, video emerged of a group calling itself a 'Muslim Patrol' shouting homophobic abuse at a man. One member of the group shouts: 'Hello mate, don't you know this is a Muslim area? Why you dressed like that for?' While another screams 'Homosexual! Homosexual!' When the victim asks, 'Why are you bothering me?', a member of the group responds, 'because you're walking through a Muslim area dressed like a fag, mate. You need to get out of here.'[5]

It is estimated that Islamic State executed forty-one gay men between 2014 and 2016. Most Muslims do not sup-port the ideology or actions of Islamic State and nor would they be harassing innocent people on the street or putting up bigoted stickers, but, based on my conversations, the idea that being gay is incompatible with being Muslim is extremely common. 'At the end of the day the religion is ordained that there is a man, there is a woman, and they only fulfill that sexual desire within a marriage,' a niqab-wearing woman in Leicester told me, 'so anything outside of that is not allowed.' A community leader in Dewsbury recalled the time a young boy came to him and told him he thought he might be gay and needed advice. 'I told him up front that in Islam it is wrong,' he told me. 'So I talked to him for a few weeks and convinced him that it is not natural. Do I think he was persuaded? Yes – I think he is getting married.' A mother in Birmingham told me: 'I think, personally, nobody's born gay, I'm sorry, I can't see it.' Almost every single British Muslim I met agreed that it was not possible to be a practising Muslim and homosexual. When I asked a father in Bradford how he would respond if one of his children announced they were gay, he said: 'I would accept them as my child, but I regard homosexuality as a sin.' The message I heard repeatedly was that Islam considers homosexuality to be a sin – no ifs and no buts.

Tahira tells me that at the Islamic girls' school she works at, 'We educate the girls that from an Islamic perspective homosexuality doesn't exist. According to the Islamic perspective Allah says He's created you as male and female, but He understands that human beings have their own temptations and their own desires. How that comes about . . . is a different journey for different people. 'It is pretty inarguable that the majority of British Muslims regard homosexuality as sinful but trying to determine the Islamic view on homosexuality is not easy. For one thing there is no single monolithic body called Islam – there are different schools of thought and thus the 'Islamic' view can vary depending on who, where and when the question is being posed. Regardless of these variables, one thing is certain: the word 'homosexual' is never used in the Qur'an. However, this is not entirely surprising since it was only coined in the late nineteenth century.[6]

Muslims who believe the Qur'an condemns homosexuality most commonly refer to the story of the Sodom and the Prophet Lot. In the conventional telling, Lot was sent to Sodom, a city populated by robbers, murderers and men who have sex with men rather than women. Sodomy was practised openly, which led Allah to ask Lot to beg the people to give up their immoral ways. They refused and rejected his appeal. Lot offered his own daughters to the townsmen, but they refused them. Allah then destroyed the people of Lot and this destruction is traditionally presented as a warning against homosexual acts. Although the word 'homosexuality' is not used in the Qur'an, there are a number of passages that do seem to support those who argue Islam is explicit about the sinfulness of homosexuality. In the Qur'an, Lot says about the people of Sodom: 'Indeed, you approach men with desire, instead of women. Rather, you are a transgressing people.' In the Hadith – the collection of stories reporting the words and deeds of the Prophet Muhammad – there are a number of sayings that appear to refer to homosexuality:

'If sodomites become common, God, the Glorious and Exalted, will wash his hands of mankind and not care in which abyss they perish.'

'God, the Glorious and Exalted, has no regard for a man who has intercourse with a man or a woman in her anus.'

'If you find anyone doing as Lot's people did, kill the one who does it, and the one to whom it is done.'[7]

These quotes seem unequivocal and reading them made me think that perhaps those who insist on the incompatibility of Islam and homosexuality have a theological point. However, these attitudes appear increasingly out of step with mainstream opinion. Legislation to allow same sex marriage in England and Wales was passed in July 2013 and took effect on 13 March 2014. It is hard, given the cultural and religious opposition they face, for most gay Muslims to be open about who they are – hence the secret lives that men like Shazad and Naz were leading. That is what makes clubs like Saathi so important in the gay Muslim community.

Saathi is a monthly club night in Birmingham aimed at gay Asians. I attended one Friday night. I was on my own and, in all honesty, felt deeply self-conscious. I was quite a bit older than most of the club-goers, who were mostly in their twenties and thirties. I worried that I looked like a dull middle-aged bloke surrounded by beautiful young things. I stood on the edge of the dancefloor where hundreds of men and women were dancing to a pulsating Bollywood soundtrack. Two women walked hand in hand, one leading the other past a heavily made-up drag queen who was deep in conversation with a sparkly-hatted man. 'This is the only place where I can truly be myself,' says Maya, a thirty-one-year-old at the club, with Eve, her twenty-three-year-old White girlfriend, who was wearing a tweed blazer with a tiny bowtie, skinny trousers and black lace-up boots. She had a silver stud below her lower lip. Maya's parents are from Pakistan, a country where same sex sexual acts are considered illegal and, a recent poll found, only 2 per cent of the population believe homosexuality should be accepted by society. Elsewhere a woman buried her face in her partner's chest before they both starting throwing their hands in the air and dancing bhangra-style, shoulders moving up and down to the music. 'It's so sad,' Maya added, 'inside this club you see Asian girls and guys dancing so extrovertly but as soon as they step outside they have to be totally different and pretend to be something they are not.'

On the last Saturday of July 2014, Naz and Matthew drove north to Birmingham. It was a strange time: a close friend had died, and they had to be back in London on Monday for his memorial service. It was also the weekend of Eid. Naz didn't like to talk to Matthew about his family. On the rare occasions Naz's family visited London, Matthew had to spend the night in a bed and breakfast. 'We had to "de-gay" the house,' says Matthew. 'That meant putting pictures of Kylie into the cupboard, Cher too – and any photo or memento that suggested a relationship had to go.' To celebrate the tenth anniversary of their first meeting, Matthew and Naz had thrown a party at a London club. Naz was now a GP as well as running his own business – three London clinics that offered Botox treatments – and Matthew was doing well working for a software company. During the party, Matthew asked the DJ to lower the music. He led Naz into the DJ booth, got down on one knee and proposed. 'He looked at me and his face just lit up,' says Matthew.

The following year, Matthew came out to his parents, who were loving and accepting of them both, but for Naz, whose family were culturally conservative Muslims, the only strategy was to keep the solid borderlines between his old life in Birmingham and new life in London. When he arrived at his family home, Naz's family were annoyed that he was late for the Eid celebrations and planned to leave early for his friend's memorial back in London. Things were said – Matthew does not know what exactly – that left Naz distraught. 'I am a good person,' Naz said, weeping. 'Why can't people accept me for who I am?' 'Is it because you like men?' his mother had asked him, out of the blue. And Naz, who had spent years hiding and pretending, to protect his relationship with Matthew, did something he had never expected to do – on the spur of the moment, he told them everything. He told this mother he was gay and had been in a relationship with a man for thirteen years and planned to marry him.

Shazad had a similar confrontation with his mother when he was living with Craig. 'The phone call came out of the blue,' he recalls. 'They said enough is enough – we want you to get married: you have been to university; you have the masters and a job – it is time to do the right thing.' Shazad felt trapped. He had spent years trying to avoid this moment, but his mother had a point – his excuses for not getting married were running out. 'There was nowhere to hide,' he says, and so Shazad did what Naz had done: he finally told the truth. 'I told them that I can't get married because I am not that way inclined,' he says. 'It was strange that such an important conversation was taking place on the phone.' Shazad told his mother that he didn't feel that way about women. 'She said, "What do you mean, I am your mum?"' he says. 'I said that is different – I love you, but I don't love other women in that other way. My mum said that is fine because she knew people in Pakistan who felt like that but once they got married they were sorted out. I told her that I didn't want to lie.' In the background Shazad could hear his dad shouting that they were going to come to his house. The phone call ended abruptly. Shazad sat down and began to write a letter to his father. He didn't feel his Urdu was fluent enough to express his thoughts verbally so he thought it would be better to write them down in English. When his father received the letter, he asked his daughter to read it first. She told him that Shazad was saying that he didn't like girls. 'Who does he like, then?' Matloob asked. 'Guys,' said his daughter. 'Oh bloody hell,' Matloob replied. Shazad and Naz's mothers did not know each other but both initially responded to their sons' revelations in similar ways. Shazad's mother tried to reassure him that marriage would 'sort him out' while Naz's mother urged her son to see a psychiatrist who might 'cure' him of his homosexuality.

In researching and working on this chapter I was aware that I had only talked to gay Muslim men, but I also wanted to hear from gay Muslim women. That was how I came to talk to Hannah, who is in her early thirties and lives in north London. She is the daughter of a Pakistani father who used to drive a taxi and Scottish-Indian mother who converted to Islam. 'I never had a boyfriend when I was growing up,' she tells me. 'I would be the one who would be chasing the girls in the playground. I was the tomboy.' She remembers fancying Sarah Connor in the Terminator films and being a sporty teenager who was worried others would notice her lack of interest in boys. 'I was very defensive about it and I was even a bit homophobic,' she tells me. 'I did not want anyone to know.' She joined a gay youth club. 'One day my mum was going through my bag – she is really nosy – and she found my application form for the club. She could see my name and the fact I had circled "lesbian" on the form. It was pretty blatant.' Hannah's mother was furious. 'She said horrible things,' she recalls. '"How you can be like this when you are so beautiful? You are going to hell. You are not my daughter." She suggested I take female hormones and see a psychiatrist – all I want is to love someone and get love from them, what is wrong with that?' It seems such a simple, almost banal, request but it can feel impossibly elusive for gay Muslims.

Shazia is in her twenties and was brought up in a tradi-tional British Bangladeshi family. The morning we met she was wearing a white hijab patterned with purple flowers.

'I do different colours because black is a bit boring,' she explains. Shazia is a practising Muslim who prays daily, fasts during Ramadan and does not drink alcohol. She is also a lesbian. 'I always knew I was different from the other girls,' she tells me, 'but I was in a massive state of denial.' She remembers going to see *Harry Potter and the Goblet of Fire*. 'All my friends were going crazy for Daniel Radcliffe, but I couldn't stop thinking about Emma Watson – she just looked absolutely stunning.' Shazia tried to ignore these urges but they persisted. She had been raised to believe that being gay was a disease and against her Muslim faith. When she finally found the courage to tell her friends she was gay, some were accepting but others warned her it was wrong and stopped speaking to her. She rang an Islamic hotline: they advised she become straight. In desperation she joined a support forum for Asian gays and attended a meet-up. 'It was such an eye-opener to finally meet people who were in the same boat,' she says. 'It made me realise that Allah created me this way for a reason and I am not an anomaly: there are thousands of others out there like me.' Shazia's current girlfriend is a brunette, privately educated farmer's daughter. 'I hold her hand in public,' Shazia says, 'sometimes we link arms.' It must attract some attention – a hijab-wearing Asian girl holding hands with a White girl? 'I'm really oblivious to dirty looks from people,' she says. 'My girlfriend notices more than I do – because I am a Muslim and of the way I dress I am used to getting looks so I don't know whether people are looking at me funny because of the way I dress or because I am holding a girl's hand.' Why not date a fellow Muslim, I asked? 'Going out with a Muslim is hard,' Shazia says, 'because the women find it hard to lead double lives. It comes to the point where the women break up with you to get married. They cave in to their families. It's happened to me a few times and it breaks your heart.'

The pressure for Muslim homosexuals to conform can be intense – the desire of families to see their children to do the 'right' thing can lead to emotional blackmail if the children do not fall in line. One strategy that some use to placate their families is to marry someone of the opposite sex who is also gay and have a marriage of convenience (MoC). At Saathi, Maya told me she had considered a MoC before deciding she could not live a lie. The Saathi website has a section devoted those desperately seeking MoC. A thirty-one-year-old Asian doctor writes that 'to avoid conflict with my loving family am looking for a MoC either for a contracted period or life-long with a girl, preferably a lesbian. No physical relationship is expected. Girl can continue her lifestyle as she wishes.' Another entry from a twenty-six-year-old woman states that she 'has no interest in men but under a lot of pressure to get married'. Twenty-seven-year-old Amir posted a request for a MoC after facing strong pressure from his family. One person who saw the post was Saima, whose family were threatening to take her to Pakistan to marry her off. Amir and Saima got married, the wedding attended by both families and the mullahs from the local mosque. That was nine years ago and both families remain convinced the couple are truly married when in fact Amir, while living with Saima, has a boyfriend with whom he spends most nights. Saima was too scared to talk to me but Amir agreed. 'It is very stressful being in a MoC,' he said. 'We have to keep the pretense up all the time and there are so many commitments, like family gatherings and putting up with each other's in-laws and all the time we have to act convincingly and look as if we are in a real marriage.' Amir told me he sometimes wishes he had told his family the truth and faced the consequences rather than live inside a sham marriage.

Hannah's parents have slowly come to some acceptance of their daughter's sexuality. When her father was told his daughter was gay his response was: 'Well, at least you're not out sleeping with every Tom, Dick and Harry and possibly getting pregnant.' When she split up with her last girlfriend, Hannah's mother even tried to get the couple back together again. 'My mum surprises me – she still says I am going to hell,' Hannah says, 'but she also says she wants me to find a nice Muslim girl.'

As for Shazia, she tells me that she has found peace with her sexuality. 'I don't see straight people cutting themselves for being straight,' she says, 'so why should I just because I am gay?' Shazia is determined she will, one day, tell her parents the truth about her sexuality. 'It would break my family's hearts if they ever found out I was gay,' she explains. 'I want to tell them one day, but I know there is a chance I won't have them in my life any more.' Her words reminded me of another young woman I met at Saathi. I had asked her what she imagined would happen if the parents of everyone in the club were to suddenly appear. She looked appalled. 'Oh my god!' she said. 'Mayhem, war: can you imagine?'

One question that has recurred while working on this book is how much things have changed – whether the challenges faced by the likes of Shazad and Naz have lessened for those a generation younger. 'I know a couple of young, gay Muslim men through work, and nothing has changed,' Shazad's boyfriend Craig told me. 'The attitudes, if anything, have stayed the same, so they might have parents who are our age or a bit older, but they haven't moved on.'

Maryam was born in 2003 and grew up in a religious household in Bradford where she wore the hijab from the age of nine, attended mosque after school every day and fasted during Ramadan. When she was around eleven she noticed that the other girls in her school would talk about the boys they had crushes on, but she didn't feel that way about anyone. When she was fourteen she got a part-time job working at an Oxfam store and met a girl called Habiba who was the same age. 'It was like we just instantly clicked and became best friends,' she says. 'We'd always do stuff like sort the books out together and that kind of stuff, and then one day it just happened.' What happened, I asked. 'I kissed her,' she says, 'and then it went on from there. I was giddy, I was so giddy, like oh my god, finally. She was the first person I ever came out to.' Maryam kept in touch by going incognito on her laptop and her parents never suspected because they were focusing on keeping her away from boys. 'It was just amazing,' she says about her relationship with Habiba. 'I was so happy and overjoyed.' The relationship lasted ten months and, not long afterwards, Maryam attended a counselling session at her school. She met a youth worker to whom she came out and the woman told her about a youth group called Colours for LGBT young people of colour. She was invited to a conference in Birmingham. 'I was shocked,' she recalls. 'I was like, "Oh my gosh, they are so many of us."' Maryam knew that she would never be accepted by her parents, so she told the youth worker that she wanted to leave home. 'It was getting out of hand,' she recalls. 'My grades had started dropping and my plan to go to university might have been ruined, so I told the youth worker, "I need to get out."' One Saturday morning in early March 2019, Maryam put her clothes in a PE bag, told her parents she was going to the Oxfam store and went to a friend's house. She left a letter for her parents and never went back. What would you say you were running from, I asked? 'The pressure, the abuse and emotional distress. I am now living in independent housing in a refuge.' We have heard versions of this story before – Ruby and Zena both ran away from home to a refuge – and I wondered how Maryam felt about the price she was expected to pay for wanting to live her life as she wished. 'When I watch TV shows or movies with the happy family, with the kids going off to college, it does hurt my heart,' she says. 'Why couldn't my family just be like that? Or just be a bit more understanding, open-minded . . . in an Asian household, if you speak back to your parents it's disrespect, if you try reasoning with them it's disrespect, no point trying – it's like talking to a brick wall.'

Naz was in a state of shock as he drove back from his family in Birmingham to his home in London. Matthew recalls Naz being distant and trying to put on a brave face. The next day Matthew got a text from his sister saying: 'Call me now'. It was early evening on Wednesday, 30 July, and Matthew was at work. He rang her and was told to go home immediately; she wouldn't say why. It couldn't be Naz – they had talked at lunchtime. Naz had called again at just after 3 p.m. and then twice after 5 p.m., but it was Matthew's first day in a new office and he had been too busy in meetings to take the calls, though he had tried to call Naz back. He wondered if there had been a bomb scare near his flat. As he left West Hampstead station, Matthew began to run. 'It was like I was running for my life,' he recalls. As he speaks, he is clutching himself tightly, his right hand gripping his biceps. 'I was pushing people out of the way and as I came round the corner I saw flashing blue lights and police cordon tape, then I saw this red blanket on the floor covering something up.' Matthew began to scream. Naz had leapt off the edge of the balcony of their top floor flat to his death. He was only thirty-four years old.

Matthew arrived at Handsworth cemetery early on the day of Naz's funeral. In the aftermath of Naz's death, Matthew had met Naz's family, but the encounters were tense and uncomfortable. It appears that they did not want to have to deal with their shame at having had a gay son, and a gay son with a non-Muslim lover. Out of respect for Naz's mother's plea not to make a scene, Matthew agreed not to ask for a major role at the funeral, which was due to take place at 3.30 p.m. With less than half an hour to go, nobody else had arrived and Matthew began to worry. In the distance he could see a burial taking place. 'I went over and asked one of the officials where Naz was being buried,' he says. 'She said, "I'm really sorry – they have already buried him."' He ran out and saw Naz's family pouring dirt on to the coffin. 'I was so angry,' Matthew tells me, tears streaming down his face. 'I could not move. My arms and legs were just clenched. I felt completely betrayed.' Naz's family had apparently given him the wrong time for the funeral.

The inquest into Naz's death took place in December 2014 in the same week that Islamic State posted a series of images showing the execution of a man accused of homosexuality. In an accompanying statement IS described the method of their killing: the man was thrown off the roof of the tallest building in the city. Following an inquest, the coroner ruled that Naz had killed himself. 'It seems incredible that a young man with so much going for him could have taken his own life,' she said, 'but what I've heard is that he had one great sadness which was the difficulty his family had in accepting his sexuality.' Naz's story is tragic and extreme but the underlying reasons for his suicide are sadly common. Given how black and white Islam appears to be on the subject, it is hard not to assume that any search for hope is going to prove futile. But searching for and believing in hope is never

futile and the truth about Islam's relationship with homosexuality is far more nuanced than it might at first appear. If
we consider the claim that Islam condemns homosexuality
to be the traditional narrative, the counter-narrative has two
strands that relate to how the Qur'an and Hadith have been
interpreted and the lived experiences of Muslims through
the centuries.

Is homosexuality a sin? I asked Alyas Karmani. 'Yes, it's
a sin,' he says. 'The simple answer is that, yes, 99.99 per
cent of Islamic clerics for 1,400 years have identified that
it is. Whatever you say, however you say it, it cannot be cir-
cumvented. It is a fundamental prohibition.' That seemed
clear enough, but he then went on to say: 'I have loads of
gay friends and what I say to them is that I'm not interested
in their homosexuality. My own personal view, and this is
the thing that is different and obviously where it brings a
lot of conflict with the Muslim community, is that your
sexuality and how you have sex and who you have sex with,
where you have sex, is your private business that no one
should really interfere with. It's between you and God. I'm
not really interested in people's sexuality. It's not important
to me.' Did this not seem a slightly tricky position to hold,
I wondered, given that he was an imam? 'There is theology
and text and theologians greater than I that engage in these
polemics,' he replies. 'What I'm more interested in is the
daily reality of an individual negotiating their own personal
challenges in their life, of which sexuality is just one. So, I'm
more interested in dealing with things on a human level.'

There is a story about Ali ibn Abi Talib, a cousin and son-in-law of the Prophet Muhammad who reigned as the fourth Caliph of Islam during the middle of the seventh century.[8] The Caliph was confronted by a group of people demanding that he simply 'apply' the Qur'an's judgment without interpretation. Ali gathered the people around him and took out a copy of the Qur'an and as he touched the book he begged it to 'speak to the people'. The people gathered around saying, 'Ali do you mock us? It is only paper and it is we human beings who speak on its behalf.' To this Ali replied: 'The Qur'an is written in straight lines between two covers. It does not speak by itself. It needs proper interpreters and the interpreters are human beings.' What this means in practical terms is that much of what Muslims believe to be stated in the Qur'an is open to interpretation and the legitimacy of some of the sayings attributed to the Prophet Mohammed has also been questioned. Those looking to find a more tolerant Islam within the pages of the Qur'an stress that while anal penetration is viewed unfavorably, the burden of proof before any punishment – which can range from mild to death, depending on the school of Islamic thought – is very high: it requires four males to witness the actual penetration or the accused to repeat their confession four times. Wading through pages of fairly dense analysis of what the Qur'an may or may not say about anal sex is a pretty strange experience. It was one thing to imagine modern scholars poring through contested phrases to try to work out what they might mean and quite another to realise that it was one family's interpretation that prompted their son to leap off a building to his death. It was also strange to my modern eyes how much attention was paid to the acts of male homosexual behaviour but not the emotions. It was all about penetration but nothing about love, and that does not reflect how any of us live or love. I could see why someone who was both Muslim and gay would find it a somewhat dispiriting experience looking for love and acceptance in the pages of the Qur'an, even after viewing it though a liberal inclusive prism.

When I talked to gay Muslims, one of the most common issues they had was how to reconcile their homosexuality with their faith. This was partly because for most British Muslims not only is homosexuality never discussed, but it has been erased from Islamic history. The somewhat surprising truth is that Muslim poets, painters and scholars frequently referred to homosexual love without any negative judgment. 'The Arabic literature of the early Ottoman period (1516–1798) is replete with casual and sometimes sympathetic references to homosexual love,' Khaled El–Rouayheb writes in *Before Homosexuality in the Arab-Islamic World, 1500–1800*. 'Much if not most of the extant love poetry of the period is pederastic in tone, portraying an adult male poet's passionate love for a teenage boy. A popular topic amongst poets and belletrists was whether beardless or downy cheeked youths were more appropriate objects for passionate love.' Some of the examples of such poetry are eye opening to read today. 'Don't censure me for I'm an old man who has regained his youth by loving a boy,' wrote one poet, while another tells that 'I was taught passionate love and the nature of infatuation by the love of a boy whose glance is more than a match for me.' A third wrote: 'to the censurer who reproached me for loving boys I professed a noble motto: I am but a son of Adam and therefore only ever fancy sons of Adam.' The poet Ahmad al-Khakaji composed the following couplet: 'since he whom I fancy visited me, he offered me drink from a mouth (as intoxicating as) wine. And his buttocks said to me from behind me: "today wine and tomorrow action."'

It wasn't only poets who eulogised homosexual love. The nineteenth-century Ottoman book *Sawaqub al-Manaquib* features a painting depicting a youth being anally penetrated by a mustachioed older man while two other men stand watching, waiting their turn. The painting is called 'Lining up to use a boy'. It was frankly rather shocking to see such explicit references and depictions of homosexuality in Islamic poetry and art, but my initial assumption was that these were artists expressing and exploring the forbidden – it was all talk. However, the more one reads about life in Muslim societies of the past, the more it becomes clear that homosexuality was often part of everyday life. The influential American historian of Islam Marshall Hodgson writes that in medieval Islamic civilisation 'despite strong [Islamic legal] disapproval the sexual relations of a mature man with a subordinate youth were so readily accepted in upper class circles that there was often little or no effort to conceal their existence.' The fifteenth-century Egyptian historian Al-Maqrizi noted that 'among the Mamluke rulers, love of men became so common that the women in the empire began to envy the men and to wear elegant hats in order to imitate them.' The British sailor Joseph Potts, writing about late seventeenth-century Algiers, observed that "tis common for Men there to fall in love with Boys, as 'tis here in England to be in love with Women.' Sir Richard Burton visited the Sindh in what is now Pakistan long before the British conquest and found a brothel of boy prostitutes in Karachi. The most fascinating aspect about these descriptions of homosexual behaviour is that those taking part did not consider themselves to be gay. The concept of the 'homosexual' appeared in Europe only in the second half of the nineteenth century, and until the early twentieth century there was no such concept in Arabic-Islamic culture. That meant that men did not feel there was anything contradictory about marrying women and having families but also having sex with other men. Trig Tarazi, a Palestinian born in Kuwait, noted that 'it's very strange to have men come up to you in bars and show you a picture of their kids and then say, "Okay let's go (have sex) now."⁹ Since nobody recognised homosexuality as even existing, they can get away with things we cannot get away with here. But if you start talking about homosexuality, they get very uncomfortable.'

In 2006, the *Guardian* carried a report of a party in Lahore where 'under a starry sky filled with fireworks, about 150 gay men clambered to the roof of an apartment building for an exuberant party. Bollywood music spilled into the streets as dress-wearing men twisted and whirled flamboyantly.' Despite the official policy of sodomy being punishable by up to life in jail, assaults on gay men are rare and sodomy laws are seldom invoked. The paper quoted one gay man saying that 'western gays are gobsmacked about how easy it is to pick up guys here, how often they are approached.'[10] Across the border in Afghanistan, the custom of *bacha bazi*, or boy play, involves wealthy Afghans acquiring young boys for the purpose of sexual entertainment and exploitation. 'The fact homosexuality is forbidden in Islam is swept under the carpet by those who participate,' noted the *Daily Mail*, 'who claim there is a loophole. They are not in love with the boys, and therefore not gay.'[11] The Pakistani journalist Talat Aslam, writing in 1994, suggested that 'in a vast swathe of Pakistan's rural areas, the Western concept of "being" gay simply does not apply, despite the widespread homosexuality prevalent. In place of the Western notion of homosexuality as a state of being, homosexuality is viewed as an activity which does not in way "make" you "a homosexual." It is this distinction – between as a state of being and homosexual as an activity – that escapes those who look at sexual mores through pre-conceived models imported from elsewhere.'[12]

'The Spanish formula "Todoshecho, nada dicho" (everything is done, nothing is said) seems,' notes the Norwegian academic Unni Wikan, 'to be a . . . strategy for maintaining absolute moral prescriptions in principle by keeping silent on the vagaries of "human nature" in an imperfect world in which "shameful acts (are) an inherent part of life.""[13] It is tempting to conclude that this is a case of having your gay cake and eating it. But the prevalence of homosexuality in both art and everyday life among societies across the Islamic world over the centuries made me wonder how different the experience of young gay British Muslims might be if they were to know that they are not as alone or as atypical as they fear. If the parents of gay Muslims knew more about the history of the faith they profess to follow, might they be less certain in their bigotry? The suggestion that homosexuality is unequivocally condemned in Islam doesn't withstand scrutiny. And yet so many of the gay Muslims I talked to spoke of their struggle to reconcile their faith with their sexuality. 'I think there is a contradiction between being Muslim and gay,' Hannah told me. 'I sometimes think that this is a test of God I have to pass by not acting on my homosexuality, but I also think I have not done anything wrong.' In searching for hope, the first place to begin, then, is the past – a greater awareness of the presence of homosexuality in Islamic societies and an appreciation that the Qur'an is far more ambiguous about homosexuality than is popularly supposed. The more recent past can also help give some perspective on how widespread homophobic attitudes were in this country until very recently.

I grew up in the eighties, when homosexuality was seen as inherently funny by television executives: Mr Humphreys in *Are You Being Served?*, Larry Grayson in *The Generation Game*; and potentially threatening to children by Conservative politicians – hence the protests around Section 28.* When I was at school, there was a boy in our class called Colin. He was very smiley, he seemed to speak with a lisp, and there was something different about him. We didn't know the word 'camp' back then, so all the boys called him a 'poofter'. The implication behind the name-calling was that there was something not quite right about being gay, something not normal. I didn't use the word myself, but I never stopped anyone else, and I did nothing to defend Colin – perhaps because I was relieved that by mocking him they were too distracted to mock me. 'We sacked people for being gay,' notes Sayeeda Warsi in *The Enemy Within*, 'we treated them like social lepers, we chemically castrated them, we tried to "cure" them through aversion and conversation therapies, we distrusted them and perceived them as a security risk, we saw AIDS as a gay disease only taking it seriously once it started affecting straight people, we rabble-roused the party faithful at conferences and meetings against them and enacted legislation to make sure we stigmatized them from birth. We created the environment where a loon took it on himself to bomb a pub in London which was frequented by "the gays", killing three and injuring more.'[14]

One month after the legislation that made same-sex marriage legal, and three months before Naz visited his family

---

* Section 28 was a law passed in May 1988 that stopped councils and schools 'promoting the teaching of the acceptability of homosexuality as a pretended family relationship'.

for the last time, Andrew Moffat joined Parkfield, a primary school in the Alum Rock area of Birmingham. The area was overwhelmingly Muslim, and the school was 98 per cent Muslim. Moffat arrived at the school with a plan. He wanted to create a teaching resource that would combat intolerance, something to encourage children to believe that no one should be considered an outsider regardless of race, religion and sexuality. Moffat came up with a school resource called *No Outsiders*. 'I sent out a letter to all the parents saying, we are doing *No Outsiders*, it's about British values, sexual orientation, disability, race, religion,' he tells me. 'I offered to meet anyone who had any questions, but no one came, so we thought everyone's fine about it and we started doing it.' *No Outsiders* ran for four years with barely a whisper of controversy and it was after reading about Moffat in a newspaper article while researching this book that I first contacted him. It seemed exactly the hopeful story – White gay teacher teaching Muslim children the importance of tolerance towards gays with the support of their parents – that I wanted to include in this book. We talked on the phone and I told him that I would like to meet him. This was autumn 2018, however, by the time I contacted him again a few months later to set a date, things had changed.

'The first sign of trouble was on Christmas Eve when a teaching assistant sent me a WhatsApp group message saying you've got to watch this film,' Andrew recalls. 'It was a video from the Islamic Unity Conference in October 2018 and a woman talking about what the RSE [Relationships and Sex Education] Government guidelines were and what it meant for primary schools. She was saying that it had a gay agenda. I watched the video, and I was horrified when I watched the video because I knew, straight away, this was going to be really big.' In the video the White muslim convert told the audience that things like *No Outsiders* were an assault on Islam and if Muslim parents did not stand up together their children would be lost. In the first week back after the holidays, Moffat was confronted by two mothers who told him they were planning a petition protesting at how *No Outsiders* was sexualising children. At one coffee morning another parent had told her that the school and Moffat was teaching their children about homosexuals. 'The kids were coming home and saying, "Is it OK to be gay?"' she says. 'There were stories of girls saying they wanted to wear their brothers' clothes and wanting to have boys names and at that point alarm bells starting ringing.'

I arranged to visit the school in early February 2019 and by then the good news story I thought I would be telling had rapidly descended into something darker and more depressing. Andrew told me that a parents' protest was planned outside the school and suggested I drive in with him early in the morning to witness the protest from the inside. I huddled in the back of his car as we arrived at the empty school and was taken to a classroom that overlooked the front entrance. It was not long before the protesting parents arrived, and by the time school was officially open, the street outside the main entrance was thronged with hundreds of parents. They were joined by their children and they were carrying placards that read: 'Preserve Innocence and Purity of Our Children', 'Our Kids, Our Responsibility' and 'Stop Confusing Our Children'. The children were chanting, or possibly being made to chant, 'Mr Moffat – out'. I wandered out to mingle with the parents and children.*

The parents were keen to stress that their concerns had nothing to do with homophobia and couched their protest as about parental rights, but it felt like a flimsy argument and each time any parent was interviewed by the media they would invariably say something that betrayed homophobic prejudice. The protests that began outside Andrew Moffat's school gradually spread to other schools as parents demanded that *No Outsiders* no longer be taught and called for Andrew Moffat to be sacked. I kept in touch with him as the pressure and abuse mounted: he told me about abusive emails and death threats he was receiving from parents. 'It was the worst time in my life,' he told me. 'I was absolutely devastated and scared as well. It was really frightening. The children would be coming down the corridor chanting, "Get Mr Moffat out. Stop *No Outsiders*", and we had to get them into the hall and calm them down. It was very difficult.' Moffat had meetings with the police, who advised him to

---

* I later learned that a WhatsApp post had been sent to a parents' group. The post featured a photograph secretly taken of me at the school gates with the message 'Do not talk to the above man he is deceptive and a liar . . . he will guaranteed twist what you say'.

get a dash cam for his car and security cameras outside his home. There were Muslim parents who supported him, he assured me, but they were too scared of reprisals to defend him publicly. A Muslim mother came to the school demanding to see him because her son was being bullied. She waited more than an hour and refused to leave until she could see him. When she finally walked into his office, she told him: 'My son is not being bullied. I want to talk to you about *No Outsiders*. You need to know I'm one hundred per cent behind you and there are many with me.'

The story became national news and questions were asked in Parliament as the issue of LGBT lessons in Muslim schools became seen as a litmus test for whose values should have priority – the school or the parents. Or put another way: the Muslim values of the parents or the secular liberal values of the school? The longer the protests dragged on, the more I worried that the good-news story I had hoped for would become another story that confirmed what many felt – that Muslims have a problem with homosexuality. In fact, what happened was that the school and the parents began a dialogue, and a parental consultation group was established. Andrew Moffat made a few subtle tweaks to the *No Outsiders* programme. The parents wanted a book called *King and King* – about a prince who married a prince – taken out, so he removed it and replaced it with another book that had a gay prince. He took out *My Princess Boy* and replaced it with a book about a transgender teddy bear. 'The other thing we did was we told the parents we were going to stop using the world celebrate,' Moffat says. 'You don't have to celebrate me being gay. I want to be accepted. I don't want to celebrate you being Muslim. I accept you being Muslim, but I don't have to celebrate it.' He also offered to put the lesson plans online and invited parents to attend lessons so they could see for themselves what their children were taught. When the parents were initially presented with these compromises, they rejected them, and Moffat had to be bundled out of the meeting for his own safety. The parents threated more protests when the autumn term resumed and warned that they would take their children out of school. Moffat went to America for a holiday during that summer. 'I can remember on my last day of the holiday I spent the day in floods of tears at the thought of going back home,' he recalls. When he returned, the promised protests failed to materialise. Despite the threats that the parents would take their children out of school, the vast majority did not, and the lessons resumed with no protests.

When I met Andrew again in the spring of 2020 to ask him why he thought a potentially explosive situation had been defused, he told me that 'what I hope happened is that people went away and looked at the lesson plans and watched the videos and thought this is not what we were told – that's what I hope happened.' I asked him what lessons he drew from the experience and he told me that one lesson was the importance of being supported by his superiors. 'I could not have done this without the school support,' he told me. 'Hazel [the headteacher] was an absolute rock and she said, "We're not giving up on this." I did, at one point, go to Hazel and say, "Is this too much? Do you think we should just stop *No Outsiders*?" She said, "I appreciate you saying that, Andy, but we're not stopping." And I never asked her again.' It was, ultimately, that courage shown by Moffat and the school that led to the parents backing down and, as a result, there will be Muslim children growing up in Birmingham who will be taught that there is nothing inherently wrong with being gay. When I asked Andrew how he felt about the fact that what he was teaching the children might be contradicted by their parents, he was sanguine, he just wanted the children to know that other opinions existed and that their parents' views were not gospel.

I would like to hope that tolerance might be infectious, and the parents might in turn catch it from their children, so that future Nazs don't end up feeling as if life is not worth living. Naz's life came to a tragic end but his partner Matthew was determined that his fiancé should not have died in vain. He set up the Matt and Naz Foundation, a charity that tackles homophobia triggered by religion, to help parents accept their children. 'It's about educating the families,' Maryam told me when I asked where she saw hope for the future. 'A lot of them are so close-minded and such homophobic, sexist, horrible people, but they're learning, and they have no choice but to accept it.' 'At the end of the day only Allah will judge me,' Shazia told me, 'but if I am going to hell then at least let me have my heaven here on earth.'

When he revealed the truth about his sexuality, Shazad's parents were, like Naz's, shocked and appalled – but there were some critical differences. 'My siblings stood up for me,' Shazad says. 'They said to my parents, "If you turn him away, we will all turn away from you." They put their relationships on the line to support me.' Shazad was also fortunate in that his mother was truly religious. 'It is because of the level of her knowledge and the fact they have read the Qur'an in their own language,' he says, 'that they can use the Qur'an as a guide to daily problems in life. The answers Mum has found have been found in the Qur'an, in the fact that there are verses that say do not judge anyone because it is between that person and God.' There was one other crucial fact: in the same conversation that Shazad revealed he was gay, he also told his parents that he was HIV+. 'Once they learnt that, the discussion moved from being gay to potentially dying,' says Shazad. 'They had to deal with the fact that they might be losing me.' And so, thanks to family support, the fear brought on by her son dying and an interpretation of Islam that stresses the importance of not judging, Jamelia made a choice: she would learn to accept her son's homosexuality.

That was why I had come to sit in Jamelia's home with Jamelia and Shazad sat opposite me, gay son and accepting mother, side by side. 'I respect Craig,' she says, referring to Shazad's partner, 'and I don't care what other people think – I leave everything to Allah.' Shazad tells me that he is conscious that he has inevitably disappointed his mother in some ways, so he works hard to make up for that by other means. 'I have compensated for the fact that there is a part of their aspirations for their child that will not get fulfilled such as marriage and children,' he says, 'so I upped other parts of my offering as a son. I will turn up to her home with flowers. I am attentive and loyal, and I will speak to my mum three or four times a day no matter where I am in the world – if I don't ring home every day she gets worried.'

I had assumed that tolerance towards homosexuality would go hand in hand with a lack of religiosity and more education – put more bluntly, I thought that those people who were culturally Muslim but not hugely observant were more likely to have less of an issue with homosexuality. Jamelia completely disproved this theory. When I try to understand why she was able to accept her son while so many other Muslim parents cannot, I think it is a combination of a number of factors. The fact that Shazad has HIV put his homosexuality into stark perspective; the fact that Jamelia is not overly concerned by what others in the community might say, the fact that Shazad was supported by his siblings; the fact that Jamelia believed that her faith led her to accept her son and not reject him. 'It's the religion,' says Shazad, when I asked him to explain his mother's attitude. 'It is the fact that she is so into the real meaning of Islam rather than the superficial practising parts that a lot of people get wrapped up into, and the root of that is don't judge and let your children make their own decisions. Her moral compass is guided by her faith not any other person or the community.' I had spent most of the afternoon with Shazad and Jamelia and I needed to get back to the train station to head home. I had one final question. I wanted to know what Jamelia would say to Naz's mother and did she have any idea why she could accept her son while Naz's mother could not. 'I am not a TP,' Jamelia told me, clarifying that TP stood for 'typical Pakistani'. 'If I ever met that woman, I would say to her: "Who do you think you are? Does you think you are Allah? Allah is up above and no one but Allah can judge anyone."'

When I was planning to write this book, I wanted to find stories that were hopeful and inspiring and in many ways the story of Shazad and Jamelia provides that happy ending – which is precisely why I am ending with it. I can't help feeling, however, that to end in such a way feels a little too neat and contrived. Jamelia *is* a remarkable person but what is truly remarkable is how few Muslim parents can bring themselves to accept or even tolerate the fact that their children are gay. The gulf between mainstream British societal attitudes and mainstream British Muslim attitudes towards homosexuality is dispiritingly wide and, frankly, I do not see many reasons to feel hopeful that it will be bridged anytime soon. I am, however, cautiously hopeful about the future. 'I really think we're moving away from this concept of a clear sexuality to sexual fluidity,' one imam told me. 'How you have sex, who you have sex with, where you have sex, what you do is all something which is based on cultural values and norms.' It was encouraging to hear an imam saying this but disappointing he did not want to be identified. I also feel optimistic that should the children of some of the younger Muslims I met while researching this book come out to their parents, they will find it easier than those of past generations. 'We're bonkers,' one young Muslim mother told me when I asked what she thought of the general Muslim attitude to homosexuality. 'The lines that we draw, that we decide on be-all-or-end-all things are bonkers. I definitely think that there are conversations to be had around why some things matter so much to some Muslims and other things are ignored.'

My wife has twin brothers. They are five years younger and identical in looks but with one difference: one is straight and the other is gay. During the last few years, I have spent a lot of time with Bridget's family and have seen first-hand what non-judgemental love looks like by watching her parents. In getting to know her brother so well, the notion that someone, anyone, would treat him differently simply because of who he chooses to love seems bewildering and insane. I used to think of gay rights as a particular cause, like women's rights or rights for ethnic minorities, but in recent years I have changed my mind: gay rights just feel like a subset of human rights. This represents something of a journey for me but, for my children, this is all they know. Laila and Ezra have an uncle who has boyfriends and they have another uncle who has a wife. My children see nothing at all strange about two men or two women marrying, it is all entirely normal to them, and that strikes me as progress.

THEY . . . LOOK DOWN ON WHITE GIRLS

'Britain has a problem with British Pakistani men raping and exploiting white girls. There. I said it. Does that make me a racist?'
Sarah Champion, Labour MP for Rotherham,
Sun newspaper August 2017

'For Rotherham'
Written on the gun cartridge used by
Brenton Tarrant during mosque shooting in
Christchurch, New Zealand, March 2019

auren grew up in a little town in Shropshire. When she recalls her childhood, she remembers sheep, tree houses and homemade swings. 'There was not really that much diversity in the town,' she recalls. 'It was all White, so there were no ethnic minorities who had different lifestyles that would clash with ours.' When she was seven, her parents split up and her mother met a new boyfriend who moved in after six months. Lauren was a friendly, lively and curious teenager. 'I was really kind to everyone,' she says, 'and I was always making jokes.'

In the first week of May 2006, Lauren left home to attend college in Telford. 'It was a converted house that had twelve flats in it,' she recalls. 'They were like bedsits, so I had a living room-cum-bedroom, a little hallway, a kitchen and a bathroom in there.' Lauren's friend William lived in one of the other flats and complained that a local gang would sometimes take over his flat and use it as a drugs den. It would also be used as a place for gang members to bring girls to have sex, forcing William to walk the streets at night. 'I felt he was being bullied for his keys,' says Lauren, 'so I said I wouldn't let them in, I will stand up to them. I told him to give me the keys.'

Lauren was in William's flat on the evening of 17 June 2006 when there was a knock on the door. It was a man called Farooq, who had recently been released from prison for breaking a stranger's jaw. 'When I opened the door, he put his foot in the doorway and forced his way in,' she says. 'He told William to leave, and I was left with this person.' With William gone, Farooq started to grab Lauren, trying to kiss her and, despite her protestations, he continued forcing himself on her. 'He was very beefed up,' Lauren says, 'like he had been to the gym and he was really strong.' Despite Lauren's desperate protestations, Farooq raped her and then threatened her to prevent her going to the police. Lauren hid in her flat, but two other Pakistani men later also forced their way in and sexually abused her. This time she did go to the police but she did not make a formal complaint of rape after officers warned her they would have to arrest her accusers. Lauren was scared of the potential consequences if her rapists learnt she had reported them. Traumatised by the attacks, Lauren found herself being further assaulted and abused as her rapists passed her phone number and address to other men. 'It's like an induced PTSD,' she says. 'They know how to traumatise you to get the results they want, because it's well-practised.' She was driven to properties to be abused by multiple men at sex parties, while other men would approach her on the street, asking for sex. 'Sexual abuse was a constant thing,' she recalls. 'It didn't even seem like abuse any more, it seemed normal life.' The abuse led to drug addiction, which led to further abuse. 'I lived in the bedsit for about four months,' she says, 'and in that time there were dozens of rapes and there were about seventy men. All of them were Pakistani.'*

On 5 January 2011, *The Times* published an investigation by Andrew Norfolk, which revealed a 'repeated pattern of sex offending in towns and cities across northern England and the Midlands involving groups of older men who groom and abuse vulnerable girls.'[1] The article noted that 'most of the victims are white and most of the convicted offenders are of

---

* Lauren wrote about her experiences using the assumed named Kate Elysia in her memoir *No Way Out*.

Pakistani heritage.' The ten years following the publication of that article revealed child sexual exploitation in towns and cities across the country, and more often than not Muslim men were the perpetrators. Telford. Rotherham. Rochdale. Oxford. Derby. Huddersfield. Peterborough. Newcastle. Bristol. The list goes on. The number of victims is hard to process: an independent report by Professor Alexis Jay into child sexual exploitation in Rotherham estimated 1,400 children were sexually exploited in the town between 1997 and 2013,[2] with 80 per cent of the perpetrators of Pakistani heritage. As many as 1,000 children are estimated to have been abused in Telford, with some as young as eleven,[3] and as many as 373 children were targeted for sex by gangs in Oxfordshire.[4]

Bridget was one month pregnant with our first child when I read *The Times* investigation. I remember feeling a sense of disgust, outrage and confusion. I simply could not understand how men who shared my heritage, and my religious background, could be responsible for such heinous crimes. It would have been bad enough if we were talking about one or two extreme and rare instances, but the scale of the abuse went far beyond the proverbial bad apple – this was a rotten orchard. In the years since the revelations of abuse in Rotherham, I became wearily accustomed to seeing newspaper reports with grim headlines about the abuse of young girls featuring rows of photographs of middle-aged Pakistani men. The men looked so . . . normal. They looked like the taxi drivers and restaurant workers they were, but appearances were deceptive, because, as the reports would describe in heartbreaking detail, these men were capable of inhumane cruelty. I found it hard to read the reports as a British-Pakistani and as a father, but mostly as a human being. The abuse had nothing to do with me, but I still felt personally offended, because these men, and I use the word in the loosest possible sense, came from backgrounds similar to mine – working-class, Pakistani and Muslim.

It was not only the profiles of the perpetrators that prompted my disgust. While the majority of the men involved in these gangs seemed to be of Pakistani Muslim heritage, their victims tended to be White girls. 'They were doing this to me because I was young and White,' says Lauren, 'they had no respect for White girls . . . [the attitude was] you're White and alone, therefore you're a slut and worthless.' I had married a 'White girl' and here were men who thought someone like Bridget or any of my other White female friends was of less worth simply on account of their Whiteness. Some claimed that the grooming scandals proved that Islam legitimised this abuse. They also concluded that child sexual exploitation revealed Pakistani racism against White girls – a racism that too many in positions of authority had been too squeamish to call out. These all felt legitimate issues to explore but, if I am being totally honest, this was not a chapter I was looking forward to writing. I even considered not writing it at all – it all felt so irredeemably grim and I was not sure I would find any reasons to feel hopeful – but that felt like a dereliction of duty. It was important that

I talk to someone who had experienced grooming and that was how I came to meet Lauren.

It was a blustery summer morning when we met outside London Bridge station. I had contacted her via social media and I was meeting her for the first time. During the course of researching this book I have met upwards of one hundred people, but I was particularly nervous meeting Lauren. I did not have much experience talking to survivors of the sort of extreme abuse she had endured. I needed, for this book, to ask her intrusive questions, but it is not a normal thing to ask someone you are meeting for the first time to describe how it felt to be raped. That was not the only reason I was nervous: the men who had abused her were British-Pakistanis and there was a part of me that wondered whether her experiences might have, understandably, affected her views about *all* British-Pakistanis. I was also worried that talking to me could trigger traumatic flashbacks. In the flesh, Lauren was not how I had imagined. I thought she might have been quiet and that it might have been hard to get her to open up. I assumed that the experiences she had endured would have left her deeply damaged and was expecting to meet someone who was serious, hardened by the evil she had encountered. This was not how she was at all – Lauren was open, chatty and with a rather wicked sense of humour. They had not broken her.

I began by asking Lauren whether she felt that the fact her abusers were Pakistani was relevant. 'Every Pakistani I came into contact with would say something sexually inappropriate to me,' she says. 'I used to hang out in this garage, and I was just sitting there one day and someone walked in, I didn't even know him, I don't know if my friends knew him that well and the first thing he said to me was: "Do you spit or swallow?"' Did she get a sense of their opinion about White people? 'They were very stereotypical about White people,' she says. 'They said a lot of racist things to me but they said I was not allowed to call them racist because racism only comes from the culture in power.'

The racist attitudes of Lauren's abusers in Telford were very similar to what Ella Hill was told by the men who abused her in Rotherham. 'As a teenager I was taken to various houses and flats above takeaways in the north of England, to be beaten, tortured and raped over 100 times,' she recalled in a 2018 article for the *Independent*. 'I was called a "white slag" and "white c***" as they beat me. They made it clear that because I was a non-Muslim, and not a virgin, and because I didn't dress "modestly", that they believed I deserved to be "punished". They said I had to "obey" or be beaten.'[5]

Haris and Henna are twenty-three and nineteen years old respectively and both live in Telford on the same street as some of the men convicted for child sexual exploitation. I wanted to talk to them to try to understand what might lead someone in their town into grooming and what the general attitude among local Pakistanis was towards White girls. 'I actually used to play football with one of the leaders of the CSE [child sexual exploitation] ring,' Haris tells me, 'but I didn't know at the time.' Haris was twelve and the man was around twenty. 'He was a bit of an odd character,' he says. 'He used to come to the park, right, he used to have his gold teeth in, he'd smoke in front of us, he'd bring his BMW to the park even though he lived two seconds away just to show off. I guess in a way he was trying to groom younger Asians into following his footsteps.' Haris says that part of the explanation for child sexual exploitation was it was an offshoot of other criminality – the men who were involved in CSE were also immersed in drug dealing and other crimes and the girls were simply another means to make money. That is not to deny other factors, however. 'There's cultural stuff in it as well,' he says. 'The way that a lot of older Asian people speak about White girls isn't great. That sort of could sink into younger generations about the way they dress and things like that. Like, calling them prostitutes in our language and things like that. I think these men treat all women badly but, in terms of taking it that step further and exploiting them, they'd exploit the White girls because they see them as of less value.' It was the girls' alleged looser morals coupled with the fact that they were vulnerable, living away from home like Lauren, or in care homes, from chaotic families and with less access to family support, which made them a target. 'I think us not being Muslim is a big part of it,' Lauren says, 'because we're not Muslim, and we're like the epitome of sin?' The irony being that it was this alleged sinfulness that attracted these men.

I talked to Henna in Telford as one of the perpetrators was the nephew of the person who taught her at mosque.

I asked how she felt when she first realised Pakistani men in her town were engaged in such crimes. 'Disgusted. I actually think it's disgusting,' she says. 'Everyone must have had a part in it. People must have been covering up for them, turning a blind eye. They would have known what they were doing, or they would have heard about it, but they turned a blind eye because it's not their daughters being affected.' 'I would say that the whole Pakistani community knew about it, but they still didn't know how bad it was,' says Lauren. 'They'd hear things, they'd see things, but the women wouldn't have guessed that their husbands were inflicting such awful abuse on another girl.'

I asked Henna how she would summarise the attitudes of the Pakistani guys she went to school with and who lived in the town towards White girls. 'The first word that comes into my head is "easy",' she says. 'They mistreat Asian girls, don't get me wrong, they do, but in terms of White girls – when they look at an Asian girl they still think, "Oh, I've got a sister at home." . . . When they look at a White girl, they don't see them in the same context. So, they would end up mistreating an Asian girl, you could guarantee a million per cent afterwards they would regret it. They would feel bad. But with a White girl, they would never, ever feel a sense of regret and that's only because they don't view White girls in the same way.' It was rather uncomfortable hearing Henna say this because I was not an objective observer – I knew exactly what she was talking about because I had heard versions of this in my own life.

It is almost a cliché that young Asian men are often encouraged to have their fun with White girls, sow their wild oats, get it out of their systems and so on before they eventually return to their cultural home and marry someone more 'acceptable'. I am reminded of what Ajaz's parents told him when he revealed he was in a serious relationship with his White girlfriend, Mary: 'You have had your fun, now it is time to come home.' The implication is that White girls are fine to have fun with – arguably more fun than Muslims – but only a fool would go any further. It's a version of what Yaseen in Blackburn told me: 'Asians will mix socially with White people and some will even date White women, but they won't go so far as marrying them.'

I was unsurprised to hear such toxic racist and misogynist attitudes towards White girls – I suspect they are sadly common in the community – but what I found much harder to process was that the girls these men were raping and abusing were just that: girls. They were twelve, thirteen and fourteen and the men were often two or three decades older. Girl A was fourteen when she was groomed in Rochdale and was later a key witness in the trial of the child sex ring. In *My Story*, she writes of her abusers that she 'reminded them that I was only fifteen. But it didn't matter to them: Daddy [the nickname of one of her abusers] kept saying that in his country they could have sex with girls as young as eleven.'[6] He was not wrong. In 2017, a ten-year-old bride in Pakistan was rescued after being forced to marry a fifty-year-old man.[7] Child marriage is common in Yemen in both rural and urban areas. Girls may be married as early as twelve or thirteen, especially if the girl is wedded to a close relative, and more than a quarter are married before the age of fifteen. In rural areas, girls may be married as young as eight.[8] Cases of girls dying during childbirth are not unusual, and one twelve-year-old bride even died from internal bleeding following sexual intercourse.[9] It is beyond justification, but how *did* the men justify it? Religion.

The supposed religious precedent is the marriage between the Prophet Muhammad and his fourth wife, Aisha. Some scholars place her at around eight or nine and claim the marriage with the Prophet, who was in his early fifties, was consummated when she was ten. It is this story that some Muslims use to justify their crimes and which some on the far right use to claim the Prophet was a paedophile. This all poses something of a challenge for someone like me who doesn't want to reject their Muslim heritage, but is deeply uncomfortable with the idea of a man in his fifties marrying a girl under ten. So, what to make of this story? 'While Muhammad's union with a nine-year-old girl may be shocking to our modern sensibilities, his betrothal to Aisha was just that – a betrothal,' writes Reza Aslan in *No God but God*. 'Aisha did not consummate her marriage to Muhammad until after reaching puberty, which is when every girl in Arabia without exception became eligible for marriage.'[10] Since 2000, Alyas has been an imam at a Bradford mosque. 'The marriage to Aisha was a marriage and they were married for ten years,' he says. 'That cannot in any way be equated to child sexual exploitation, which is essentially the rape of a child. People will say, "How can a child consent?" Well, this was 1,400 years ago and this was the norm and today we have different norms around these issues. Therefore, we have to conform to the social and legal parameters that we have now.' The point about changing norms is a good one: when Eleanor of Provence married King Henry III in 1236, she was thirteen and he was twenty-eight and she had never set eyes on him, and when King Edward II married Isabella of France in 1308, he was almost twenty-four and she was twelve.[11] So, we might understandably find it questionable, but child marriage was not just a Muslim thing. It is also important to acknowledge that scholars disagree on how old Aisha was and estimates of her age range from nine to nineteen.[12]

In June 2013, Alyas was among the Muslim leaders who condemned the sexual grooming of children in a sermon during Friday prayers. The condemnation was organised by Together Against Grooming (TAG), set up by Ansar Ali, whose story we have also been following. 'It was around 2013 when a few of these cases started hitting the news,' Ansar says. 'A lot of people said: "This was so rife in your community in your area, you must have known." I knew that the media was going to use these cases to bash the Muslim community so maybe we should engage in this work.' Ansar started to research the evidence. 'The conclusion I drew was that part of this is to do with sex but it's a lot more than that,' he says. 'A lot of it is to do with gangs and criminality and drugs. So, although paedophilia isn't disproportionately represented in our community, sadly it's present in all communities, for the people involved in these gangs and drugs, a disproportionate amount were from our community.' This prompted him to start speaking out – to show that Muslims were not collectively burying their heads in the sand. 'We have been horrified by the details that have emerged from recent court cases and, as Muslims, we feel a natural responsibility to condemn and tackle this crime,' Ansar told the BBC. 'The Qur'an exhorted Muslims to act against evil and injustice and create just societies. We are united in our stand against sexual grooming and, as Muslims, we are leading the effort to rid society of this crime.' I asked Alyas what he told the worshippers. 'What I spoke about in the sermon was first the Islamic imperative around child protection,' he says. 'We have very strong rules around child protection in Islam, which recognise that the child has to be protected from many forms of abuse. So, the concept of every child matters and the concept of child protection is an Islamic imperative.'[13]

I felt reassured that child sexual exploitation was not a Muslim problem but was it a Pakistani problem? In 2011 Jack Straw, the former Labour home secretary, suggested there was a cultural element to the phenomenon of grooming gangs. Straw made his comments after two Asian men who raped and sexually assaulted girls in Derby were given indefinite jail terms. 'There is a specific problem which involves Pakistani heritage men ... who target vulnerable, young White girls,' Straw told the BBC's *Newsnight*. 'We need to get the Pakistani community to think much more clearly about why this is going on and to be more open about the problems that are leading to a number of Pakistani heritage men thinking it is OK to target White girls in this way ... these young women, White girls who are vulnerable, some of them in care ... who they think are easy meat.'[14] Straw's suggestion was echoed six years later by Labour MP for Rotherham Sarah Champion in a controversial column for the *Sun* newspaper: 'Britain has a problem with British Pakistani men raping and exploiting white girls. There. I said it. Does that make me a racist? Or am I just prepared to call out this horrifying problem for what it is? For too long we have ignored the race of these abusers and, worse, tried to cover it up.'

Abrar Javed is forty-one. He is a member of the Rotherham Muslim Community Forum. He was born and bred in the town and has the stocky physique of someone who spends a lot of time in the gym. Abrar has been active representing the families of men who have been charged with grooming offences but insist they are innocent. I travelled to Rotherham to meet him to find out how local Pakistanis felt about the accusations levelled against the community. 'As one of her constituents, for her to be putting a stamp on it and legitimising the narratives of the far right, it was almost like a nail in the coffin for us,' Abrar told me. Sarah Champion later tried to distance herself from the column, claiming the piece had been altered and should 'not have gone out in my name' and was 'stripped of nuance',[15] but the damage had arguably already been done. Rotherham became inextricably associated with 'Muslim rape gangs' and this drew the attention of far-right groups. The English Defence League held marches in the town, which they labelled the 'Islamic paedophile capital of Britain.'[16] A BBC report in 2017 revealed that 'since 2012 16 protests have been held, the majority organized by far right groups such as the EDL and Britain First'.[17] Mushin Ahmed, an eighty-one-year-old grandfather, was walking to his local mosque in August 2015 when he was murdered by Dale Jones and Damien Hunt. During the trial, jurors heard that Jones attacked Ahmed after accusing him of being a 'groomer'.[18] The protests and the killing led the Muslim community in Rotherham to launch a neighbourhood protection group in 2020 after three mosques were targeted by the far right.[19] 'There were so many groups turning up every other week and it created a sense of fear,' recalls Abrar. 'There was a sense of paranoia and a rift was created in communities that had lived side by side for so many years.'

In March 2019, twenty-eight-year-old Brenton Tarrant murdered fifty-one worshippers in shootings at two mosques in Christchurch, New Zealand. Tarrant posted a seventy-four-page manifesto entitled 'The Great Replacement' the morning before the attack to explain his motivation. He wrote that he carried out the mass shooting to avenge Muslim terrorist attacks on the West, as well as the Rotherham child sex ring.[20] A picture of an ammunition clip he allegedly posted to Twitter before the attack showed the words 'For Rotherham' written in white ink.[21] The far right may have weaponised the grooming scandals, but that does not mean that their central claim – that Pakistani men are hugely over-represented in them – is not true. When you look at the figures, I said to Abrar, Sarah Champion had a point. 'The headline is always Pakistani men rape White girls and they're the only ones that do it,' he says. 'Whereas if you look at child sexual abuse, grooming is a sub-category of child sexual abuse. People have forgotten that there are other types of abuse like online grooming, and it is proportionally White men who commit the majority of these crimes, and what she's done is shine a torch on one particular area. And that has become the focal point of child sexual abuse. It's always easy to go after minorities.' This was something that had been on my mind because I was in Rotherham in the same month that newspapers were full of revelations about the sex crimes of financier and prolific paedophile Jeffrey Epstein. In all the reporting I read of Epstein's crimes, there was plenty about how he used money and influence to recruit young girls and evade justice, but I don't recall reading anything that suggested his crimes could be explained by the fact he was Jewish. I don't recall anyone mentioning that Harvey Weinstein is Jewish or that Jimmy Savile was a devout Catholic when seeking explanations for their criminality.

Britain's worst ever paedophile was Richard Huckle, who was believed to have abused as many as 200 children. During his trial in 2016, it was revealed that his computer contained more than 20,000 indecent pictures and videos of his assaults. Commenting on one of his victims, he boasted: 'I'd hit the jackpot, a three-year-old girl as loyal to me as my dog and nobody seemed to care.' Huckle was convicted of seventy-one counts of serious sexual assaults against children and handed twenty-two life sentences. The reason I mention this is because Huckle groomed children while doing voluntary work in Kuala Lumpur with a church-based charity. In Britain he was a regular worshipper at Ashford Baptist Church, he attended a congregation in London[22] and worked as a Sunday school teacher at a church in Kent.[23] That might all merit describing Huckle as a Christian, which is why it is rather telling that the BBC referred to how he 'presented himself as a practising Christian'[24] while the *Independent* suggested he was 'posing as an English teacher and Christian volunteer'[25] – the same word used by the *Guardian* and *Sun*. There is no suggestion that his religion explains his crimes, rather the inference is that a real Christian would never do what he did. Muslims are rarely accorded such nuanced reporting.

We met Nazir Afzal in Chapter 1 when he was growing up in working-class Small Heath. He avoided an arranged marriage because of his academic talents and worked as a solicitor in Birmingham from 1988 until moving to London in 1991, where he became a Crown Prosecutor. In 2001, he became the youngest person, and first Muslim, to be appointed assistant Chief Crown Prosecutor. In 2011, he was appointed North West Chief Crown Prosecutor, covering Greater Manchester, Cumbria and Lancashire. It was around then that he started paying attention to Andrew Norfolk's articles in *The Times*. Afzal asked his team to investigate, and successfully prosecuted eight British men of Pakistani origin and an Afghan man for raping and trafficking White girls in Rochdale. I asked him what he made of the fact that so many of the men involved in these gangs were Pakistani. 'I've prosecuted bad guys from sixty-four different countries,' he says. 'I've prosecuted cases involving victims from fifty-plus different countries, so you're not going to tell me that this is just a south Asian issue. Predators hide in every community and child sexual abuse takes very many forms. It most often happens within the family, it happens online, it happens in institutions like the BBC and places of worship.' Street grooming is only one form of grooming and, he says, it is often connected to the night-time economy – taxis, takeaway restaurants – which tend to be run by Pakistanis. 'The victims are looking for transport, they're looking for food, they're looking for money for substances and all of that can be found in the night-time economy,' he says, 'and in places like Rochdale and Rotherham, British-Pakistani men are involved in those kinds of things.'

I am in the living room of a terraced house ten minutes from Rotherham train station. I am meeting a man I will call Abdul although that is not his real name. He is wary of talking to me and of having our conversation recorded. He starts by asking me whether I am Muslim or not, which is another way of asking how much of a Muslim I am. He then wants to know what I think of the grooming story. I try to come up with something exceptionally bland. He seems reassured. Abdul is thirty-five. He is the youngest of seven children to a father who came from Pakistan in the late 1950s to work in a steel factory. 'My father always wanted me to be either a doctor, lawyer or dentist,' he says. 'Unfortunately, it didn't go that way.' Abdul did well at school but at college he became involved in a fight that led him to getting thrown out. He married his first cousin at the age of twenty-two and soon started driving a taxi. 'I had a wife and kids to look after,' he says, 'driving a taxi was an easy way to earn money.' Abdul was at work one snowy February morning in 2017 when his mobile rang. It was his wife telling him that the National Crime Agency was at the door. 'I parked my cab up, got out and they jumped on me,' he says. 'They put handcuffs on me and explained I was under arrest.' Abdul was arrested and charged with two offences of sexual assault and rape. Were the people you are accused of assaulting and raping underage, I asked. 'That's what they're saying,' he says, 'they weren't sure of the age, but they said twelve, then it went to thirteen, then it went to fourteen, then it's come to fifteen.' Abdul categorically denies the offences. 'I couldn't understand why somebody would say something like that has happened when it actually hasn't,' he says. 'Why would somebody ruin somebody's life? I knew of this person, she was a friend's girlfriend, but why would somebody say something has happened when it hasn't?'

I had no way of knowing if Abdul was telling the truth or not, so I asked him what he thought more generally of the

Rotherham grooming scandal. 'Don't get me wrong, there's definitely some truth in it,' he begins. 'I'm not going say that everybody that's come forward are all full of shit. But to be honest, I think the numbers have been exaggerated. When I was in school there were guys that were sixteen, seventeen who were with a girl that were fourteen, fifteen. It was just a normal thing, like a relationship, boyfriend-girlfriend. And all of a sudden now it's like groomers but back then they were friends.' I heard a version of this from other Pakistanis in Rotherham. 'I believe bad things did happen, without a shadow of a doubt,' says Abrar, 'but I believe that was in a minority of cases. In the majority it is not the way grooming has been portrayed to the rest of the world – that these were gangs who were forcing girls to do things against their will and being taken from point A to point B and being drugged, and the girls were unconscious and forced to sleep with so many men. What you would find in most cases, you would find men generally three or four years' older thinking they're in relationships with these girls and vice versa – it was consensual, even though it was illegal. I do believe that is closer to the truth.' You have met some of these perpetrators, I say. What are they like? He laughs. 'These are guys that you could bump into at your local bar or your local takeaway and have a conversation with,' he says. 'They don't have narcissistic, psychopathic, sociopathic tendencies. These guys don't look at these girls as victims. Whether they've actually done something wrong to the girls – forced her to do this or that – a lot of them would deny that because they'd say it wasn't like that. It was more a relationship.' Have you ever met anyone and later thought he was a monster? 'I met one or two guys where I've got to find out a little bit more about their cases,' he says, 'and I have no doubt what some of the victims were telling us was not exaggerated. One hundred per cent. I can say that.' The important point for Abrar, however, is that these minority of men were criminals who happened to be Pakistani. 'If you take a set of circumstances and give it to a Black guy or a White guy nothing would be different,' he says. 'These guys have been embroiled in drugs, violence – generally never done well at school. No ambition. Unstable families. Probably their father was into drugs and in and out of prison. If you take those factors into account, I don't care who you are. Those factors could affect anybody. Race, faith and everything else just go out the window. And culture plays absolutely no part. You could be the Pope, mate. It's going to affect you in an adverse way.'

Abrar clearly did not believe culture played any part in the grooming, but the woman who helped expose child sexual exploitation in Rotherham disagrees. 'I don't think any of what happened in Rotherham between white girls and Asian men is connected with religion,' Jayne Senior writes in *Broken and Betrayed*. 'However, I do believe there are some cultural issues around abuse ... I believe there is an issue around respect for women, and particularly young white females, coming from some members of the Asian community in this country.'[26] Lara McDonnell was twelve when she was groomed, abused and trafficked by the Oxford sex ring and writes in her memoir that 'while there are paedophiles in every race and religion, I do think the gang behaved in the way they did because of cultural differences in how they viewed women. Statistically there are more white male paedophiles, but the structured gang set-up seems to be something to do with Muslim men and I think that stems from a lack of respect for women within a certain section of men.'[27]

In earlier chapters we heard from Sajid, who grew up in Rochdale – the location of one of most notorious grooming gangs – and spent his teenage years working in his father's corner store, where he would often have to clean off the racist graffiti that had been daubed by the local skinheads. In Chapter 2 we learnt of how Sajid met Laura and how they played the long game to win the approval of his parents. Sajid embarked on an eighteen-year career in banking with Chase Manhattan and later Deutsche Bank. In 2009, he left Deutsche and in an audacious attempt to become ever less popular, moved from banking into politics. He had long been an admirer of Margaret Thatcher – even having her image on his teenage bedroom wall – and in 2010 he was elected to Parliament. In April 2018, Sajid Javid was appointed Home Secretary. 'When it comes to gang-based child exploitation, it is self-evident to anyone who cares to look that if you look at all the recent high-profile cases there is a high proportion of men that are of Pakistani heritage,' Sajid Javid told BBC Radio 4, adding 'there could be – and I'm not saying there are – some cultural reasons from the community that those men came from that could lead to this type of behaviour. For me to rule something out just because it would be considered sensitive would be wrong.'[28] In suggesting 'cultural reasons', Javid was echoing the views of Sarah Champion, but the fact he is of Pakistani heritage made his comments more noteworthy.[*]

'Let's put it on record – he's a bloody coconut, mate,' says Abrar, when I asked him what he made of Javid's comments. 'He tries too hard to be something he'll never be accepted for. If you live in a working-class area like I do, you accept who you really are in society. I don't hide away from that fact. If you try too hard to fit in and assimilate you are going to be reminded of who you really are.' The accusation levelled at Sajid Javid was that he was highlighting these so-called 'cultural reasons' in a bid to curry favour with White voters. I asked him to expand on his comments – how had he felt when he first heard about the grooming gangs? 'I thought it was a disgrace to my heritage and it angered me,' Sajid tells me. 'If you look at child sexual exploitation as a whole, there's no ethnic cluster, but if you look at group-based child sexual exploitation and look at the conditions that have happened in recent years, it is disproportionately ethnic minority. It is, in fact, disproportionately British-Pakistani

---

[*] In November 2020, Sajid Javid was announced as the Chair of the Child Sexual Abuse and Exploitation Commission. Among the other commissioners were Shaista Gohir, Nazir Afzal and Sarah Champion.

and because that is my heritage as well, there is a personal side to thinking, "What the hell?"' How did he explain it, I asked. 'The authorities for a number of years turned a bit of a blind eye,' he says. 'They didn't want to take it seriously enough because ... whether they were police or others ... they didn't want to be accused of racism. That was part of the problem. I think people in the community – not the community – but those abusers may have felt that they could get away with it.' This all feels persuasive to me – the nervousness around being accused of racism coupled with a sense that the girls were unlikely to be believed or taken seriously. It was a point Lauren had also made. 'The police were racist,' she told me. 'They labelled the girls as "Paki-shaggers". Pakis are the scum of the earth, and these girls are sleeping with the scum of the earth and therefore they are even lower than them. They thought they were doing it consensually, they said that it was a lifestyle choice, and they were choosing to be prostitutes, and they were blaming the girls for the messes they got themselves in. I don't think that they were afraid of being racist. Maybe they were afraid of being caught out as racist because they are racist, and they don't want anyone to actually know that.'

I feel like we have so far established that child sexual exploitation has very little to do with Islam and the religion does not condone child abuse. The fact that the perpetrators of street grooming tend to be Pakistani is related to them being over-represented in the night-time economy and the interconnectedness of the night-time economy, criminality and the availability of vulnerable girls whom the authorities failed to protect. A Home Office report published in December 2020 on child sex abuse gangs concluded there was not enough evidence to state that they were disproportionately made up of Asian offenders. It found that while offenders come from diverse backgrounds, groups tended to be of men of the same ethnicities. Money and sex were motivations as well as a sexual interest in children and misogyny.[29] The report was described by some critics as a whitewash. 'The grooming report has provided a case study in the way the British Establishment continues to thwart any attempt to finally get a grip on an issue that shames our nation,' wrote Dan Hodges in the *Mail on Sunday*.[30] I don't believe there is anything in 'Pakistani culture' that justifies the abuse of young White girls, or of any girls, but I do believe that many Pakistanis in Britain view White girls differently to Muslim or Pakistani girls. And I find it hard to believe that this played *no* role at all in the crimes of the grooming gangs.

There was another factor that I repeatedly heard cited, and it had to do with what more than one person referred to as 'toxic masculinity'. When Haris was growing up in Telford, he recalls that older Asian lads would force the younger ones to fight. 'It was just for their entertainment to see who the hardest kid was,' he says. 'I was nine, maybe ten years old and I would have to fight one of my friends. Looking back, obviously something like that is a bit strange, it was all about showing how masculine you were.'

Years later, when Lauren was being abused, she experienced another manifestation of toxic masculinity. The local British-Pakistanis would introduce her to men who had recently arrived from Pakistan. These men would be virgins and would be introduced to Lauren to have sex with her. 'They would force him to lose his virginity because they believe that he's not a man until he's lost his virginity,' she says. Sometimes she would meet men who did not want to have sex with her but were forced to by the local Pakistanis. 'They enjoyed embarrassing the man,' she says. 'It was like a ritual into their gang but if the guy didn't want to have sex, I would pretend to have sex with him and then I'd say, "Don't worry we can tell everyone that we had sex, but we don't have to have sex."' The scene Lauren was describing was heartbreaking – it was hard not to feel sorry not only for Lauren, but for the virgins expected to have sex with her for the amusement of other men. This felt like the dictionary definition of toxic masculinity and it made me wonder what shaped the perverted values of these men.

'We have a generation of men who have poor role models,' says Alyas Karmani. 'We have issues around identity, mental health, family conflict and cultural conflict. We have negative role models and absent fathers or fathers you wish were absent, and we are exposed to very toxic models of masculinity and a pornified culture, which is profoundly misogynistic. We don't have any counters to that in terms of developing a masculinity which is based on emotional intelligence, compassion and empathy. These are not unique issues to the Muslim or Pakistani community but where they become more problematic in our community is that we just don't talk about stuff.' These are difficult conversations that go beyond simply blaming a community or faith. 'It is up to us to have some engagement with our generation of young men growing up and be quite direct about the wider issues that affect Muslim men: about toxic masculinity, around porn, around how we see women, the issue of respect, the issue of values and what is a healthy relationship,' Abrar says.

These are clearly issues not only for the Muslim community, but it was striking how often when I talked to the men in this book about their relationships with their fathers they described them as distant and deferential. 'There wasn't much of an emotional connection,' says Abrar, 'Dad worked in a factory fourteen hours a day. We wouldn't do any social activities together.' When I asked if he was someone to whom you could confide, he laughed. 'No chance, mate,' he says. 'Those types of conversations never took place. There were never any moments with my old man where I could sit down and tell him what school was like or how I was feeling.'

I could not talk to my parents about my feelings and I certainly could not discuss matters of the heart. In Chapter 2 I talked about the pressure to get married, but even before marriage was discussed there was a strict rule – never stated but always understood – never to talk about girls at home. I obeyed this rule not only as a teenager but even into my twenties. I had to pretend I never talked to girls and it meant that if I wanted to relate an incident that happened in my social life, I would have to change the genders of my friends. You would have thought, based on my conversations with my family, that I lived, worked and socialised only with men. I had to maintain this fiction because girls, particularly White girls, seemed to possess some sort of radioactive energy to my family – it was as if in admitting I talked to them I was opening up the possibility that I could or might be doing more than talking. I am not suggesting a direct causal link between this sort of upbringing and the crimes committed by grooming gangs – both Abrar and I managed to survive our fathers without turning to vile crimes. I do, however, wonder whether there is something in the argument that part of the explanation for the actions of the grooming gangs – and most explanations will be partial – could be the taboos surrounding love and relationships. It was telling how often in the memoirs of grooming survivors the abuser would try to frame the abuse as an actual relationship. There is a scene in Girl A's memoir where she is raped by a man in his fifties while still underage. 'All the time he was saying, "Don't cry",' she writes, 'and "You're beautiful" and "I love you."'[31] In Sarah Wilson's memoir, she describes being raped at the age of twelve by a Pakistani doctor in his twenties. '"One day, I'll take you to meet my family." He promised,' she writes, '"Then we can get married and have children."'[32] Holly Archer, a survivor of the Telford sex ring, describes her abusers as 'sex deprived and lonely: immigrants who knew no one in the UK and couldn't meet women because of the language barrier, and older men trapped in loveless marriages and communities which frowned upon divorce.'[33] None of this is to excuse their behaviour, but if we believe that monsters are made not born, it is worth exploring the worlds from which these men emerge. 'The men would have had arranged marriages, but they didn't love their wives,' Lauren says. 'Sometimes their wives didn't speak English and they were actually from Pakistan not raised in Britain, so they had a completely different culture to them. So maybe they thought the sex [with White girls] was OK because they're not in love with their wives and the sex at home was just for making children.'

Alyas and Abrar both raised the issue of toxic masculinity and suggested that it was only by confronting it that things would improve. Henna suggested that if Pakistani men believed there was even a possibility they could end up with someone White that might mean they would not have turned to abuse. 'There is a chance it maybe wouldn't have happened because they would have grown up with that little bit respect for women,' she says. 'They would look at someone, whether she was White, Black, Asian, non-Muslim, whatever and think, "She could potentially be my wife one day." Whereas at the moment, a lot of them they will date a White girl and in the back of their minds they'll be thinking, it's not like my family will let me marry this girl. I'm going to marry a Pakistani girl anyway, so it doesn't matter what I do to this girl. It doesn't matter how much I hurt her.'

Lauren told me she thought part of the explanation for the men's actions was that they had grown up segregated from all girls, particularly White girls. 'The men generally have less understanding of women in general,' she says. 'Not just White women but all women, so they never get that practice of having a conversation with women.' I asked her whether she thought that if Pakistani culture was more relaxed about gender mixing, especially with White girls, it would have had an impact on the scale of the abuse. 'I do, yeah. I think that if it was more relaxed then it wouldn't happen,' she says. 'If Pakistani men were able to communicate with White people and you could bring your White girlfriend home and introduce her to your mum and your mum would be cool, they'd naturally have more respect for you because they'd be able to get to know you better.' I found the fact that she could view her abusers with any degree of empathy, and possibly even sympathy, quite extraordinary. 'I pity them because it's hard for them,' she says. 'They have no idea what White women are really like and the only interaction that they get with White women is having sex with a woman who has been groomed and raped and abused. I feel sorry for them – they're actually socially deprived people.'

This led me to a question that I had long wondered about these abusers. It is a version of one that I have asked in different forms throughout this book – if there was more integration between communities, if Muslims and non-Muslims had the opportunity to see and get to know each other better, would the chances of such abuse have been reduced? I believe it would. I believe that it is easier to treat people cruelly if one objectifies and dehumanises them. The victims of the grooming gangs were, I would suggest, dehumanised on account of being non-Muslim and objectified on account of being White, but it is harder to dehumanise and objectify someone when you truly know them. I asked Haris, who had encountered some of the abusers, if this theory had any merit. 'The way it's targeted at White girls would probably change,' he says, 'but in terms of it happening, because I believe it's mainly economic, I still think it would occur, the patterns would just be different. They wouldn't mainly be targeting White girls. It would probably be less discriminatory. They'd probably just target girls of all ethnicities.'

So far I have focused on Pakistani male abusers and White female victims. That is the most familiar narrative – the one that the media has most fixated on and the far right have exploited. But is it the whole story? In August 2013, the Muslim Women's Network UK published a report called 'Unheard Voices – The Sexual Exploitation of Asian Girls and Young Women'.[34] 'The media and public attention has mainly focused on White British female victims of sexual exploitation and Asian offenders,' the report began, 'suggesting that the motivating factors behind such cases of abuse are to do with race, faith and ethnic culture.' The report revealed that Asian/Muslim girls were also vulnerable to grooming and sexual exploitation. There were some clear parallels with the abuse White girls faced. 'A striking feature was that in 86% (30 out of 35) of the case studies the victim was being passed around and prostituted amongst many other men, whether they were friends or loosely connected associates within a group or network,' the report found. 'Sometimes the victims were drugged to such an extent by alcohol and drugs that they were unaware of the extent of their abuse and of the different ways in which they were being violated or by how many men. The grooming and abuse of the girls and young women took place in various locations including vehicles, parks, flats, house parties, school, takeaway food outlets/ restaurants, alleyways and hotels. Evidence of trafficking also emerged, which included movement within cities or towns, between nearby cities and towns and also between regions.' This sounded very similar to the Lauren's experience and tallied with evidence from survivors in other grooming cases. The report also found, however, that 'Asian/ Muslim children have specific vulnerabilities associated with their culture which are exploited and also constitute a barrier to disclosure and reporting. Blackmail connected with shame and dishonour appeared to be a key and unique method of control for victims of Asian and Muslim backgrounds. A key driver for targeting Asian and Muslim girls could be that they were considered as a "less risky" option because they were unlikely to seek help or report their abuse due to "shame" and "dishonour" issues. The findings could indicate that Asian/Muslim girls are possibly more vulnerable than white girls to exploitation by predatory Asian/Muslim men.' I found this report eye opening because it upended some base assumptions in the coverage of grooming scandals – that it was only White girls being abused and it was their Whiteness that made them targets.

The lead author of the 'Unheard Voices' report was Shaista Gohir. 'Muslim girls, Pakistani girls are also groomed,' she tells me, 'but for some reason there seems to be a hierarchy when White girls are sexually abused by men of a different background, Pakistani men, then people are really angry. Yes, you've got CSE victims, but children are victims of sexual abuse from people that are known to them, family and friends. Children and young girls are sexually abused in temples by people in the community. There's no community that can claim the moral high ground – this is happening in every community, but no one cares about women's rights, but as soon as a man from another ethnicity or background or faith abuses a girl in your community, suddenly it matters.' The fact that Asian and Muslim girls were abused, and that the majority of abusers are White, still does not get away from the fact that when it comes to street grooming, a high proportion of offenders are Pakistani, and that made me wonder what efforts were being made among Pakistani communities to confront and combat this issue.

Having open conversations about toxic masculinity was part of the solution, but what else could be done? 'I never say to my girl, "Don't talk to boys" or to my son, "Don't talk to girls",' says Shaista. 'I don't have an issue with my daughter when boys call her. I think, as a parent, I think it's really important to give your children lots of attention, love and affection. It's not just about putting food on the table. When you don't get that love and affection, you seek it from other people, and it's usually from other older boys because they are the ones who are trying it on.' The old answers – talk to your children, show them love and affection and give them your time – still hold true. Haris had talked to me about why some men in his town had become abusers, but I had a different question for him – why had he not? He told me it was all about his mother. 'Other parents would let their kids roam about the streets at night and therefore get influenced by other people who are already part of the night economy,' he says. 'I wasn't allowed beyond the park by my house after 8 p.m. My mum would always check on me to see what I was doing. She would buy things like English books and give me extra tuition at home to help me in education.' What would have happened if your mother had not been so strict about you staying out, I asked. 'I probably would have ended up the same [as the gang members and abusers], to be honest,' he suggests.

Lauren left Telford to study nursing at university in Essex aged nineteen and soon after arriving had a feeling she describes as pure euphoria. 'I felt like somebody had scooped me out of the toilet, put me in a bowl of clean water and washed me,' she says. 'It was like I had been picked out of hell and put back into normal life.' Lauren arrived in Essex during the Muslim month of Ramadan and met some Muslims from Jordan. She had always been interested in faith, if not any particular religion, and decided she would fast during Ramadan as a way of thanking God on the anniversary of her escape from Telford. During this time, she started to read more about Islam. 'I tried to read the Qur'an because that's what you do in Ramadan, but it was too complicated,' she says, 'so I read a book called *Teach Yourself Islam*. I wanted to see what Muslims do, and think about it in the way Muslims think.' The more she read about Islam, the more certain Lauren became that her abusers were not true Muslims. 'They were not really Muslim,' she says, 'the only thing they do is eat halal from horrible chicken shops, because that's how they identify themselves as Muslim, but that's literally the only thing they're doing that's Muslim.' Lauren recalled that her abusers never spoke about their religion and when she tried they had always gotten angry. She realised that they didn't want her to know because knowing would make her human in their eyes and thus reduce their power over her. Lauren was invited to celebrate Eid in Trafalgar Square and it was there, in October 2008, that she decided to convert to Islam. I was, I have to admit, a little shocked to hear about her conversion but also a little sceptical that it was genuine. It was hard not to be suspicious that it was a version of Stockholm Syndrome, where hostages or abuse victims bond with their captors. 'I didn't get groomed by a man telling me about Islam who was trying to convince me to convert,' Lauren says in response to my scepticism, 'I literally did my own research and ended up liking it myself.'

During her final year in Essex, Lauren had a work placement with a criminal justice mental health team. It was June 2010, and one meeting during this placement was attended by senior police officers who talked about high-risk individuals out of prison on license. 'There were paedophiles and rapists and, as the police started reading out the profile of these men, I started feeling like a burden of responsibility,' Lauren recalls. 'I know men who have done these things and these men are dangerous. Suddenly, I felt guilty for not reporting it.' Immediately after the meeting, Lauren went to her local police station and told them everything. The police were already investigating child sex abuse offences in Telford in an investigation called Operation Chalice. 'As soon as I reeled off some names to them that they were already investigating they were all over-excited,' she says, 'they did a massive interview with me and then arrested them all.'

I ask Lauren what the lasting impact of the abuse has been. She starts tearing up. 'I still have PTSD and I struggle with my relationships,' she says. 'I don't think they're ever going to be normal. I wanted to have children and a family. I haven't got that. I'm on my own. I feel, at the moment, like I will be for ever. I'd have to have IVF if I was to have children because I've so had many infections that one of my fallopian tubes is blocked.' She is crying so much that I feel bad for having asked the question. I apologise for having upset her. 'I am OK,' she says, drying her eyes. 'I just have to live my life a bit crooked. Like not everything is like a porcelain doll. Some things have got cracks in them. I live my life the way I do, the way I can.'

The week after converting, Lauren started wearing a head-scarf. She found that whenever she returned to Telford she would start getting messages from Pakistani men trying to pull her back into the world she had left. 'I was finding it really difficult to prove to men I wasn't going to have sex,' she says, 'so I thought if I wear a headscarf, then no one will even ask me, and it worked, it actually worked. I called my hijab my "Big fat fuck-you".' She laughs. 'I found that when I had God on my side it gave me the power to say no,' she says. 'I had something telling me this is how God sees the world, and this is how you be a good person.' Lauren tells me her Islamic faith remains strong. 'My knowledge of Islam helps me in everyday life,' she says. 'I do believe that Islam saved me in the end.' She now works in London as a senior mental health nurse. I asked what she would say to the men who abused her. 'I don't think I'd want to say anything to them,' she says. 'In an ideal world I'd tie them to a chair, and I might have a hand drill and slowly drill it into their knees or something like that.' She laughs. That doesn't sound very Muslim, I say. 'Well, I could burn them,' she replies laughing. 'I could burn them at the stake – yes, I'm sure I could do something Muslim to them.'

The central question I wanted to explore in this chapter was how much ethnicity and religion are factors in explaining the horrific crimes committed by abusers like Lauren's. I do not believe religion plays a key role in excusing or explaining the grooming gangs' actions. 'They weren't "Muslims" in the true sense of the word – just in name only,' Lauren says. 'Islam had nothing to do with how they were, and their behaviour was contrary to the teachings of their religion. They were misogynists who thought of young White girls as inferior to them.' I was dreading working on this chapter. I knew it would mean having to confront the evil that these men did and the religious and cultural justifications they employed. I was also concerned that because so many in the community denied there was any issue was anyone actually doing the hard work of having difficult conversations inside the community? This was a story with so much horror but where was the hope?

Naz Kazmi from the Keighley Association Women and Children's Centre has also been active in tackling child sexual exploitation by working with the families of perpetrators. 'The families of the perpetrators were often in denial,' she says. 'They could not accept what their sons had done. I know one mother who has two sons both in prison for CSE and she is still in denial.' She tells me about another local man, a taxi driver in his sixties, who was sentenced for child sex crimes. He has two daughters, one of whom ran away because she found it so hard to accept what her father had done. Since the revelations about child grooming emerged, Kazmi has been working with the community to raise awareness. Her group has trained local women – dubbed the Auntie Network – how to look for and report any signs of abuse. She has also spoken out on the subject at local mosques. 'The gist of the message was that grooming children is wrong and unacceptable and hurting a child is unacceptable,' she says. 'Afterwards I was approached by a number of elderly first- and second-generation men who said they were proud of me for having the courage as a woman to stand in front of an audience of men just after Friday prayers to say what I did.' It did take courage to talk about such uncomfortable matters: not long after she spoke her offices were torched and the windows of her home were smashed. 'It's sensitive stuff, isn't it? – how dare I go out and speak in the mosque about those people grooming?' she says. 'But I didn't stop – parents need to be aware that young girls are being used and abused.' I asked Kazmi what her theory was about why such crimes took place. 'It comes back to nurturing,' she says. 'Do you have a daughter? Then you show her respect and if you have a son, that son will see how you respect your daughter and your wife. It's learned behaviour.' I found Kazmi's courage truly inspiring – she is a textbook example of the Fred Rogers quote that begins the book, that for all the terrible things that go on in this world there are also good people trying to help.

I have struggled with how much the fact that so many of the abusers were of Pakistani heritage is relevant. It is true, as Nazir Afzal says, that these crimes occur in all communities and are perpetrated by all ethnicities, and that the Pakistani abusers are a tiny minority of a tiny minority. My worry is that this still feels like a handy cop-out that prevents some in the Pakistani community from confronting deeply troubling views towards White women, such as the suggestion that White girls are fine for 'fun' but not for marrying. It was telling that whenever I tried to make enquiries to try and talk to Pakistani perpetrators, I would be offered case studies of men who were falsely accused and had had their lives turned upside down. These stories are worth hearing but they deflect from admitting that there were many, too many, Pakistani men who *did* take part in abuse. The fact that the issue of grooming has been exploited by the far right and the Islam haters makes it particularly sensitive, but it needs to be addressed for the sake of the thousands of victims, and to help ensure there are fewer victims in the future.

THEY . . . WANT TO TAKE OVER OUR COUNTRY

'Whatever England is now, it's not what it was and it's lamentable that we've lost so much. England is a memory now.'

Morrissey, *NME*, 2007

'It's all about immigration. It's not about trade or Europe or anything like that, it's all about immigration. It's to stop the Muslims from coming into this country. Simple as that.'

Barnsley resident who voted to leave the EU, Channel 4 News, 2016

On 10 March 2009, 200 soldiers from the 2nd Battalion The Royal Anglican Regiment paraded through Luton town centre. They had just returned from a second tour of Iraq and the march was part of the British army's policy of morale-boosting parades for the troops when they returned home. The soldiers were on their way to Luton town centre when they were met by around twenty Muslim protestors. The protest was organised by former members of Al-Muhajiroun, the banned group founded by the radical preacher Omar Bakri Mohammad, and the protestors held aloft banners that read 'Anglican Soldiers: Butchers of Basra' and 'Baby Killers', while they chanted 'Burn in Hell'. The protestors were confronted by locals waving Union flags and chanting 'Eng-er-land'. My mother had recently returned from a trip to Pakistan, and I had been planning on going to see her and the rest of my family on the day of the protest. I ended up changing my plans, but when I read the reports of the protest my initial reaction was that it was simply another stick with which people could beat Luton. The number of protestors was less than two dozen, but they had secured nationwide coverage while the quiet majority of Luton's Muslims, who remained opposed or indifferent to the loudmouths in the town centre, would be overlooked. I was used to Luton having an unenviable reputation as a hotbed of Islamic radicalism, and my assumption was that most outsiders would watch this with frustration but little surprise.

Later that same evening, Ivan Humble was sat in the living room of his council house in Lowestoft. He was thirty-nine, a single dad of two young children and on the dole. He was also, although he didn't openly talk about it, the victim of domestic violence at the hands of the mother of one of his children. 'It went on for eighteen months,' he says. 'I had two hospital visits, it used to be now and then, but then it got more regular, the more she started drinking. She was one of them that used to go out drinking – she'd go out on a Friday night and I wouldn't see her 'til Sunday and then she'd come home and just batter me. I've been hit with plates, fists, knees, feet. I just took it because of the kids. I didn't talk about it, but it made me feel like I weren't a man any more – it stripped me of my masculinity.' While he was looking for work, Ivan volunteered with the Royal Anglicans and met some young soldiers who had returned from Basra and were marching in Luton. 'My perception of the army was that they were good,' he says. 'They were in Iraq to improve things.' While sat in his living room, Ivan saw a report on the local television news about the events in Luton. 'I saw what the Muslims were saying about child murderers and the butchers of Basra,' he recalls, 'and I got so angry I put up a rant on Facebook.' It was not long after he posted that Ivan received a message from someone saying that he agreed with him. He also told Ivan that there were other like-minded individuals who were about to form a group, and he should consider joining. And that was how Ivan Humble came to be among the first recruits to the English Defence League. The organisation had been established by Luton-born Stephen Yaxley Lennon – who went by the name Tommy Robinson – as a direct consequence of the protests in his hometown. Ivan became an administrator on the first EDL fan page. 'It gave me a purpose,' he says. 'I was a single dad, lonely, sat at home a lot online, so it gave me something to do during the day when my kids were at school instead of sitting there watching telly. At first, I was against the radicals, but then slowly I became stereotypical of them.' By 'them', he, of course, meant all Muslims. Having grown up in Suffolk, Ivan had never meaningfully encountered any Muslims – no one on his street or at his school – but he seemed to have a firm idea of what they were like. 'Bad people,' he says, 'who wanted to get rid of people like me and change our way of life, change our country.'

So far I have focused largely on the stories of British Muslims, but in this chapter I want to explore some of the issues that incite anti-Islamic hostility among non-Muslims. I want to examine how legitimate the fears are of those who, like Ivan, worry that Muslims want to change their life and country, and how much these anxieties are rooted in ignorance and stoked by the media.

The initial target of Ivan's hostility was Anjem Choudary, the spokesman for militant extremist group Al-Muhajiroun, whose willingness to make incendiary statements made him a ubiquitous figure at the time. 'He was the one I would see on the news,' he says, 'he was on the TV, the papers and everywhere.' I am around the same age as Ivan and I too remember when Choudary was ubiquitous on television news and current affairs programmes. It used to enrage me that such an attention-seeking rabble-rouser could in any way be mistaken for representing the Muslim community. I was a journalist myself and so I recognised why he was booked by television producers – he was guaranteed to make incendiary claims that would rile up audiences and, given a choice between a fiery hothead and someone offering a more nuanced commentary, it was not hard to predict which was more likely to produce good television. The trouble was that what was good for television was not always good for broader society. In the absence of a range of Muslim voices, it was hardly surprising that cartoonish characters such as Omar Bakri Muhammad, also known as the Tottenham Ayatollah, and Abu Hamza, the one-eyed, hook-armed hate preacher who had previously been a womanising and hard-drinking, strip-bar bouncer,[1] became the faces of British Islam. Anjem Choudary, who had been known as Andy at university and had a reputation as a notorious party animal who would get stoned with friends,[2] was dismissed as a joke by most Muslims but reinvented himself as a bearded self-styled cleric. 'It was the loudest voice,' says Ivan, 'so I just accepted that Anjem Choudary was the voice of the whole Muslim community.' The media gave Choudary exposure, and he was treated as both comical and threatening – when he appeared on the BBC's *Newsnight* in 2010, Jeremy Paxman's first question to him was: 'How's the campaign to move Britain over to sharia law coming along?' Choudary was a reliable rent-a-quote, happy to offer up reliably ridiculous and outrageous statements. It was almost funny, except it wasn't, because people like Ivan took him seriously and thought he had great legitimacy among Muslims, when in fact he had none at all. Choudary's outlandish prophecies about how Britain was set to become an Islamic nation worried Ivan. 'We thought Muslims would change all the laws,' Ivan says.

'We thought we wouldn't be able to drink alcohol or be able to have a bacon roll.' When I ask him if he was ever tempted to do any research into Islam, he shakes his head. Instead of taking the time to meet Muslims, Ivan began meeting fellow EDL members on marches across the country. 'When you meet them face to face – it's like you've known them your lifetime,' he says. 'There's an instant connection, an instant brotherhood, it was just something that I hadn't felt for a long while. A sense of community – these were people like me.' I was talking to Ivan only a few weeks after my conversations with former Islamist radicals and it was fascinating to note the parallels between what Ivan was telling me and what they had said. Ivan used the phrase 'an instant brotherhood', mirroring Alyas Karmani's description of the radical Islamist group he joined as 'a solid brotherhood'. Both cases were stories of weaponised grievance – someone who was lost and vulnerable being offered the chance of reinvention by a group that claimed to be defending a way of life that was being threatened. For people like Ivan, Islam seemed to be an existential threat to all they held dear, which in his case seemed to be alcohol and bacon rolls. Muslims were transforming the face of the nation, meaning that the native population felt like strangers in their own land.

It isn't only right-wing demagogues like Tommy Robinson who have shared this fear. 'London is no longer the London I used to know,' declared the actor Terence Stamp in a 2015 interview. 'I do think a multicultural society can be a good thing, but when it's at the cost of your own culture and history, then it's gone too far and it would be very sad if London stopped being predominantly English.' The novelist Martin Amis, no stranger to eyebrow-raising comments about Islam, suggested that 'the great thing about America is that it's an immigrant society and a Pakistani in Boston can say "I'm an American" and all he's doing is stating the obvious. But a Pakistani in Preston who says "I'm an Englishman" – that statement would raise eyebrows, for the reason that there's meant to be another layer of being English. There are other qualifications, other than being a citizen of the country, and it has to do with white skin and the habits of what is regarded to be civilised society, and recognisable, bourgeois society.' And then there was Morrissey, who in 1992 draped himself in the Union Flag during a notorious concert at Finsbury Park, prompting accusations of racism. 'Travel to England and you have no idea where you are,' he told the *NME* in 2007. 'Other countries have held on to their basic identity, yet it seems to me that England was thrown away. Whatever England is now, it's not what it was and it's lamentable that we've lost so much. England is a memory now.' The worlds that Morrissey, Stamp and Amis inhabit are very different from Ivan's but there are unmistakable similarities in their sentiments, and it has to do with a fear and sadness about a lost England and a suggestion that *they* want to change the country from the red, white and blue of Great Britain to the green of Islam. 'They [the far right] believe that the traditional values that have always been there around pride, religion, family and culture are degenerating now,' says William Baldét, who works for the Home Office in anti-radicalisation, 'and they claim Islam is the problem. They fear that we are being "Islamised" by stealth.' The ways that Britain would be 'Islamised' by stealth, the means by which Muslims would, in Ivan's words, 'change our way of life, change our country' had to do with, among other things, mosques, halal meat, immigration and sharia law, and I want to discuss each of these in turn.

The big news among Luton's Muslim community when I was ten was the imminent opening of the first large, purpose-built mosque in the town. This was the early eighties and the mosque that my father and I would usually visit was actually a small, terraced house. I remember taking my shoes off in the hallway, walking up the steep stairs and going into one of the bedrooms filled with worshippers attending Eid prayers. If any White people lived on that street, I imagine they would have found the whole thing rather disrupting. It was always a very cramped affair and so the prospect of a brand-new mosque was enormously exciting. It was located in the heart of Bury Park, with a minaret stretching into the Luton sky, and built from clay-coloured stone with a large green dome, on top of which was an Islamic crescent moon. The opening of the mosque felt like a declaration of confidence and intent from the town's Muslim community. That confidence was shaken when racists hung a pig's head on top of the mosque in its opening week. I remember reading about the attack in the local paper. I am not going to pretend to remember my precise thoughts, but I imagine the incident would have made me wonder if my father had a point when he told me that us that Muslims would never be fully accepted.

That was forty years ago, but scepticism and outright hostility towards mosques has far from abated. 'Mosques don't fit in with the scenery around them,' Ivan says. 'They make the area look a bit different, it's that difference, it's change, people don't like change.' Forty per cent and 60 per cent of the mosques, Islamic centres and Muslim organisations in the UK have suffered at least one attack that has or could have been reported to police as a hate crime since 9/11, according to research published in 2010. 'Attacks include petrol bombs thrown into mosques, serious physical assaults on imams and staff,' the *New Statesman* reported, 'bricks thrown through mosque windows, pigs' heads being fixed prominently to mosque entrances and minarets, death threats, other threatening and abusive messages – sometimes verbal, sometimes written – and vandalism.'[3] In September 2001, two days after the 9/11 attacks, a man dumped eight pigs' heads and fake blood outside an Exeter mosque;[4] a former soldier tied a pig's head to the gates of a Cheltenham mosque in 2012[5] and vandals threw two pigs heads and urinated inside a mosque in Manchester in 2017.[6] It was not only criminal-minded thugs who had concerns about mosques. In 2018, Richard Dawkins tweeted the following: 'listening to the lovely bells of Winchester, one of our great mediaeval cathedrals. So much nicer than the aggressive-sounding "Allahu Akhbar." Or is that just my cultural upbringing?'

My cultural upbringing enables me to appreciate the sound of church bells *and* the call to prayer. I can be angered and appalled by attacks on mosques while recognising why some non-Muslims might feel that a mosque – particularly a large one – might be seen as dominating the landscape. It is reasonable for everyone to have a place of worship but sometimes the size and style of mosques can feel like an admission of cultural insecurity and a resistance to accepting that twenty-first-century Britain is not eighth-century Arabia.

The other issue often mentioned by those fearing Britain is being 'Islamised by stealth' is halal meat. Morrissey is a tediously passionate vegetarian* and fierce opponent of halal meat. In an interview published in 2018, the singer described halal meat production as 'evil'. He also claimed that 'halal slaughter requires certification that can only be given by supporters of Isis'[7] – which I found somewhat surprising given that Muslims were eating halal meat hundreds of years before the emergence of Islamic State. Morrissey also, in the same interview, threw his weight behind For Britain, the far-right party set up by former UKIP member Anne Marie Waters, saying he was supporting the party because 'they have the best approach to animal welfare'. At the time this interview was published, I was following Anne Marie Waters on Twitter, a somewhat masochistic activity as her feed consisted of a stream of anti-Muslim claims and diatribes. I was

---

* This should not be interpreted as a criticism of vegetarians, or the music of The Smiths.

nevertheless fascinated by Waters – a woman Nigel Farage considered too extreme to lead UKIP – who called Islam 'evil' and claimed the religion has turned Britain into a 'fearful and censorious society'.[8] Her tweets routinely focused on claims of Islam's alleged appalling treatment of women and animals. I wondered whether she would agree to meet me and contacted her via Twitter, and somewhat to my surprise she replied quickly and agreed to talk to me.

I was surprisingly nervous as I walked with Waters from the train station to her home. I unsuccessfully attempted to make small talk, but sensed a strong chill in her presence. We reached her home and I sat across from her as her dogs lolled around. My secret hope in talking to this woman notorious for her antipathy to Islam was to find out if I could find anything in common with her. Waters' party is called For Britain. 'Britain has an identity,' she says, 'it has a history, it has a heritage, it is not just a bit of land. There is still a majority culture, and it has a specific British identity and (there needs to be) respect for that, joining in with it, obeying the laws and not making demands upon the British that they change their culture to suit you.' I couldn't help noticing that Waters, even as she was singing Britain's praises, had a strong Irish accent. She first came to Britain at the age of twenty and became a British citizen in 2006, around thirty years after me. I asked her to expand on what she felt defined British identity. 'I love the sense of humour, I love the friendliness,' she says, adding 'it's a fantastic country, I'm proud to be part of it.' I felt I could get on board with this and so I followed up by asking what respecting the majority culture might entail. 'It means engaging in everyday life,' she says, 'engaging in pleasant conversation as British people.' This was going better than I had feared. It was only when the subject turned to Islam that my earlier hopes began to fade. Waters was certain that she truly knew Islam and nothing I was going to say was going to sway her. 'There is unique cruelty towards women in Islamic states,' she says, 'the more Islamic they are, the more adherent they are, the more brutal. That's an objective observable truth. I understand that not all problems are caused by Islam. I understand that there are cultural aspects as well but what I'm saying is the religion is a problem. It is. What it teaches is a problem.' I tried to suggest that the problem was about people feeling so certain as to what Islam taught but I could tell she was not really listening. In her mind Muslims, it seemed to me, could only ever be *they* unless they renounced everything that was meaningful to them about their faith. I asked her what it was about Islam that so concerned her, and alongside the rights of women she mentioned, as I expected, halal meat. 'It's the minority imposing on the majority,' she says. 'There may only be a five percent Muslim population but everybody in schools and NHS hospitals is eating it.'

She was referring to repeated reports in newspapers about how unsuspecting non-Muslims were being sold halal meat. 'Britain Goes Halal (. . . but nobody tells public)' yelled the front page of the *Mail on Sunday* on 26 September 2010. 'Britain's biggest supermarket chains are selling halal lamb and chicken without telling unsuspecting shoppers,' the paper revealed, later quoting Mike Judge from the campaign group the Christian Institute, who told them, 'the idea of having Islamic ritual said over meat would be objectionable to some Christians. I would find it objectionable, so it should be labelled as halal.' This narrative – that non-Muslims were being forced to eat halal – was one that certain newspapers, in particular the *Daily Mail* and the *Sun*, would return to repeatedly. In January 2011 the *Daily Mail* ran the headline 'Halal Britain: schools and institutions serving up ritually slaughtered meat', with an accompanying article reporting that 'all beef, chicken and lamb sold to fans at Wembley Stadium has been secretly prepared in accordance with strict Islamic law. And hundreds of pubs and restaurants in Britain, as well as top racecourses, schools and hospitals, now only serve chicken that has been ritually slaughtered according to Sharia Law.' On 8 May 2014, the *Daily Mail*'s front-page splash was 'Millions are eating halal food without knowing it'. The story followed a *Sun* front page the previous week that had led with 'Halal secrets of Pizza Express'. 'Britons are unknowingly eating Halal meat that is being sold without a label', was a *Daily Mail* headline in February 2018. The gist of these stories was that millions of ordinary – meaning White – folks were being duped into eating halal meat because supermarkets and restaurants were selling halal-certified meat to unwitting customers.

A kind explanation for this obsession over halal meat is that those commissioning this coverage are devoted animal lovers who find the idea of ritual slaughter so terrible that they want to warn readers. I'm not completely convinced by that. I am more persuaded by the argument that shoppers have the right to know if the meat they are buying is halal, and I can see why some people might feel put out if they felt they had no choice whether or not to eat halal meat. The danger with such relentless coverage, and with reporting that aims to amplify outrage rather than reassure readers that halal meat tastes the same as any other meat and eating it won't turn them into Muslims, is that it feeds into the narrative that 'they' are taking over. 'They' are riding rough-shod over all that 'we' hold dear and trying to change 'us'. 'Muslims should not be imposing halal on anyone,' Waters says, 'it's causing antagonism and separateness. People on the non-Muslim side are drawing away and becoming hostile with these constant demands. A lot has to change from the Muslim side in order to integrate. We're always told it's us that have to change.' If you fear that your country is being stolen, the attraction of a party or group who are willing to defend it – whether it's the EDL, Britain First or UKIP – is obvious and a political slogan that promises to 'take back control' is likely to appeal.

On 23 January 2013, Prime Minister David Cameron pledged an in/out referendum on the question of EU membership. Just as the controversy around halal meat was outwardly about animal rights but actually about anxiety around Islam, the referendum was officially about deciding Britain's relationship with Europe and perhaps for some that is truly what they were voting on, but my own suspicion, however, is that talking about the threat from 'Europe' was an acceptable code for some to express anxieties about immigration, multiculturalism and, ultimately, Muslims. This was an anxiety that Fazila Aswat encountered on the streets of Batley during the referendum campaign. Aswat was the daughter of Ghulam Maniyar, whom we first met in Chapter 3. By the time of the referendum campaign in the spring of 2016, she was knocking on doors and talking to people. 'The whole thing was about leaving Europe but actually it became about something else,' she says. 'When we were doing door to door and street talk, you didn't hear people talking about EU law or policies. I don't think people even understood that. I think a lot of people were more bothered about taking our country back, taking the control, protecting our borders, not letting foreigners in and a lot of it was around the immigration position. It became less about Europe and more about a race issue.' Fazila was working for the Labour Party as the office manager for the local MP Jo Cox. 'Her background was very similar to mine,' Fazila says. 'She worked for Oxfam and several other charities and so there was that mutual understanding and bond there and our thought processes were the same.' Fazila often accompanied Jo on constituency business, and so she was with her in a car heading to a surgery meeting at Batley library on the afternoon of 16 June 2016.

It was 12.51 p.m. when the car arrived at the library and Fazila, Jo and a case worker called Sandra Major got out.

As they climbed from the car, the women noticed a man approaching. He had a gun. He raised his arm and shot Cox in the head and then pulled a knife from his bag and started stabbing her while she was lying on the ground. Fazila tried to fight him off with her handbag. 'Get away from her,' she shouted at him, 'she's got two little children.' When Bernard Carter-Kenny, a seventy-seven-year-old passer-by, tried to intervene, the man stabbed him too. He then stepped back a little, as if he had finished. But when he heard Cox warn her two assistants to flee – shouting "Get away, let him hurt me, don't let him hurt you!" – he stood over her and shot her twice more, and stabbed her again. He raised his sawn-off rifle and shot her. Then he pulled her to the ground, dragged her between two parked cars, and stabbed her repeatedly with his dagger. 'Jo, you need to run,' Fazila told her, but Cox told her that she could not run as she was in too much pain. She said: 'I can't run, I'm hurt.' Sandra Major would later recall Cox shouting, 'Get away, get away, you two – let him hurt me – don't let him hurt you'. Jo Cox died in Fazila's arms. Her last words were, 'I can't make it, I'm in too much pain.' She had been shot three times and suffered fifteen stab wounds. She was forty-one and had two children, then aged five and three. She had been elected in 2015, and supported the campaign to remain in the EU. After he murdered Jo Cox, Thomas Mair, who would later be arrested and convicted for the killing, was reported to have said: 'Britain first, Britain will always be first. This is for Britain.'

Who and what radicalised Thomas Mair? Reading through the extended profiles published after his conviction, the portrait that emerges is of a loner, obsessed with neo-Nazi iconography, who believed that White people were facing an existential threat. 'The White race,' Mair wrote, was about to be plunged into 'a very bloody struggle.' His greatest obsession was those White people he considered 'the collaborators'. Jo Cox was someone who been vocal in speaking out on global issues, such as the plight of Syrian refugees, and she was a strong supporter of the Remain campaign. Those fighting to leave the EU had, during the course of the campaign, made a series of increasingly provocative claims about the possible impact of a remain vote: 'swarms' of immigrants would enter the country, it could lead to mass sexual attacks and, only hours before the killing, Nigel Farage unveiled UKIP's 'breaking point' anti-immigration poster. 'Jo Cox had voted in favour of increased immigration, so Mair decided that he would murder her,' says William Baldét, 'because she was the one that was at fault, it was very similar to the Anders Breivik view, which is don't kill the immigrants, kill the politicians who are voting for the situation.'

I wanted to ask Fazila about her thoughts but I was really nervous about broaching the subject. She had not talked in detail to anyone and knowing that she had witnessed a brutal murder, with her close friend dying in her arms, I did not want to ask her anything that might trigger traumatic memories. So, when we talked I did not ask her, as I had originally planned, to recall the day Jo died. I frankly didn't have the heart to ask her to relive such an awful experience so instead I asked her what she thought had radicalised Thomas Mair. 'I don't think anyone can be radicalised instantly,' she told me. 'He must have harboured some hate and anger from the beginning anyway, but I think what the whole Brexit campaign did was it magnified the whole thing massively. It became almost like a one-agenda item campaign about immigration, protecting our borders, taking our country back. The narrative that the Brexit campaign chose was very toxic. It was an extreme action [the murder of Jo Cox] but it was the tip of the iceberg and below that you could see the mountain that had built up of bigotry and hate over the past year. That guy [Thomas Mair] probably woke up in the morning and everything he read in the newspapers and saw on the TV was hate filled and anti-immigrant. The whole campaign was very toxic and where certain views had once been contained Brexit lifted the lid on those views and it led to a tsunami of hate.' The referendum campaign was briefly suspended in the immediate aftermath of Jo Cox's murder but, come the actual vote, the worldview espoused by Cox, who famously used her maiden speech in Parliament to argue that 'we have far more in common with each other than things that divide us', lost and Britain voted to leave the European Union.

The trauma of witnessing her friend's murder and the subsequent win for Leave deeply affected Fazila. She remembers attending a meeting almost three years later, attended by a man who didn't realised she worked with Jo Cox. 'He made a comment, "It's people like that Jo Cox that I don't like, because they're the worst kind. They're the traitors,"' she recalls. 'It was so stark, and I think what he said was almost a reflection of perhaps what that man [Thomas Mair] felt on the day – perhaps what he said embodies what some people do think and perhaps that's what Mair thought and that's why he targeted Jo. They are worse than the immigrants because they're the real traitors to their own kind.' Fazila was diagnosed with Post Traumatic Stress Disorder (PTSD) and felt overcome with a sense of despair and despondency. 'I could only see the negative stuff,' she says, 'I couldn't see the positive. I remember reading somewhere that there were 60,000 tweets celebrating her death and things like that really stuck with me.'

I stayed up to watch the BBC coverage of the referendum results and sometime in the middle of the night Bridget wandered into the living room. She had not been able to sleep, and asked me how it was looking. When I told her that it was looking very likely that Leave would win, she burst into tears. It was not that we were huge fans of the European Union but rather that the vote suggested that the battles we thought had been won around multiculturalism and belonging were not as settled as we had assumed. I was reminded of the feeling I used to have as a boy watching the likes of Norman Tebbit on television: the fear that no matter what people like me did, they would never accept us.

Shabnam, Selina's daughter, whom we met in earlier chapters, was at home in Keighley. 'I had a pretty good

idea that people in my neighbourhood would vote leave,'
she says, 'though we never talked about it. You could see
lots of Union flags and St George's flags hung out.' When
she woke up the day after the referendum and checked her
phone, she saw a friend had texted her with the words: 'Fear
won today.' 'I couldn't believe the majority of the country
had voted out,' she recalls, 'it felt like a punch in the gut and
like the world had gone mad. I was sad that the xenophobic
rhetoric had played such a huge part with the majority of
voters, as it obviously had. It felt like Britain was showing her
true face, and that hurt. I felt like life would get that much
harder for people like us, for visible minorities from now
on.' Ruby, who had grown up in Crewe but run away from
home, learnt of the results from her home in Scotland. 'It
was a chance for all the racists to vent and feel their bigotry
was at last legitimised,' she says. 'I had a feeling of rising
shock and incredulity that this could happen and my feeling
concerning its impact on Muslims was that of impending
doom. *Daily-Mail*-reader types and the ageing population
sold their children and grandchildren down the river in
terms of free access to jobs and education in Europe. Just
to recapture the feeling of "Englishness."'

It had taken years for me to feel that I had the right to call
myself British without embarrassment and I still dared not
call myself English. I now had a White wife and two young
children born in this country. I had deep roots in Britain
and in my life choices I was thoroughly integrated, but in
the end perhaps none of it really mattered, perhaps there

was nothing people like me could do to be truly accepted by some of my fellow countrymen and women who voted Leave. In days after the vote, Channel 4 News broadcast a report from Barnsley, seventeen miles south of Batley, in which they asked a voter why he had voted to leave the EU. He was a middle-aged White man with greying hair and glasses, and was refreshingly honest in his analysis. 'It's all about immigration,' he told the reporter, 'it's not about trade or Europe or anything like that, it's all about immigration. It's to stop the Muslims from coming into this country. Simple as that.' How to process that there are people in this country who feel that way? My approach was to remind myself that I did not live in Barnsley.* It made me feel grateful to live in London – the borough where I lived had overwhelmingly voted Remain – but it also made Bridget and me feel like our options for where we could live were limited. I remember seeing a map of Britain showing the parts that had voted Leave and Remain – vast swathes of the nation felt out of bounds because the likes of me would not, I feared, be made welcome. 'I have felt like that, where I started to ask if this country is for me and my children,' recalls Sajda, the 7/7 survivor we met in Chapter 4. 'I have sat here and thought, "Is this a place where I could actually bring up my two daughters safely?" But then where would we go? And then I just get back to Britain again, because

---

* It also made me feel somewhat grateful I did not live in Luton, which voted 54.6 per cent to leave the EU.

when you think further, there's no real place I can call home and nowhere else I could go.'

In Blackburn, Aziz Hakim was watching the result and it reminded him that he had noticed 'the trend of older Muslim voters who voted leave because it seemed to them that there was too many foreigners with easy access to the UK, they felt the influx has had an impact on the quality of healthcare that they are currently receiving which would deteriorate further if we were still in the EU.' In the aftermath of the Brexit vote, Sajda noticed a rise in Islamophobic attacks. 'You read about this in the media, but I see it in my work,' she says. 'We hear how women are saying their hijabs are being pulled off; they've been spat at. We went into our centre one morning and we had EDL signs all over our centre and the windows.'

One year to the week after the murder of Jo Cox, my family attended a local street party as part of the More in Common initiative established following Cox's murder as a way of honouring her legacy and giving neighbours the chance to get to know each other. It was a hot Sunday afternoon, and the road was closed to allow children to play while adults ate, drank and chatted. There was live music, a baking competition and a hotly contested round of musical chairs. Londoners are often accused, by those who don't live in the city, of being unfriendly, but that has not been my experience and, sitting with friends and neighbours chatting while our children played, it felt like all was well in the world. It was only later that night, after we had put Laila and Ezra to bed, that I first heard the whirring sound of helicopters. By the time I awoke on Monday, Finsbury Park, a ten-minute walk from where I live, had mutated from a neighbourhood to a hashtag. My Twitter timeline revealed that there had been an attack on a mosque – a man had driven a van into worshippers leaving Ramadan prayers and apparently been overheard saying he wanted to kill all Muslims. The man's name was Darren Osborne, an unemployed father-of-four from Cardiff with a history of violence, who had served two years in prison for assault and suffered from depression, alcohol and drug abuse. Osborne had left his home the previous day in a rented van and driven to London looking for Muslims. When he reached Finsbury Park, he asked for directions to the mosque before speeding his van into a crowd of worshippers. One man would later die from a heart attack. Osborne was arrested and charged with terrorism-related murder and attempted murder. He was found guilty and sentenced to life imprisonment.

So who or what radicalised Darren Osborne? According to those who knew him well, Osborne did not have a long history of racism or antipathy towards Muslims. The turning point, the trigger, was when Osborne saw the BBC drama *Three Girls*, which told the story of the Rochdale child sexual exploitation scandal. 'Darren Osborne was radicalised by *Three Girls*,' says William Baldét. 'He was angry at what he saw, and he felt that Muslims had been responsible for grooming and the state, the police and local government had not stood up for these girls – that was where his anger came from.' Osborne became obsessed with Muslims and started seeking out online material, including posts from Tommy Robinson and Britain First. 'We know the algorithms on Facebook and YouTube will be shaped by what you've already viewed,' says Baldét, 'so if you've viewed something that is anti-Islam, the next set of news feeds that the algorithm will think you need to see will be anti-Islam. They're not designed to give you an opposing view, they're designed to keep feeding you what you've already consumed.' Reading about Osborne and the way he was radicalised, I could hear echoes of Ivan's story. Ivan never engaged in or supported violence towards Muslims but both Ivan and Osborne were radicalised by a specific event – the Luton march, the television drama – which led them to have a negative view of Muslims, which was then amplified and reinforced by what they consumed online. There was another parallel. Ivan was vulnerable around the time he joined the EDL, having recently become an unemployed single father. Osborne was also out of work and his wife had recently thrown him out of the house. 'That was the underlying issue that triggered all of this,' argues Baldét. 'That's when the process started for him. He had seen the drama, his rage was increasing, there was then this defining kind of negative life moment with his wife kicking him out and he just spiralled out of control over the next three weeks, which ended with him doing what he did in London.'

The Finsbury Park attack unsettled me in a way that the murder of Jo Cox, the Manchester Arena bombing and even the London and Westminster Bridge attacks had not. The sheer proximity meant that it quite literally hit home. I could not so easily dismiss it as something that was happening elsewhere and it meant that my wife and I had to consider such practicalities as how to keep the news of the attack from my daughter. On Monday morning, not long after learning of what had taken place, I dropped Laila off at kindergarten and took the bus to Finsbury Park. Costa Coffee was like an international newsroom, with young women editing video footage on laptops while television reporters scribbled notes and made calls. I looked at the massed ranks of television cameras and reporters. I saw local White residents spontaneously approaching Muslims to offer sympathy, hugs and flowers. I heard more than one White person apologise to a Muslim for what happened at the mosque. They had nothing to apologise for, of course, but their actions reminded me, as did the vigil in Finsbury Park on Monday evening, that one consequence of tragedy is to highlight how much decency and kindness human beings are capable of. I had to take Laila to her violin lesson that afternoon and usually it would mean passing where all the reporters were amassed, but we took a different route. I knew that one day she would learn of the hatred that men like Darren Osborne, Thomas Mair, Manchester Arena bomber Salman Abedi and their kind harbour, but my daughter was still little, and I wanted her to believe that the world was mostly populated by people who are kind and good-hearted. Hell, *I* wanted to believe that. The trouble was that it was getting ever harder to remain optimistic about the direction that the country was heading. And it wasn't only this country.

Five months after Britain voted to leave the EU, the United States elected Donald Trump as president. Our son Ezra was born twelve days after Trump's victory. Ten days after his inauguration, on 27 January 2017, President Trump signed an Executive Order that banned foreign nationals from seven predominantly Muslim countries from visiting the country for ninety days, suspended entry to all Syrian refugees indefinitely and prohibited any other refugees from coming into the country for 120 days. It was a policy that Anne Marie Waters believed Britain should also adopt. 'It's a very harsh position,' she says, 'it's one that 47 per cent of this country holds according to one poll, which is an enormous thing. If half the country feels like that, it's something that should be discussed.' The 'Muslim ban' provoked protests across the United States – in New York, Los Angeles, Boston, San Diego, Chicago, Dallas and Kansas City. In the words of someone who tweeted me after the Finsbury Park attack, 'crisis brings out the good in all of us. The few mindless individuals are lost in a sea of good, kind-hearted people.' It was possible to dismiss one or two individuals' actions and to comfort myself that they were not representative, but it was hard not to be unnerved by the fact that anonymous letters were being sent to Muslims in six communities in England about an upcoming 'Punish A Muslim Day', where points would be awarded for varying acts of violence, from pulling off a woman's headscarf to bombing a mosque. Tommy Robinson, founder of the EDL, was being described in the media not as a Muslim-hating demagogue but as a journalist and activist. He was hired by UKIP leader Gerard Batten in late 2018 as an advisor, saying that people respected Mr Robinson's 'stand on things'. When Robinson was jailed for breaking contempt of court laws, thousands of protestors descended on Trafalgar Square with placards bearing his face covered in a mask and #FreeTommy. The sight of this former football hooligan being treated as a lionised political prisoner and champion of free speech was bewildering and depressing, as was the daily coverage from Westminster, where Brexit-supporting Tommy Robinson fans would abuse and antagonise Remain-leaning MPs and accuse them of betrayal or worse.

I was starting to no longer recognise the country I called home. The tone of political debate was harsh and ugly, and amplified by social media. I had grown up with fascists marching on the streets, but this felt different because back then the fascists always felt like they were on the fringe – frightening but far from power and influence. Now they felt more numerous and inching towards respectability. I remember watching coverage of the Free Tommy marches and hearing the chanting move from 'We Love You Tommy' into 'En-ger-land, En-ger-land, En-ger-land', and speakers refer to him as a civil rights hero and a modern Braveheart. 'Jesus died for our sins,' wrote one commenter below a YouTube video of the protests, 'don't let them crucify Tommy for our freedoms.' The 'En-ger-land' that these men and women were singing for – and I use that word in the loosest possible sense – was not one, I suspected, that openly welcomed someone who looked like me or my children, and they might well consider my wife to be a traitor to her people.

It was during times like these, when the news was so relentlessly grim, that I felt blessed to have young children. Immediately after the Finsbury Park attack, I did what I had done after Manchester Arena, after London Bridge, after Paris, after the elections of Donald Trump and Boris Johnson: I immersed myself in the world of my children. I played with them, read them stories and hugged them often, and the truth was that I was doing it as much for myself as I was for them. One of the less pleasing consequences of having children with dual heritage is that they will one day learn that there are people who are White like their mother who viscerally loathe brown-skinned Muslims who look like their father, and there are also people who look like their father who consider non-Muslims like their mother to be infidels. Moreover, both groups might well consider both their parents to be traitors to their race, religion and culture. Given all this, was it any wonder I preferred to lose myself in *The Smartest Giant in Town, Paper Dolls* and *The Tiger Who Came to Tea?* I needed, for my children's sake, to not fall into abject despair. I reminded myself that one month before the EU referendum, London, the city I lived in, had elected Sadiq Khan – a British Muslim of Pakistani heritage – as mayor with 57 per cent of the vote. Eight months before voting for Brexit, Nadiya Hussain, a headscarf-wearing Muslim born in Luton, won *The Great British Bake Off.* One month before the Finsbury Park attack, Saliha Mahmood-Ahmed, a British-Pakistani junior doctor, won the BBC's *Masterchef*. This was also England. My hope was boosted when I read about the imam of the Finsbury Park mosque, who chose to defend Darren Osborne from the retribution of worshippers and insisted that the law should deal with him. This was also Islam, and this was also England.

It was unsettling to have terror arrive so close to home, but even here there was one thing to be grateful for: at least this attack was not perpetrated by Muslims – at least this one could not be considered 'our' fault. When I talked to Fazila about how she had tried to move on from utter despair following the murder of Jo Cox, she told me that she was grateful that the killer had not been Muslim. 'If [the killer] was Muslim it would have been fifty times worse,' she says. 'I dread to think of the backlash that would have happened.' Fazila, like me, found a medicinal benefit in spending time with her young daughter. 'She was the one who anchored me back down to the here and now,' she says. 'Playing cricket in the garden anchored me back down to the present in looking for the simple pleasures in life.' Fazila told me that it took time, and it is still a journey she is on, but she made a conscious decision not to be negative. 'Once you get into that mindset that it's beyond repair, you're allowing those people to win,' she says. 'I remember talking to a friend of mine who worked in social services as a psychologist, and she said always look for the good. And I keep telling myself that. Look for the good! Look for the good!'

The good, for me, resides in the surprising and the hopeful and in the times when we are reminded of the ways that, regardless of where we originally came from or which faith we follow, we are all British. The former Conservative party chairwoman Sayeeda Warsi raised this issue in 2015 in a speech arguing for a 'quintessentially British' form of Islam. 'Islam is different whenever and wherever it is found. If Islam always takes its cultural references from where it finds itself, British Islam must take cultural reference points from where it grows.' Part of this, she said, meant building quintessentially British mosques. She argued that minarets, towers built alongside mosques from which the call to prayer is broadcast, were not culturally necessary in modern Britain. 'There is no need for a minaret. There is no need for a mosque to look like it doesn't fit into its environment. It doesn't need to be like that. I would love for there to be English-designed mosques.'[9]

I heard this point repeated by two brothers in Aberdeen. One told me he thought a mosque looks like 'an alien building that doesn't really belong, it just doesn't fit in', while his brother agreed that 'a vast majority of mosques can be a bit loud and possibly offensive'. These men were not members of the EDL or any far-right group, but British-Pakistanis – a reminder that these debates are not quite as polarised between Muslims and non-Muslims as they might first appear. Brothers Sarfraz and Iftikar Ali grew up in 1970s Huddersfield before moving to Aberdeen in 1982 when their father bought a local clothing business. The mosque was a converted bank and over the decades the community bought the adjoining properties, but it was still too small to cater for the community, and many were forced to worship outside. So the search began for a new mosque.

In July 2011, Sarfraz and Iftikar, by now prominent members of the Muslim community, started to plan the construction of a new mosque. The brothers were determined that it would not follow the usual dome and minaret template. 'We were very particular about a couple of things,' says Iftikar. 'It was really important that it was sympathetic and non-offensive to our neighbours. In Islam, our neighbours are very important, so it had to fit into the landscape. Its identity also had to be very Scottish, and it had to appeal to women because we thought they were often overlooked when it came to mosque designs.' The brothers hired Shahed Saleem, a London-based architect, to translate their vision into reality and his plans were unveiled in 2013. The mosque that he designed doesn't look like any mosque I had ever seen. There is no dome or minaret and the mosque resembles a grey rectangle block built from granite to reflect local tradition. It is adorned with ceramic stars made by a female Muslim designer. In a statement released when the plans were unveiled, Saleem said his design was 'based on our vision of Britain's Muslim communities as progressive and creative members of society and we want the building to reflect this spirit. The new Aberdeen mosque speaks of being fully Scottish, fully British and fully Muslim all at the same time. In this way we hope the new mosque represents and reflects the spirit of Aberdeen's diverse communities and serves as a symbol around which understanding and interaction can happen.'

If we want to build a bridge across the divide and challenge the fears stoked by the far right, this bridge will be built from greater understanding and interaction. In May 2013, the elders of York Mosque learnt that the EDL were planning a protest outside the mosque. Muhammad el-Gomati, a lecturer at York University, decided to take the initiative. 'We realised that we did not fully understand the EDL stance in York and, from what we could make out, they did not fully understand us either,' he wrote in an opinion piece for the *Guardian*. 'It was up to us to provide an atmosphere that was representative of our culture. When I say "our culture", I mean all of us, including the EDL and the members of the mosque. We all think of sitting down with a cup of tea as something quintessentially English, so we thought that offering a cup of good old-fashioned Yorkshire tea and hospitality would be a start.'[10] He decided to organise an open day to coincide with the EDL protest. Around 200 local residents accepted an open invitation to the mosque to enjoy tea, biscuits and a chat with their Muslim neighbours. A small gathering of EDL members also arrived to protest outside the mosque. They were eventually approached, and a heated argument ensued. After a short while, a tray of tea and biscuits was sent over and EDL members accepted the invitation to join the others for a drink. With cups of tea lowering tensions, a few members of the protesting group were invited into the mosque and shown around. 'When we listened, we realised the EDL may have thought that we supported extremist behaviour and the Taliban,' el-Gomati wrote. 'We pointed out that we condemned both in the strongest terms. Assumptions are dangerous, untested assumptions can be lethal. They were surprised, and they understood. The day ended in a game of football.'

Interaction and understanding. I started this chapter with Ivan's story of joining the EDL. In 2012 he learnt that the Muslim community in Ipswich had bought a church and the rumour was that it was going to be turned into a so-called mega mosque. Ivan decided he would pay the leader of the mosque a visit. 'I went up to him and said: "I'm Ivan Humble from the EDL. I'm the regional organiser for around here. You've just bought a church and I've heard it's going to be a super mosque – can you prove me wrong?"' The man he contacted was Manwar Ali. 'He told me there's a council meeting that I've got to go to about this community centre,' Ivan says, 'he said, "You can come along – some of your lads can come along." So eight of us went to this meeting. Manwar was telling me the truth. The church was going to be a community centre for everybody so because he told me the truth I wanted to learn more, so we just started talking.' Ivan and Manwar begun a conversation that would last two years, the pair meeting every fortnight, with Ivan sharing his concerns and Manwar explaining they were misconceptions. He associated sharia law, for example, with barbaric punishments involving dismemberment. I could hardly blame him – for years that was what I believed sharia law meant.

I assumed 'sharia' was a synonym for 'barbaric' or 'medieval', when it actually refers to the system of laws that determine how Muslims lead every aspect of their lives. The word 'sharia' has been weaponised by the far right, who claim that Muslims want to impose sharia law in their adopted homelands. A 2019 poll revealed that two-thirds of Conservative Party members believed parts of Britain operated under sharia law.[11] 'For most Muslims [sharia law] is about births, marriages and deaths,' writes Sayeeda Warsi. 'Britain has been accommodating Sharia law and religious practice for Jews, Hindus, Sikhs and others for decades.'[12] I am no Muslim scholar and I had not believed I had any personal involvement in sharia law, but then I remembered that I had had a nikah – Islamic wedding – so perhaps that counted as adhering to sharia law. When my children were born, I found someone with more Muslim knowledge than me to whisper some words from the Qur'an in their ears. I was told this was a ritual that Muslims did, so perhaps that too was following sharia law. It is hard to scare folks with the benign reality of these examples, which is perhaps why they are not better known. 'I'm not bothered by it any more,' Ivan says. 'I now realise sharia law is a way of life – it tells you how to cut your fingernails and everything. Cutting off your hands (the punishment for stealing) is after about twelve other chances – it's the final, final act they can do. Realising that that's not going to come here and be affecting me was a big thing.'

The more Ivan talked and listened, the more he began to question his views on Islam. 'When I was talking about the religion [in the EDL], I was cherry-picking verses of the Qur'an,' he says. 'It is like the same as extremists do on the other side, they cherry-pick the Qur'an.' He recalls attending a demonstration in Slough towards the end of 2013. 'I remember walking on it and thinking this ain't for me no more. Some of the chants people were saying – I thought I can't say this shit no more because I now had Muslim friends and it felt disrespectful to say some of them things now.' So, Ivan made a decision: he left the EDL.

The reason he left, in short, seems to be that he actually met some real-life Muslims who were able to correct him on some of his prejudices. I am around the same age as Ivan and it made me wonder if we had lived on the same street as children, if we had played sport on the street and he had gotten to know me and my family as neighbours who also happened to be Muslims, how likely did he think it was that he would have joined the EDL? 'I can't say I wouldn't have done,' he says, 'but it would've helped me a lot. I wouldn't have stereotyped all Muslims if I had that better understanding.' It is hard to have that better understanding without interaction and a willingness to engage. Cultural nationalists such as the EDL believe that the role of the family and religion are being eroded. 'I spent an awful lot of time sort of in and around Muslim communities and in their homes,' says William Baldét, 'and some of the sort of family values and traditions that I was seeing in those houses are things that White supremacists should probably celebrating, not attacking.' Ivan now works to try and combat radicalisation. 'A lot of the people on the far right have had something happen to them like maybe having a fight with an Asian group or something and that has pushed them that way,' he says. 'The hardest bit is listening properly – listening with an open mind and somehow imagining yourself in that person's shoes when they're telling you their story because if not you'll never understand their struggles or where they're coming from. I'm hopeful because I'm passionate about change, I refuse to give up on anybody and I know there are some people that won't be changed and won't be helped but we're not going to find out until we have conversations with each other.' Darren Osborne was reported to have said 'I've done my bit' after he was arrested for the Finsbury Park attack. The only way to ensure that Osborne, Mair and those who side with them do not win is if the rest of us do *our* bit and remember that hope and change are possible. Ivan has two tattoos, one on his right bicep and another on his left forearm. One reads 'EDL East Anglian Division'. The other repeats Jo Cox's celebrated speech in Parliament: 'we have far more in common than that which divides us'.*

---

* A few days after we met, Anne Marie Waters was permanently suspended from Twitter for hate speech.

NINE

THEY . . . DON'T BELIEVE IN OUR VALUES

*'48% of the British public believe there is a funda-
mental clash between Islam and the values of British
society.'*

Savanta ComRes poll of 2,000 adults,
August 2019

'Islam is reviving British values'

Rowan Williams,
former Archbishop of Canterbury, 2014

On 9 May 2007, Abdullah Rehman was standing on the
concourse of Birmingham New Street Station. Abdullah
was a thirty-seven-year-old community activist based in the
Balsall Heath neighbourhood and was waiting for a man
called David, who was travelling to Birmingham to learn
more about the lives of ordinary Muslims. 'It was kind of the
norm for us to have people staying,' Abdullah says. 'It was

part of my work working with churches and local groups. They would say, "We have someone who needs to stay over." I drew the short straw, so it was agreed that David would stay at my house with my family.' David slept in one of the spare rooms and in the morning he had breakfast with Abdullah, Abdullah's wife and their three young children. 'It was the morning that Tony Blair was resigning as Prime Minister,' recalls Abdullah, 'so we watched that together in my living room and it was kind of surreal, but he was such a nice guy. He made me feel so comfortable and so relaxed.' Abdullah created an itinerary for the next few days so that David could meet people at the grassroots in the Muslim community and they could tell him the issues that mattered most to them.

David appeared very interested, but Abdullah suspected he had not spent much time among Muslims. 'He was really interested but it did seem he hadn't had much past experience with Muslims,' Abdullah says. 'All of the questions were like, "What is your life like? When do you pray? Who do you pray to?" He was really, really interested.' David was forty and had been raised in a White, English, middle-class family, and was particularly impressed by the strong sense of family he witnessed. 'He said, "We don't see our relatives for years and years and here you have relatives who all support each other." He was very impressed . . . with the hospitality that he received, not just from my family but from all the residents that he met. He said if we were to learn anything from the Muslim community it would be hospitality. You know how we love to feed people as well.' I asked Abdullah if he toned down the spices for his guest. 'Actually, we didn't, and he thoroughly enjoyed himself,' he says, adding, 'he did have a sweat on, but we did everything traditionally – the curry was maximum spices. He loved it – he loved the cauliflower curry.' Having spent a couple of days immersed in the Muslim community, David thanked Abdullah and his family and promised he would keep in touch. David later wrote about his time with Abdullah's family and he reflected on what it had taught him. 'Asian families and communities are incredibly strong and cohesive,' he wrote, 'and have a sense of civic responsibility which puts the rest of us to shame. Not for the first time, I found myself thinking it is mainstream Britain which needs to integrate more with the British Asian values of life, not the other way round . . . If we want to remind ourselves of British values – hospitality, tolerance and generosity to name just three – there are plenty of British Muslim values ready to show us what those things really mean.'[1]

When Abdullah read David's comments, he was deeply moved. As a Muslim he had become accustomed to criticism that Muslim values were somehow in conflict with British ones. In a speech the previous year, Tony Blair had talked about how immigrants had a 'duty to integrate, to stress what we hold in common'. In the speech he claimed that 'for the first time in a generation there is an unease, an anxiety, even at points a resentment, that our very openness, our willingness to welcome difference, our pride in being home to many cultures, is being used against us – abused, indeed, in order to harm us. Our tolerance is part of what

makes Britain Britain. So conform to it; or don't come here.'[2]
That sentiment was repeated in a speech made by the Prime
Minister in 2011, where he talked about how there were
British Muslims who 'may reject violence, but who accept
various parts of the extremist world-view including real hostility towards western democracy and liberal values ... We
have even tolerated these segregated communities behaving
in ways that run counter to our values ... We need a lot
less of the passive tolerance of recent years and much more
active, muscular liberalism.'[3] When Abdullah read these
words, he was bitterly disappointed – yet again a politician
was singling out Muslims and accusing them of having
values that conflicted with British values. There was another
more personal reason for Abdullah's disappointment: the
British Prime Minister who had made this speech was the
same man who visited Abdullah and his family four years
earlier, David Cameron.

A 2018 study revealed that seven in ten Muslims rejected
the idea that Western liberal society is incompatible with
Islam. This contrasts with what non-Muslims believe: a
2016 study suggested that over half the public disagreed
with the statement 'Islam is compatible with British values'
and another survey that same year found that 56 per cent
of the public agreed that Islam poses a serious threat to
Western civilisation. A 2019 survey found that almost half
of all British adults believed 'there is a fundamental clash
between Islam and values of British society'.[4] Meanwhile, 83
per cent of Black and Asian Muslims agree it is important

that people of their ethnic group should maintain their own values, beliefs and traditions. So, what are British values? What are Muslim values? And why do so many believe the two are in conflict?

Prime Ministers love talking about British values and when defining them they perhaps inevitably settle on a suspiciously flattering list. In 1993, John Major referred in rather misty-eyed prose to a nation of 'long shadows on county grounds, warm beer, invincible green suburbs, dog lovers and pools fillers and – as George Orwell said – "old maids bicycling to holy communion through the morning mist".'[5] In 2000, Tony Blair suggested British values included 'fair play, creativity, tolerance and an outward-looking approach to the world.'[6] Gordon Brown referred to 'British tolerance, the British belief in liberty and the British sense of fair play.'[7] David Cameron listed 'a belief in freedom, tolerance of others, accepting personal and social responsibility, respecting and upholding the rule of law', while his successor, Theresa May, talked about 'fundamental British values, including democracy, the rule of law, individual liberty and the mutual respect and tolerance of different faiths and beliefs.'[8] The preoccupation with defining British values often stems from a fear that these nebulous values are threatened – for John Major, the potential threat was membership of the European Community, and for prime ministers since the threat was multiculturalism, and more specifically Muslims.

I have always found the definitions offered by politicians, such as those suggested by various prime ministers, to be rather unconvincing and self-serving. They arguably tell us less about who the British are and more about how they would like to be – they are not so much values as aspirations. In *The British Dream*, David Goodhart suggests that the essence of British values can be summarised as 'pragmatism, empiricism, moderation and readiness to compromise; indirectness, obliqueness, a desire to not cause offence; sense of humour and ability to make and take a joke; love of sport and competition and gambling; skeptical verging on cynical about political power but law abiding and relatively uncorrupt; dislike of swagger and pomposity and support for the underdog; independent, individualistic and suspicious of bureaucracy but also ready to help those in need.'[9] It is an impressive list, but Goodhart is honest enough to admit that 'many of these are commonplace in other countries too and there are lots of British citizens, and even large groups of them, who do not exemplify these attitudes or preferences very strongly'. The British government has defined British values as 'democracy, the rule of law, individual liberty, tolerance and mutual respect, aversion to conflict and preservation of human rights'. These are all laudable aspirations, but there are plenty of examples in history and the recent past where Britain has vividly flouted these supposed values – a recent one being when Boris Johnson's government was accused of flouting international law, albeit in a 'very specific and limited' way, when it sought to override parts of the Brexit withdrawal agreement.[10]

There is a version of this chapter where I take each of the values considered British and examine how they align with Islam as it has been practised throughout history. When the Prophet Muhammad died, he deliberately did not appoint a successor and left it to the Muslim people to select who should replace him and that, it has been argued, set a precedent for the democratic process. The Qur'an states that 'let there be no compulsion in religion', suggesting that tolerance and freedom are not incompatible with the faith, and Muslims are ordained by Allah to protect the rights of all human beings regardless of their religion. There are also numerous references in the Qur'an that speak to the peaceful nature of Islam, and the religion does not allow Muslims to fight except in self-defence. It is possible to engage in a textual study of the Qur'an and Islamic history and find examples where so-called Muslim values tally with so-called British ones, thus confirming what David Cameron wrote after visiting Abdullah, or what the former Archbishop of Canterbury Rowan Williams suggested when he claimed that 'Islam is reviving British values.'[11] I could write that chapter, but I won't. I want instead to ask: *why* do so many people think that Muslim values are in conflict with British values? The answer to that, I suspect, is not to do with the abstract concepts of pragmatism and empiricism, or concepts such as the rule of law and fair play, but rather a generalised suspicion that *they* are not quite like us – put bluntly – *they* want to follow their own rules in *our* country: they don't want to do what is needed to fit in, and the fear that this difference might have unpleasant consequences.

The Muslim migrants whose stories I have followed throughout this book have largely been from working-class backgrounds. Arif Qawi has a different story. His parents were doctors, and his uncle was the editor of a prominent national newspaper in Pakistan. He went to the same elite boarding school that the cricketer turned Prime Minister Imran Khan attended. He arrived in Britain in 1973 as a nine-year-old, went to prep school and later attended Harrow. He did not share the experience of young Muslims during the seventies who ran from racists. 'I was completely protected against all that,' Arif tells me. 'The only racism I ever felt has been from fellow Pakistanis and Asians. I've never felt any racism from Whites.'

Arif left Harrow to study engineering at Oxford and married an Indian Catholic. The marriage lasted fifteen years and the couple had two daughters. Arif went on to have a career in management consultancy before retiring early. In early March 2016, he was looking at potential schools for his son. 'He was around ten years old and . . . I didn't want to send him to Harrow because it was too traditional and male,' he recalls. At a school open evening, Arif met Neena Lall, head of a school in east London. They talked and she invited him to visit the school. 'I think she was looking for people to join her governing board,' he says, 'but she didn't mention that at the time. She said, "Come visit us", so I went along – and the minute I walked in there I fell in love with the place.' St Stephen's is a primary school in Newham and, out of a population of around 830 children, less than a handful were White – the rest were Asian and Black. 'Every class I walked into there was a boy that looked like me,' says Arif. 'The discipline, the way she ran the place, the teachers, everything was fantastic.' Lall soon invited Arif to join the school governing body – as a former management consultant, she felt he might be able to help run meetings and make the organisation of the school more efficient.

Arif started in March and within three months had become chair of the governors. I asked him what he made of the other parents. 'I thought the parents were quite scared,' he tells me. 'The majority were living as if they were in the same village they came from. They were obviously far less educated than me – they hadn't had the advantages I've had. They hadn't assimilated into modern Britain and the mullahs were guiding them.' The mullahs would see the children at the mosque every day after school for two hours of Qur'an classes. 'The reason they sent their children to mosque was that parents were not really very good at being parents,' claims Arif. 'For them it was free babysitting: you pick the kids up, get them chicken and chips for a quid and at four you take them to the mosque 'til six so you don't have to deal with them. The problem is the majority of our parents don't speak English so they can't even communicate with their kids, so they just got rid of two hours, you know, for ninety quid a month or whatever the mosques charge them.' The fact that the parents were sending their children to the mosque meant, Arif suggests, that the mullahs were able to influence the parents and that led to them interfering in the school curriculum. 'They were dictating to the parents anything that seemed mildly un-Islamic,' says Arif. I asked for an example. He told me that during Ramadan five- and six-year-olds would be passing out from an eighteen-hour fast and so the school banned fasting. The children were expected to eat lunch at school and fast at the weekend. 'I had several mothers come to see me in full niqab and they were so relieved that their children weren't having to fast because we had taken that responsibility away from them,' he says. 'This is a patriarchal society – the mullahs dictate to the fathers, the fathers dictate to the mothers, the mothers dictate to the kids, that's the chain.' The fasting ban led one senior local mullah to meet Arif and challenge the ban. 'He came in gleaming white robes and misquoted the Qur'an,' recalls Arif. 'I asked him, "Where does it say in the Qur'an that children of six should fast?" He pulled out a fancy iPhone and quoted a hadith, but what people don't realise is that I grew up in a very conservative Islamic household. I said to him there are hadiths and hadiths, and I quoted six books of hadiths to him, out of two hundred and seventy-three, and he was so shocked. I told him: "Son, I have forgotten more than you'll ever know." So that pissed him off and he went away.'

The controversy, however, did not go away and only grew when the school instituted a ban on girls between four and eight wearing a headscarf. 'The reason behind the ban was simply that the teachers were getting very nervous that these kids were on climbing frames and the cloth can get stuck,' Arif says. The ban only affected a handful of girls, but was met by opposition from parents, incited, he claims, by outsiders. He remembers one father coming to meet him in a T-shirt that read: 'Hands off my hijab'. Arif told the parents that St Stephen's was a secular school and a hugely successful one – under Neena Lall's leadership, it had become the top primary school in Britain.[12] Arif told disgruntled parents that their children were lucky to be attending such a great school and if they wanted to leave there was a waiting list of hundreds. It was perhaps not the most conciliatory approach, and led to the school receiving widespread abuse. 'There were tons of emails and there was constant picketing of the school, so it became very uncomfortable,' says Arif. 'We got zero support from the outside world because the Muslim vote is very strong in certain communities and they were too nervous about losing the block vote.'

The opposition to the headscarf ban became national news in January 2018 when *The Sunday Times* published a story on it.[13] The pressure on the school continued to grow and Lall reversed the policy and Arif resigned as the head of governors due to what he referred to at the time as a 'highly orchestrated abuse and intimidation campaign from Islamic extremists'. 'I left because Neena decided to reverse the hijab ban,' he told me. 'It became really difficult for the teachers and the staff in the school. One hundred and eight people working in school, who live in the community and they were walking through the streets, and they're getting yelled at.' I remember reading about the headscarf ban and its subsequent reversal but at the time I assumed that the vast majority of the schoolgirls wore the headscarf, however the truth is that out of around 800 children, it was only around sixty parents who were particularly vocal and forced the school to back down. I wanted to know why that was – why did the minority win?[14] 'The majority of parents were sheep,' Arif tells me. 'A lot of parents don't exercise the voice they've got, because they're still living in that cocoon. The majority of parents haven't left the four or five streets around their home – the only time the children got to see any other part of London was when we took them on school trips.' That geographic insularity contributed, he suggests, to an ideological and cultural insularity. It was something I had heard when I explored the issue of segregation. 'Asians prefer living amongst themselves,' he claims, 'but the problem is they bring Asia into it – so they open up halal shops everywhere, there'll be mosques everywhere, people wander around in hijabs. The men are in these semi-bastardised Saudi robes that look ridiculous and make people feel uncomfortable – it makes *me* feel uncomfortable. There'd be these, you know, brown lads in robes and they speak one sentence in Arabic to me. I'm fluent in Arabic so I will reply to them and they say, "Brother, that's all we know, bruv." So given the environment, Whites won't feel comfortable. If the average beer-drinking West Ham supporter was coming out of the pub and was confronted with this shit, he'd become sober immediately. When you give tolerance to people that don't appreciate tolerance you end up with the mess we're in because these people have grown up in countries where there is no tolerance, and when you give them some freedom, they will grab whatever they can, and that's what happened.'

It is shocking to read Arif's words written down in black and white. I admired his honesty but also wondered if he realised that he sometimes sounded as if he was quoting Tommy Robinson and his tribe. It was pretty clear that Arif remains frustrated and bitter about his experience at St Stephen's. 'I live in Chelsea, so I have no reason to come to East London,' he says. 'It was always for the kids and simply because I really wanted to see those kids succeed. But it's the mullahs that have got a stranglehold on that community and there's no reasoning with people like that. Dealing with mullahs is like playing chess with a duck: they'll make some completely ridiculous moves, crap all over your board and then piss off. And that's exactly what happened.'

There are parallels between what Neena Lall and Arif faced at St Stephen's and what Andrew Moffat faced at Parkfield – in both cases a progressive school head found themselves in conflict with a conservative Muslim community. That conflict can be reduced to a clash between British and Muslim values. Lall told *The Sunday Times* that she was concerned about the pupils' lack of identification with Britain, recalling how she had asked them to put their hands up if they thought they were British and very few had done so. The headscarf row could be viewed as a clash between a Muslim community who wanted to turn a nominally secular school into a faith school and a head worried that this would negatively affect the children's sense of belonging. I find it interesting that in the end the parents won – not least because Lall and Arif failed to secure support from politicians nervous about alienating Muslim voters. I use the word 'interesting', but a more honest word would be 'disappointing', because when I read about the school's climb down I felt disappointed and frustrated. It was disappointing that few politicians wanted to be seen publicly supporting Lall – and that silence threatened to embolden the mullahs and enrage non-Muslims already wary of Muslims who they felt were a threat to British values.

Those views could be on homosexuality or the rights of women, or on something as minor as teaching music. 'They don't like children playing the recorder,' the head of a Luton primary school tells me. 'They just say it's for religious reasons, but other people tell me it's because they think it's calling the devil. They don't like drama, they don't like children dancing, and swimming can be a bit of an issue sometimes.' The school is in Bury Park, the head is White and her students were nearly all Muslim. The parents at her school, like the parents at St Stephen's in Newham, had views that were in conflict with the school and, as in Newham, argued that it was their religion that shaped their attitudes towards music, art and swimming. (Swimming was controversial because of reasons of modesty.) 'People are frightened to say things for fear of being called racist,' the head told me, 'but you have to ask the questions because how do you learn if you're too frightened to ask questions.'

I wanted to know why the school could not just insist that all children learn music and art. 'That wouldn't work in this country,' she says. 'We're too laid-back, I think. Let's take queuing as a prime example. There are quite a few communities that will not stand in a queue. So, wherever there's a queue, they're at the front. Britons will moan about it, but they do nothing more than moan, they stand in the queue still and let the others go in front, that's just us.' If these are examples of Muslims seemingly espousing values different to the mainstream, does that mean those in the survey who believed there was a contradiction between British and Muslim values were right? And what can Muslims do to win over the doubters? I travelled to Dewsbury in search of answers.

Dewsbury is not necessarily associated with successful integration. The town has an unenviable reputation as a hotbed of Islamic radicalism. It was home to Mohammad Sidique Khan, the leader of the gang of four bombers who attacked London on 7 July 2005, claiming fifty-two innocent lives. Hammaad Munshi, another Dewsbury resident, was arrested in 2006, aged just sixteen, and became one of the youngest people ever to be arrested for terrorism. Munshi's brother Hassan, seventeen, secretly travelled to join ISIS with his neighbour Talha Asmal, also seventeen, who became Britain's youngest ever suicide bomber in Iraq. I met Farook Yunus in a community centre in Savile Town. He has lived in the area all his life – he was born in 1966 and still lives in his childhood home. He remembers his father keeping chickens in the cellar so that they had halal meat. 'Dewsbury is very segregated now,' he says, 'if you look at Savile Town it is a hundred per cent Muslim.' Yunus set up an organisation to help empower young people to be better Muslims and to develop better relationships between Muslims and non-Muslims. What I found inspiring about the work his organisation does is that it is very practical and community-based– it is not about textual similarities between the Qur'an and the Bible – it is about living Muslim values. One thing the young people do is visit local old people's homes to talk to residents, who are often rather sceptical about Muslims. He recalls one time around 2009 when he brought ten teenage Muslims to meet twenty older people. 'We prepared a presentation, we took some samosas and pakoras and we went down,' he says. 'We opened the door, walked through, and a lady, ninety-three-year-old, turns around and looks at us, and goes, "Are you fucking Pakis? We don't like Pakis here."' The teenagers became nervous and wanted to leave but Yunus told them to smile, continue with the presentation and to share the food they had brought. They encouraged the older people to ask questions, which they did – about terrorism, the hijab and other contentious issues. The young people told them that they wanted to help, and they were true to their word. 'From that first meeting onwards, we would do clean-ups in the garden and we played games with them,' he tells me. 'We ended up building a really good relationship after that. They even came to the mosque and we changed their whole perception from hatred, and we made it into a really nice thing.'

The projects that Yunus' organisation gets involved with are about reaching beyond the Muslim community and demonstrating what he believes to be true Muslim values. 'There are people who are scared of us,' he says. 'Why is that? What would the Prophet do if he were here? He would reach out to them and show them true Islam. Some people say that they won't accept us but my response to them is: "Are you doing your bit? What are you doing to help out and be a good citizen?" We keep it very simple: love thy neighbour and help thy neighbour. Simple.'

In the winter of December 2015, Yunus was at home when he started seeing reports of flooding caused by Storm Desmond affecting homes in Cumbria. The region had more than twice as much rain in 24 hours as it would normally expect for the entire month. Six thousand homes were flooded, causing around £500 million in damage. 'I said to the young people, "What are we gonna do?"' recalls Yunus. 'They said, "Let's go and help!" So, we just put out an announcement: "We're going, we've got two minibuses." We had a problem. Too many kids wanted to go so we couldn't take everybody. Then we had other people coming in cars. So, we took fifty, sixty people over, not once but a few times.' Yunus' group was not the only Muslim charity to help the victims of Storm Desmond – hundreds of Muslims from a range of charities came to Cumbria.

The helpers waded through thick mud and chest-high water to clear people's homes and possessions. They helped the army to pull down ruined outbuildings and sheds, clear

gardens and pile up debris to be taken away by relief vehicles. 'I remember seeing the mud damage and looking at it
and thinking it is not possible to clean it up,' Yunus recalls.
'I don't know how but the help from Allah came and we
cleaned it all up. The owner came, and he just looked at
everything, and he just started crying. He hugged me and
he just started crying.' But six months later the residents
helped by those Muslim volunteers voted by 62 per cent to
38 per cent to leave the EU.

I remember reading about the help Yunus and his organisation provided and was struck by the fact that he was based
in Dewsbury – a place more associated with radicalism than
charity. It fascinated me that Yunus could have grown up
in the same community as men arrested for terrorism and
yet his interpretation of his faith was about helping the local
community and building bridges of understanding. 'We do
a lot of mosque visits,' he tells me, 'and when they come
in sometimes it is because they've been told to come by the
council, or their school, and you can sense the fear. Then
they stay for an hour and half and they leave laughing. They
were scared because they don't know you – and when they
get to know you, they think "Actually Muslims, Christians,
we're all the same."' When I think about the work that
Yunus' organisation does it strikes me that it is all about
being good citizens. The impulse behind it all, however, is
faith – for Yunus the work embodies true Muslim values,
but I am sure they could easily be considered British, or
simply decent human values. 'We don't even bring religion

into it,' he tells me. 'Islam teaches you to love thy neighbour, help thy neighbour, but when there's someone that needs help, whether they are Christian, Muslim or whatever, you help them.'*

It is lovely and important to hear the stories of those Muslims demonstrating that Muslim and British values can exist happily alongside each other; it supports the argument of those such as Rowan Williams, the former Archbishop of Canterbury, who has suggested that 'the setting-up of British values against any kind of values, whether Muslim or Christian, just won't do.'[15] But in my desire to amplify positive stories, I don't want to ignore the real challenges that remain, and this is particularly true when we consider the British, or Western, value of free speech. We have already seen the impact of the 1989 fatwa following the publication of Salman Rushdie's *The Satanic Verses* on Alyas Karmani, and how it prompted him to embrace radicalism. I was eighteen at the time and watching the book burnings in Bradford left me feeling bemused. I suspected most of the folks burning the books were not big readers of magical realism and the anger they displayed left me wondering

---

* One of the things I have learnt while writing this book is that there are no 'good' and 'bad' guys – Yunus was also the person mentioned in the chapter on homosexuality who, when asked for advice by a young boy who suspected he might be gay, told him homosexuality was wrong and advised him that getting married would sort him out.

whether there was something wrong with me because I was not so furious. My baseline position was that people should, on the whole, be able to write what they like and those who did not like it could exercise their right to not read it. The idea of being offended from a religious viewpoint never made much sense to me – surely a faith that was thousands of years old and had conquered nations and civilisations could withstand a *book*?

On 30 September 2005, the Danish newspaper *Jyllands-Posten* published twelve cartoon depictions of the Prophet Muhammad. It is considered blasphemous to visually depict the Prophet Muhammad but one of the cartoons depicted the Prophet with a bomb in his turban. Another showed the Prophet in heaven, remonstrating suicide bombers with the words, 'Stop, stop, we have run out of virgins!' Protests against the cartoons were held around the world. 'On February 4, 2006, the Danish and Norwegian embassies in Syria were set alight,' reported *The Atlantic*, 'a day later, a mob burned down the Danish embassy in Lebanon. In total, 139 people were killed amid demonstrations against the cartoons from Nigeria to Pakistan. One minister in the Indian state of Uttar Pradesh promised a reward of $1 million for anyone who beheaded one of the Danish cartoonists.'[16]

Ten years later, on 7 January 2015, two Muslim brothers, Saïd and Chérif Kouachi, forced their way into the offices of the French satirical weekly newspaper *Charlie Hebdo* in Paris. The brothers identified themselves as belonging to Al-Qaeda and, armed with rifles and other weapons, killed twelve people and injured eleven others. In the aftermath of the attacks, an estimated 1.5 million French people took to the streets of Paris in a unity march to reaffirm France's commitment to freedom of speech. The reaction to the publication of these cartoons struck me as outsized and seemed to confirm that there is a clash of values on the subject of free speech between some Muslims and non-Muslims.

In a British poll conducted in late January 2015, 93 per cent of British Muslim respondents believed that Muslims in Britain should always obey British laws, 78 per cent were offended when images of the Prophet Muhammad are published but 68 per cent agreed that violence against those who publish images of the Prophet Muhammad was never justifiable.[17] More worryingly, 24 per cent disagreed with the suggestion that violence was never justified. My own view has not changed since I was a teenager watching what I considered to be the over-reaction to the publication of *The Satanic Verses*. I maintain that if Muslims want to reassure the rest of society that Muslim values do not clash with Western one, Muslims need to accept that free speech sometimes means reading things, and teaching things, that offend. That said, while I believe writers and cartoonists have the right to mock Islam without fearing they will be killed, that does not mean they should do it. Context matters. 'The cartoon controversy should be understood against a backdrop of rising Western prejudice and suspicion directed against Muslims, and an associated sense of persecution among Muslims in many parts of the world,' noted a 2006 Human Rights Watch report. 'In Europe, rapidly growing Muslim communities have become the continent's largest religious minority but also among its most economically disadvantaged communities and the target of discriminatory and anti-immigration measures.'[18] The over-reaction of Muslims is, in other words, at least partly explained by a sense of defensiveness about their faith and culture, which stems from feeling discriminated against. The road to overcoming this has to involve Muslims feeling that they are fully accepted but also appreciating that the price of acceptance is occasionally having to tolerate things that they might find offensive.

I was raised to believe that the values with which I was raised – usually shorthanded to Muslim values – were not the same as mainstream British values. It was that friction that I fled when I left Luton for Manchester, and by settling in London and marrying Bridget, I was in effect signalling that I wished to sail under the flag of British values. I did not believe there was such a huge difference between the two – but I *had* to believe that. It was the only way I could be comfortable about marrying Bridget. From the moment we realised we would be parents, Bridget and I began to construct an alternative and more positive narrative where the important thing was not the particular faiths my wife and I were raised in but the values we both shared. Our children would not be lost in the space between being Christian or Muslim – they would be both; they would not be stranded between being Scottish or Pakistani – they would be both. It was an enlarging and intoxicating vision that implied that our children were blessed rather than cursed to be the product of two cultures. It would mean that Laila and Ezra celebrate both Christmas and Eid, that they wear traditional Pakistani clothes from my family and from Bridget's. When it works, it feels like a deeply hopeful version of a thoroughly modern British family. It is, however, not the whole story and, as the children have grown older, I have become more aware that Bridget and I have differing attitudes towards parenting. It is not easy to disentangle culture and class from religion, but I do think that some of those differences are due to our different religious backgrounds. When Bridget and I discuss the issues around raising children in a mixed-faith and mixed-race family, she concedes that she was perhaps a touch naive (her word) in her initial optimism. I am grateful for her naivety since it helped give me the confidence to marry and have children, which despite its challenges is the most rewarding thing I have done.

I grew up in a time, and in a family, where children obeyed parents. When my father told us to do something – told not asked – it was not an invitation for an extended discussion on the rights and wrongs of what he was asking us to do, it was an instruction. When my parents were talking it was understood that children did not interrupt. My father never hit us and I hardly recall any incidents where he even threatened to. We obeyed him because that was how we were raised and it was how generations of children from my background were raised too. The contrast between how my wife and I are raising our children is almost comical. My daughter recently turned nine and, put simply, she barely listens to a word we tell her. Trying to get her to tidy her room is less about issuing an instruction and more about us descending to pitiful begging, which is routinely ignored. The notion that she should listen to us simply because we are her parents is not one that she accepts. In this she is entirely representative of her age and generation, but I find it much harder to accept this behaviour than my wife. Bridget argues that it is a function of growing up, that children inevitably rise up against parental authority, and she will regale me with colourful incidents from her own youth when she behaved appallingly. The implication is that this is just how it is and all we can do is accept it with good grace. I disagree, and I point out examples not only from my own youth but the experiences of my brother raising his children. Why is it, I ask, that his children continue to respect their father when they are in their late teens and early twenties while our children are under ten and are already refusing to listen to us? The discussion often becomes polarised and could be described as a clash between my wife's middle-class White values and my working-class Pakistani-Muslim ones. Is my desire for children to be more deferential to parental authority a product of my cultural heritage? It is true that when I talk to other parents from south Asian backgrounds they instantly recognise my complaints and frustrations, but it is also true that the style of parenting my father and his like practised is sometimes referred to as Victorian, which makes the claim that it is culturally specific less persuasive. That said, I still associate the liberal child-focused parenting that my wife prefers as being imbued with 'British values', whereas the style of parenting I would practice were it entirely my choice would not be as authoritarian as the manner in which I was raised, but could be reasonably described as following Asian, Pakistani or Muslim values.

It isn't only in the way we are raising our children that I have become aware of the distance between British and Muslim values. One thing I hear often from my White friends is the idea that they never want to be a burden on their children in later life. Bridget's parents are already clearing out the attic in their home because they don't want to put their children through the emotional ordeal of having to go through their belongings after their deaths. The starkest example of not being a burden concerns what White parents expect from their children when they become too old to live independently: they expect nothing. This was not how I was raised. I was brought up to believe that there was an unwritten contract between parents and children: the parents take care of their children and then, in time, the children look after their parents. The concept of 'burden' was never entertained. My mother is, at the time of writing, eighty-seven years old. She is extremely frail and forgetful, and looking after and living with her is a huge challenge. Since my father's death my mother has lived with my older brother and his family. It is not easy, but for my brother there is literally no question of putting our mother in an old people's home. He remembers the sacrifices she made for us when we were little – the way she would forgo meals to ensure that her children had enough to eat. He recalls, like I do, the trauma she endured of losing her husband just as they were preparing for retirement, and he is aware, as I am, of how the foundations of our success were laid by our mother. That is why, despite the challenges, he would never countenance putting her in sheltered accommodation. I see what my brother and his wife do as representing the very best of Muslim and Pakistani values, but I also know that it is easy to applaud such values when I am not called to live them. Since I left home at the age of eighteen, I have been a fairly free agent largely unbound by family obligations. The hard work of looking after our mother fell first to my younger sister and later my brother. So perhaps my warm words are worthless, but I still believe that the values embodied in my brother's actions are praiseworthy. I also still believe that it is no sin to raise one's children to believe it is their role to take care of their parents when the time comes. I want that to happen, and I believe in those values, but I am not sure it will happen.

I am married to a woman who grew up with different values and we are raising our children in a society where my wife's values are dominant. I had assumed that my pessimism was due to the fact that my wife is not Muslim and was not raised with my values. Do you think your children are going to look after you? I asked Ruby, who grew up in a working-class Pakistani family in Crewe and married a White man. 'Asian families cannot fathom why White parents want the kids to move out of the family home at the earliest opportunity, there is the feeling that they don't love their children as much as Asian parents,' she says. 'They are also quite disparaging about the elderly parents not getting looked after by sons and daughters who do not have their parents living at home with them. It seems pretty much standard that elderly parents get put into homes and that does concern me. I try to instill a sense of duty around that with my children, by indirectly informing them that we give up aspects of our lives, make enormous sacrifices to have a certain lifestyle, put them through university and so on. I'm trying to get them to understand, without actually saying it, that it should be a two-way street.' I put the same question to Abdullah in Birmingham. 'My wife and I have already had that conversation,' he says, adding, 'probably not. I don't want to be a burden on them either. I want them to live their lives.' These were the things I usually heard White people say. I asked Abdullah if he was unusual in assuming his children would not look after him, and he told me he would canvas opinion at the mosque. The next day he reported back. 'Many said exactly what our parents said to us, that our children should look after us,' he tells me. 'However, the word "should" kept being used and the people I spoke to all agreed that it probably will not happen as the culture has shifted to a more European way of thinking in our children.'

I am aware that in describing my values I have referred to them variously as Asian, Pakistani, working-class and

Muslim. That feels accurate – when I was growing up my parents were much more likely to talk about us being Pakistani than Muslim, and it hardly needs stating that there are plenty of non-Muslim communities that share some of the parenting habits I have talked about. The hard question in trying to identity what it is uniquely or specifically Muslim about any of these values is what is uniquely or specifically Muslim about me? It is true that I identify as a Muslim but what sort of Muslim am I – and am I a Muslim at all?

This is a question I have struggled with throughout much of my life. When I was growing up, I could deny my faith about as much as I could deny my brownness – both were self-evident. I was a Muslim because . . . well, because my parents were, and I was from Pakistan and everyone from there was Muslim, and because I read the Qur'an and went to mosque for Eid, and because we didn't eat pig meat. I was a Muslim because of the things I did and did not do rather than what I did or did not believe. The belief part was always more challenging but I never explicitly and deliberately turned my back on Islam. When I went to university it would have been very easy to start drinking and eating non-halal meat, but I never did. I still haven't touched a drop of alcohol, eaten pig meat or intentionally eaten non-halal meat. In part that is out of respect for my mother and my late father, but it is also because my identity as a Muslim hangs by those two threads – meat and drink. The implication is that if I ever started to drink or eat non-halal meat I would no longer feel I had the right to call myself Muslim. The irony here is that I have plenty of Muslim friends who drink and eat non-halal meat who have no doubts about their right to say they are Muslim. I am reminded of two Pakistani migrants cited in Rex and Moore's study of Birmingham in the early sixties. One 'regards himself as a good Muslim . . . he goes to mosque for the main Muslim festivals. He drinks whisky on doctor's orders [he has a pain in his chest] and has a few drinks in the pub with his friends in the evening. This he feels in no way runs counter to Islamic teaching.' The authors met the second man in an Irish pub. 'He explained to us that Islam always adapts to the culture in which he finds itself. Soon it would give way on drinking. Thus he saw himself in the "Black Horse" as in the vanguard of ideological reform.'[19] I have friends who have gone on pilgrimage to Mecca but who also enjoy a glass of wine. I remember the first time I visited Pakistan for professional reasons. I was attending a literary festival in Karachi and I was invited to a number of swanky social events where, to my surprise, I seemed to be the only person *not* drinking. I used to think that the difference between them and me was that they were hypocrites and I wasn't, but I am no longer sure that is true. I now think that my reliance on my meat and drink choices to define my faith is a sign of insecurity rather than strength – an indication of nervousness rather than confidence about my right to say I am Muslim.

The question of how important it is to eat only halal meat is something that has repeatedly arisen in my marriage, particularly after we had children. When I used to visit my in-laws for Christmas, they would cook a turkey or chicken for the family but make a vegetarian dish for me. It was deeply thoughtful of them and in later years my mother-in-law would prepare for my visit by visiting a Muslim butcher to source a halal chicken. My wife would sometimes ask me why I was so insistent that the meat I ate was halal. I would say that was the rule, but she wanted a better explanation. She would say that she was happy to tell our children they could only eat halal meat so long as the reasoning felt logical. In her mind it was better to eat organic meat than halal meat from animals that she suspected had been pumped full of drugs. I accepted she made a good point, and my only response was that for me Muslim values meant appreciating the importance of having meat that was halal. 'The Qur'an teaches you that if you go to the homes of the people of the book you should eat their food,' Dilwar Hussain, chair of New Horizons in British Islam, tells me. 'That's because what the Qur'an is trying to do is encourage social interaction.' Did this not contradict the requirement that meat must be ritually slaughtered, I asked. 'The Qur'an lays down two conditions,' he says, 'it should be lawfully slaughtered – halal – and wholesome. There is a caveat, which is that when you are interacting with people, you don't want food to be a source of impediment in that social interaction. If you look at the way that food is used in Islam, it's hospitality, it's about generosity, it's about encouraging people to meet and talk in society and breaking down differences. Now we can't then turn that on its head and make food a point of departure because you are actually doing the opposite of what the spirit of Islam is trying to encourage you to do.'

I found this illuminating because it reveals how people like me focus on the rituals of a religion and in so doing miss the wider point. It also hints that what Muslim values mean and how they are practised is not fixed – it is about nuance and interpretation. I was never taught these nuances, so have remained nervous about challenging the importance of halal meat and not drinking alcohol because I have always worried that were I to look too deeply into Islam I would not like what I saw. I feared that were I to delve too deeply my fears about Islam would be confirmed. It would be revealed as a religion that demands unquestioning obedience. I suspected Islam was, at its core, intolerant and illiberal, misogynist and backward. I did not want to have to confront this and I did not want to worry that I would be unable to reconcile Islam's values with my own, and so I took the easy path of not thinking, and not drinking.

Naveed Idrees is the head of Feversham Primary in Bradford. I visited in spring 2019 to meet Naveed who arrived at the school in September 2009 on secondment as a deputy head. When he arrived, the school was having serious problems. 'The staff were leaving, and parents were not engaging in the school,' he recalls. 'The kids' behaviour was atrocious – if you visited then you would have seen fights in the corridors and kids flinging chairs.' The school was put under special measures following an OFSTED inspection and Idrees was appointed head in 2013. 'We had low staff morale, parents not happy with the school, results were poor, and nobody wanted to come here,' he says. 'We needed to do something dramatic.' Idrees began with a simple question: what did the children need? It was then he came to a realisation. 'I started to think that the reason the children had behaviour issues was that their souls were not being reached,' he says, 'and that made me ask, "How do you connect with someone's soul?" It is through music.' Idrees decided he would focus the school's resources on music by hiring a full-time music teacher. The children would receive three practical music lessons each week and there would also be after-school clubs every day and every lunchtime so children could access up to eight hours of music a week. This would be impressive for any school but bear in mind this is an inner-city Bradford state school that is 98 per cent working-class Muslim. The teacher I spoke to in Luton told me that she found it hard to persuade the parents at her school to allow their children to even play the recorder but here was a Muslim majority school where children were learning Beatles' songs and playing a variety of musical instruments. I wanted to know how Naveed had done it, so I asked him to tell me more about his own past.

Naveed grew up in nearby Halifax, his family were from Mirpur, and as a boy he attended mosque after school and had memorised the Qur'an by the age of fourteen. 'I spent a lot of time in the mosque, but I learned nothing,' he says. 'It was all in Arabic and I knew nothing and that was when

I started to learn Arabic and started to research the history of Islam.' He became interested in Islam as it was practised in Turkey and Spain. 'The Muslims of Spain invented the do-re-mi-fa scale,' he says, 'so that's always been part of our tradition, but the arts have completely disappeared from our cultural landscape because the people who arrived in the sixties weren't educated so they never were into the arts even though the arts were in our tradition. And so, art, culture, music and poetry all disappeared.' This felt joyously persuasive to me and confirmed how much my ideas of Islam were shaped not by the religion but by class.

The generation that travelled from the subcontinent to Britain in the fifties and sixties were, put bluntly, largely ignorant about the ways that Islam had informed art, music, poetry and science and therefore could not pass this rich heritage on to their children. That partly helps explain why some Muslim parents are so wary of their children studying music and art in school. How did Idrees manage to overcome this scepticism? 'We had a discussion and debate with the community,' he tells me. 'I asked them: "Who says that music is haram? Is it Allah, is it the Prophet or is that man with the beard over there?" In our community people look up to religious authority but they don't use basic reasoning. So, when people talk about religion they immediately refer to the bearded crowd, but a lot of these imams might be living in Britain, but their mindset is still very much a village mentality, and these are the people who are representing Islam to them.' Idrees also had the advantage that unlike many parents he understood Arabic. 'I can access the original text of the Qur'an,' he says, 'so the moment anyone made a false claim I could say that was not true.' His Qur'anic knowledge conferred credibility and meant that they did not raise any objections to the music lessons.

I visited the home of one girl who attended the school. She lived in a terraced house a few minutes away. Her father was a taxi driver, and her mother wore a face veil. It was in many ways a family like so many others in Asian communities across the country, except that this teenage girl had a drum kit in her bedroom and her parents were happy for their headscarf-wearing daughter to pound the drums at home. When I asked her father if he had any concerns about his daughter playing music, he told me that so long as her studies were not affected he was not worried. That is the second part of the story of this school. The change in culture and the focus on music turned the school around: the school is now in the top 2 per cent nationally and the most recent OFSTED inspection awarded it 'outstanding' status, noting that 'the head teacher has been pivotal to the success of the school. He is uncompromising in his determination to instill in all pupils the belief that they can, and will, achieve their best.' *The Times Educational Supplement* noted how a school that 'lies in one of the most deprived areas in the UK, with high levels of unemployment and crime, and low levels of literacy . . . and was once a run-down, unloved building with unhappy staff and a dry curriculum is now a place where children achieve beyond their wildest dreams.' It named Naveed Idrees Head Teacher of the Year 2019.

'Critical thinking is part of our tradition,' Idrees tells me. 'There is a saying from the Prophet that "unexamined faith is useless" – if you have just been born a Muslim you haven't chosen that. What does it mean to be Muslim? Is it just wearing the T-shirt or the badge, or is it something like a deeper understanding of going to the depths? If you just say, "I have got the badge because I was born with it", then you have not gone through that process.' The implication was that the parents in Bradford who might have objected to their children studying music, like the parents who objected to their daughters not being able to wear a headscarf in Newham, were happy to wear the badge of religion without properly examining what this truly meant. One societal con- sequence of this lack of examination is that wider society tends to see Islam depicted through the actions and attitudes of 'badge-wearing Muslims', which perpetuates the idea that there is a clash between British and Muslim values.

The impression is often given that Islam is somehow unique in having followers with views that might be consid- ered outdated. As Sayeeda Warsi writes: 'I have yet to see a politician go to a synagogue, gurdwara, temple or church and address the Jews, the Sikhs, the Hindus, the Christians or indeed any other group and talk British values. I've yet to see a policy announcement on British values which is directed at a specific ethnic or religious group other than "the Muslims", despite the fact that many a Jewish girl in

London isn't permitted to study beyond sixteen ... many a Sikh girl has suffered physical and emotional abuse for simply daring to marry the man of her choice ... many a child has been branded a witch and abused with the Church's knowledge, and many a "cure" has been developed by evangelical Christians for the immoral and sick gays.'[20]

There is a certain knee-jerk reaction I have observed from Muslims whenever they are challenged with difficult questions around extremism or grooming or homophobia, for example. Their instinct is rather than confronting the issue head on, to resort instead to blaming the media for spreading scurrilous lies about Islam. I have worked in the British media for more than twenty-five years and my instinct is to resist blaming the media because it so often feels like a lazy way of evading responsibility, but in this particular case I do feel the media bears some responsibility. A 2019 study from the Muslim Council in Britain of 10,000 articles and clips referring to Muslims and Islam found that 59 per cent of all articles associated Muslims with negative behaviour and over a third of all articles misrepresented or generalised about Muslims.[21] Is it hardly surprising, then, that large swathes of the public believe Muslim and British values are locked in an inevitable conflict? According to a 2016 report, although nearly 5 per cent of the UK population is Muslim, just 0.4 per cent of British journalists are Muslim.[22] The percentage in senior roles as editors and commissioning editors is therefore a tiny fraction of a tiny fraction and this has real-world consequences when it comes to representing Muslims and Islam.

This is why we so often end up with a distorted picture and hysterical headlines: 'Muslim Plot to Kill Pope'; 'Now Muslims Get Their Own Laws in Britain'; 'Keep Out, Britain is Full Up' and 'Fury at Police in Burkas'. Every single one of these was splashed on the front page of the *Daily Express* – a newspaper whose anti-Muslim agenda was matched only by its devotion to bad weather, the benefits or otherwise of statins and the disappearance of Madeleine McCann. The worldview of the *Daily Express* was perhaps most succinctly summarised in a November 2010 front page that read 'Muslims tell British: Go To Hell!' It was only in the body of the report that it was explained that the story was about a protest that involved *three* Muslims.[23] (There are estimated to around three *million* Muslims in Britain.) I assumed that a hateful *Daily Express* was an uncomfortable part of life and had little hope that things could change, but in March 2018 the paper changed editors. The new editor, Gary Jones, made a decision that the newspaper would no longer run anti-Muslim front pages. 'I went into my first news conference,' Jones tells me, 'and I just sat down and said, "Look, I know none of you in this room are going to say you're racist, but we're not going to publish this stuff again because it's fundamentally wrong."' Overnight the newspaper changed, but, and I found this fascinating, the journalists remained the same and circulation was unaffected. 'People almost want to feel fear at times,' Jones says, when I asked him why so much of the press coverage around Muslims is negative. 'If you fail to accept that this is a tiny minority of a minority then you want to be fearful.' I asked him why he had chosen not to indulge this need for fear, and he told me about a conversation with his son, who was twelve, when he told him he was moving to a new job. 'I'm the new editor of the *Daily Express*,' Jones told his son, to which his son replied, 'I feel sick. I hope you're not doing this to pay my school fees.' Jones was somewhat shaken by his son's reaction. 'I found myself saying, "I promise you I'm going to try and put things right. Hopefully you will respect what I'm doing in the future."' In some ways this is a hopeful story – an example of how one person can make a difference – but it is also a little dispiriting if the fate of Muslim representation in the press rests on the children of newspaper editors guilt-tripping their parents.

I started my journalism career writing opinion pieces where I would be commissioned in my unqualified role as 'professional Muslim', but I always felt uncomfortable writing in that voice. I would stress that I was expressing my own personal view, but it was hard not to conclude that I was being commissioned to speak as the voice of all Muslims, which I clearly was not. I did it because I wanted my voice heard, because it was nice to see my face in a paper and because, regardless of whether I spoke for all Muslims or not, I felt I had some worthwhile things to say. In time I began to feel uneasy about opining and started to write more first-person pieces where my religious background was less relevant, pieces about being a new father or having lost my own father. I preferred this style of writing not only because it was warmer and less preachy but because it was showing rather than stating the commonalities between people regardless of their religious backgrounds. I was trying to hint that we had more in common than that which divides us and yet it is a measure of just how ingrained these attitudes are that when I started working on this book I would broadly have agreed with the sentiment that there are such things as Muslim values and British values. I would have agreed that Muslim values were basically old-fashioned and somewhat backward, and British values essentially progressive. It has been somewhat humbling to realise how wrong I was. What has been so enlightening is the realisation that Muslim values can also be deeply progressive, sometimes in surprising ways, while British values have in the past been deeply regressive. I inadvertently bought into the myth that British values have remained steadfast throughout history when in fact, as Sayeeda Warsi notes in *The Enemy Within*, Britain has 'been sectarian, racist, sexist and homophobic . . . and each time our behaviour has in our view been consistent with our Britishness . . . We, in the not too distant past, have done and said things which flew in the fact of our current version of British values, which include individual liberty and mutual respect and tolerance. We speak about these so-called British values as if they have always existed the way we define them today. Each generation asserts its own British values based on the society that makes up Britain at that time. Britain is on a constant journey where it defines and reaffirms its values.'[24] I had not fully absorbed this, and

I had also accepted the notion that there was something inherently regressive about Muslim values. I think this was in part because many of the values I was raised with *were* old-fashioned and there are instances of regressive attitudes among Muslim communities in Britain. The mistake I made was to generalise from these instances and assume it told me something about Islam when it is more accurate to say that it tells us about the attitudes of largely uneducated immigrants from the subcontinent. In other words, I confused working-class south Asian attitudes with Muslim values. I did not allow for the fact that these attitudes can and do evolve over time, which is why Abdullah Rehman is resigned to the fact that his children will not be looking after him and his wife in their old age. 'My children are growing up in this country and they want the same things, and they have the same values as everyone else,' he says. 'Britain has changed them – they have a different culture to our culture and they have different values.' Abdullah was using 'they', I noted, to refer to his own children.

TEN

THEY . . . DON'T LOVE OUR COUNTRY

*'A large proportion of Britain's Asian population fail
to pass the cricket test. Which side do they cheer for?
It's an interesting test. Are you still harking back to
where you came from or where you are?'*
Norman Tebbit, politician, 1990

'There were no Pakis at Dunkirk.'
Bernard Manning, comedian, 1998

1962 was the year of Bob Dylan and Marilyn Monroe. Dylan released his self-titled album in March and Monroe was found dead in her Los Angeles home in August. It was the year that *University Challenge* and *That Was The Week That Was* first aired on television. It was the year Brazil beat Czechoslovakia in the football World Cup Final and it was the year that the Pakistan cricket team arrived in England for a five match test series. It was also the year that saw the arrival of men from the Indian subcontinent, men whose stories we have followed during the course of this book. Among these arrivals was Mohammed Jamil. He was twenty-one and arrived as a student on 2 May, only days after the Pakistan team. This was only a few months before the Commonwealth Immigrants Act, which removed free immigration from the citizens of the member states of the Commonwealth, was due to come into effect. The first Test commenced on the last day of May at the Oval in south London. England won the toss and elected to bat first. Jamil was in the stands to watch the match. 'I started following the tour,' he recalls, 'I saw them in Birmingham, Leeds and London. There were very few Pakistanis in the audience but a lot of the West Indians supported us at the time.' Jamil recalls that the Pakistan team played dismally. 'I'm afraid to say they didn't leave a good impression. Individually they were very good players, but as a team, they didn't perform very well. I was watching the match at the Oval and Pakistan were doing really bad. It was almost an embarrassment.' Pakistan would end up losing the series with four defeats and one draw.

They returned in 1967 – with Jamil again among the spectators – and in 1978. The first Test began on 1 June 1978 in Birmingham. At the beginning of the year, Margaret Thatcher, leader of the Conservative Party, had told a TV programme that 'people are really rather afraid that this country might be rather swamped by people with a different culture'. On 4 May, one month before the series commenced, a young Bangladeshi textile worked called Aftab Ali was walking home from work when he was attacked and stabbed to death by three teenagers. Two of the teenagers – Roy Arnold and Carl Ludlow – were seventeen and the third unnamed boy was sixteen. The murder was racially motivated and random – they did not know Mr Ali and did not care who he was. 'No reason at all,' said the sixteen-year-old boy, when a police officer asked why he attacked Mr Ali. 'If we saw a Paki we used to have a go at them,' he remarked. 'We would ask for money and beat them up. I've beaten up Pakis on at least five occasions.'[1] The day Aftab Ali died was also the day of local elections in England. The far-right National Front ran in every Tower Hamlets ward that year and gained nearly 10 per cent of the vote.

This was the first Test cricket series that I can recall watching, as a seven-year-old boy. My most lingering memories of 1978 are Boney M's 'Rivers of Babylon', my older sister's love of *Grease*, the football World Cup Final between Argentina and the Netherlands, and watching the Test series between Pakistan and England. I am not going to claim I can recall precisely what I thought about identity and belonging all those years ago, but I do know that as a boy the few times I would have seen brown-skinned people on television would have been on comedy shows like *Mind Your Language* and *It Ain't Half Hot Mum*, both of which were hugely popular. The Asians in these shows offered comedic light relief to White audiences, and some were even portrayed by White actors.[2] It must have been such a welcome shock to see players who did not just look like me but, in the case of Sarfraz Nawaz and Javed Miandad, even had my names.³ I did not have to be told to support Pakistan – it was beyond obvious – and as a teenager I had posters of Pakistani cricketers Mohsin Khan and Imran Khan on my bedroom wall. Pakistan returned for a Test series in 1982, only months after the end of the Falklands conflict, and again in 1987.

I turned sixteen on the last day of the first Test in 1987; two days later Margaret Thatcher won her third successive general election. I remember Thatcher waving from a Downing Street window with a smiling Norman Tebbit, who masterminded her campaign, at her side. In the spring of 1990, Tebbit gave an interview to an American newspaper. The interview was supposed to be about his opposition to a proposal to admit up to 250,000 immigrants from Hong Kong after the colony reverted to Chinese rule in 1997. He was concerned that a large-scale influx would be a threat to the national character, and unworried that such concerns might be dubbed racist. 'That's a very foolish thing to do,' he told the *LA Times*, 'because if you say to a lot of people out there in the street that Tebbit is racist, they'll scratch the back of their head and say: "Well, so am I. If that's what being racist is, then I'm one as well."' In the interview Tebbit moved from expressing reservations about immigration from Hong Kong to worrying about the loyalty of Britain's Asian communities. He told the interviewer that it was still common among British Asians to search for husbands and wives in the family's native country but, he warned, 'You can't have two homes.' Although he was talking

to an American newspaper, Tebbit encapsulated his apprehension by referring to a sport about which most Americans
were, and still are, only dimly aware. 'A large proportion' of
Britain's Asian population, he told the paper, failed to pass
what he called the 'cricket test'. 'Which side do they cheer
for?' he asked. 'It's an interesting test. Are you still harking
back to where you came from, or where you are?'

The 'Tebbit test' was my generation's 'Rivers of Blood'
speech; another example of a darkly charismatic Conservative
politician expressing misgivings about the consequences of
immigration on the character of British life. It cast a shadow
over my generation just as Powell's speech had for immigrants a generation earlier. I was in my first year at university
in Manchester when Norman Tebbit coined the 'Tebbit test'.
I remember the anxiety it prompted because I knew that
the test was calling into question my right to call myself
British, since when it came to cricket I unequivocally failed
the Tebbit test. In a contest between England and Pakistan,
I would unquestioningly support Pakistan and this support
was given so instinctively that, before Tebbit, I am not sure
I even asked myself why I was so wholeheartedly cheering
for a country I left at the age of two.

'We grew up supporting Pakistan without even realising
it,' Amir, Mohamed Jamil's son, tells me. 'It was just normal.
Everybody we knew supported Pakistan. It was not even a
question. It wasn't as if we made a conscious decision.' In
Bradford, Zulfi Karim, whom we last saw helping rescue
the local synagogue, also grew up supporting Pakistan.

'We can't help it,' he says, 'we're better at entertaining. We're better at partying. Food smells better and looks better. There's no real comparison.' Humayun Ansari, who arrived in London in 1962 – the same year as Mohammed Hussain and the Pakistan cricket squad – has been a cricket fan since he was a young boy in Pakistan listening on the radio. 'There was no television in Pakistan until 1964, but it didn't matter,' he says, 'while the ball-by-ball cricket commentary was on the radio there was nothing else we cared about.' Ansari arrived as a fourteen-year-old and continued to support Pakistan. 'I keep asking myself why and on a rational level I can't come up with a response,' he says. 'The only way I can think about it, is that this is what I was socialised into until the age of fourteen and so one becomes emotionally attached to the idea of Pakistan.' In Birmingham, Shaista told me she cheered on Pakistan because 'Pakistan are not very good at many sports so when they're good at something, I want to cheer them on. It's a bit like supporting the underdog.' It wasn't just the Pakistan cricket team who were the underdogs – it was us. The seventies and eighties were decades of in-your-face racism and it would have taken more resilience than I possessed to feel proud to be British. Britain did not accept the likes of us, and so it was natural for people like me to retain some attachment to Pakistan.

My affection was not for Pakistan as a place – which I barely knew – but for Pakistan as an idea. The idea that it was the one place in the world that would not deny me.

In Britain or any other country that I moved to, I would always be considered a foreigner and an outsider. Pakistan was the one place where no one could tell me to go back to where I came from. Those of us from Pakistan were used to being mocked and growing up it frustrated me that there was so little about my heritage about which I could feel proud. Britain had once ruled the world, but Pakistan was younger than my parents. We were so desperate for heroes that we even pretended to be interested in squash because Jahangir Khan – generally considered among the greatest squash players of all time – was Pakistani. This was where cricket came in because here was something invented by the English at which Pakistan were actually good. There were no internationally successful film stars from Pakistan; there were no huge globally famous Pakistani pop stars or authors, but we *did* have Imran Khan.

Imran Khan was the best of us. He was indisputably a great sportsman, but he was so much more: he hung out with Mick Jagger and dated glamorous women. 'We were in awe of him,' recalls Zulfi Karim, 'he was just the ultimate. He was the icon and he made Pakistan trendy.' 'I loved seeing him playing,' says Mohammed Jamil, 'he was a hero for every Pakistani. He cast a magical spell wherever he went. Everyone wanted to see him and especially see him play.' Munir Ali, son of Shafayat and Betty, who we met in chapter two, remembers seeing Imran Khan play in the seventies and eighties in Birmingham. 'He was very dedicated and serious guy,' he says, 'and he was a winner.'

In the spring of 1992, a fortnight before the Conservatives won a fourth successive general election, Pakistan won the cricket World Cup final against England. I was in my final year studying in Manchester and I listened to the match on the radio hooting and cheering with delight. Amir Jamil was in his final year at high school and took the day off to watch the match. 'I went in late, and the teacher said it was very sus-picious that I was off on the day,' he says. 'The teacher asked me why I supported Pakistan. I said, "When people see us at school, they don't think of us as English." We were Pakistani to them. They used to treat us like Pakistanis so was it any surprise that we would support Pakistan?' Humayun Ansari recalls going to see Pakistan play England at Lords in 1992. It was a hot Sunday afternoon and having bowled England out cheaply, Pakistan needed 138 to win. 'As the sun shone, drinking grew apace,' he says. 'As Pakistan's batting began to collapse, so rose the volume of insults; baiting England spectators surrounding Pakistan supporters, belching out abuse – to the latter's chant of "Pakistan zindabad"(Long live Pakistan), they retorted, "Pakis in the pub, Pakis go home." I felt intimidated, emotionally vulnerable, as the atmosphere became increasingly, aggressively ugly.' It was such taunting reminders that people like me were not really English that reinforced my support for Pakistan.

I was not born in this country and I felt I would be a fraud if I tried to claim that Britain was truly my country. I had no right to take pride in the Britain that preceded my father's arrival when that was not my history. I also did not think modern Britain accepted that people who looked like me could be fully British. This produced an ever-present anxiety about my place in the world, and this was an anxiety reinforced by countless encounters in childhood and adulthood.

I have a memory of going on a day trip to France as an eleven-year-old sometime around 1983 and going through Calais. In my head I was just another young British boy with my mates. I can still remember the keen interest the French officials took and how they spent longer staring at me, and the way it made me feel so self-conscious. It was almost as if the official was communicating via his insistent glare: 'I know the truth, you might act as if you're just like your friends, but I know you are different, and you know it too.' I could not share these anxieties with my friends during my teenage years and it was unimaginable to discuss them with my parents. I wrote poems instead:*

WILL YOU EVER KNOW

Will you ever know, my friends
What it is like to not have a face
To be mocked, ridiculed and despised
And all because of your race

---

* I was warned by one alleged friend that to include childhood poetry risked the accusation of over-indulgence, but I feel relaxed about taking this risk – if you cannot be a little indulgent in your own book when can you?

Will you ever know, my friends
What it is like to have an infinity of worries to drown
In concealed tears and silent rage
All because your skin is white and mine is brown

Will you ever know, my friends
How it feels to be denied an equal chance
To be continuously harassed and attacked
To always take the defensive stance

Will you ever know, my friends
Or will you remain in glass
Cubicles, detached from the present
And still living in the past.

I first visited the United States in the summer of 1990, to
sell encyclopaedias door to door in California. I was advised
that my chances of success would increase if I told folks on
the doorstep my name was Steve and not Sarfraz. When I
returned to the United States in my twenties and thirties, I
would meet Americans who found it similarly hard to connect
my accent with my face. They thought British men looked
and sounded like Hugh Grant and the idea that someone
could legitimately call themselves British and look like me felt
funny to them. I remember being in a store in Amsterdam
and the shopkeeper, a smartly dressed, middle-aged woman,
asked me 'Where are you from?' 'Where do you think I am
from?' I asked her with a smile. She looked at me, thought

for a second and then said, 'Well, you *sound* English . . .'
She didn't need to complete the sentence. There were other
enquiries – most often when I would arrive at foreign airports
and be led towards secondary inspection when I would be
habitually reminded that my British passport does not necessarily mean others see me as British. I remember a work
trip to Israel. Immigration officials led me away the moment
I disembarked from the plane at Tel Aviv airport. Once they
had interviewed me, I was free to line up at the immigration
desk where I was again led away for more questioning. I
explained I was in Israel for the British Council to talk about
the power of theatre to change perceptions. I told the official
I was due to make a speech. She asked me to deliver the
speech to her – which I duly did.

I mention examples from around the world because it
reflects what others perceived as being British: each time
someone asked where I was from it felt like my hold on my
British identity was loosened. It was not only White people
who would ask. It is hard to get into a taxi and strike up a
conversation with the driver – invariably Muslim – who will
ask that same question. I have been asked it by cab drivers
in Luton, New York and Melbourne and if I dare answer that
I am from London or Luton they look at me as if I have not
understood the question. They want to know where I am
really from and the only acceptable answer is to tell them
which village in Pakistan my family hail from. The message
from both sides was the same – you might live in Britain but
don't kid yourself that this is really your country. I think all

this also played into why, when it came to cricket, I found it so difficult to support England and why it felt right to support Pakistan. I might have left when I was two and had no dream of returning but it was the one place that would never deny me, and it is hard to love a country that you believe does not love you back. Norman Tebbit tapped into all these conflicted emotions when he coined his cricket test. George Orwell famously described sport as 'war minus the shooting'. In November 2014, fourteen years after he had suggested sport as a way of gauging loyalty, Norman Tebbit offered another test for would-be British citizens. 'One test I would use,' he told the BBC's *Newsnight* programme, 'is to ask them on which side their fathers or grandfathers or whatever fought in the Second World War.'

Mohammed is ninety-six but could easily pass for some twenty-five years younger. He has a full head of hair and a neatly trimmed white beard and military-style moustache. He was wearing a cream-coloured plaid shirt and a neckerchief when I met him in his home in Windsor in July 2019. He greeted me in English, but when he realised I could speak Urdu his conversation slid between the two. Hussain was born in pre-partition India in a village in Rawalpindi and when he was sixteen he ran away to enlist in the British Indian Army during the Second World War. 'My father's older brother and my mother's brothers had fought in the First World War,' he told me, 'so it was a family tradition to join the army.' Hussain's grandson Ejaz would sometimes helped clarify what his grandfather was saying. 'There were multiple incentives to join the army,' Ejaz says. 'The British had promised independence to India, it was also a way out for people who had low education but there was also a genuine loyalty towards Britain.' Hussain joined the Army in 1941 and was sent to fight in Italy in 1943. 'There were three Indian Army divisions in Italy,' he says. Hussain joined as the machine gunner on an armoured car and fought in the battle of Monte Cassino. He spent two years in Italy and when VE Day arrived in 1945 he and his comrades advanced into Austria and learned of the German surrender alongside Bulgarian allies. After the war, he returned to Pakistan but following a serious car accident in 1958 he retired from the army and decided to come to Britain. I had come to meet him because he was one of the few living British Muslim veterans of the Second World War and thus one of the last links to an often overlooked chapter of history.

'By 1945 India had sent 2.5 million men,' writes Rozina Visram, author of the excellent *Asians in Britain – 400 Years of History*, 'in a war of conscripted armies, the Indian army was the largest volunteer army on the battlefield. India provided doctors and nurses, personnel for armoured units, gunners, signallers, sappers and miners, air mechanics and wireless operators. More than 8 million were engaged in auxiliary work for the armed forces and another 5 million in war industries, producing machine guns, field guns, bombs, mines and small arms. The Indian army saw action in all theatres of war – in the Middle East, North and East Africa, in Singapore, Malaya and Burma, and in Europe.' Their contribution has not always been fully recognised – hence the comment made by the northern comedian Bernard Manning while filming *The Mrs Merton Show* in 1998 that 'there were no Pakis at Dunkirk'. I remember watching that episode. I was saddened by Manning's language but assumed that his assertion was true, and that made me sadder. Manning was simply reminding me of the fragility of my claim to be British. What I didn't know then, and have only learnt very recently, was that his comment was not only offensive but it was also untrue: there were Muslim soldiers from the land that would later be named Pakistan at Dunkirk.

On 28 May 1940, thousands of British soldiers lined up on the beaches of Dunkirk awaiting evacuation. The majority were White but 300 were Muslim Indians from what is present-day Pakistan. These were the men of 25th Animal Transport Company of the Royal Indian Army Services Corps, who had travelled 7,000 miles with their mules to help the British Army. They were part of the so-called 'Force K6', also known as the 'Indian Contingent'.[4] Force K6 had come to man mules to carry supplies to the frontline, and brought with them everything from cooks to act as halal butchers and prepare dhal and chapattis, to tailors, bootmakers and an imam. As strict Muslims, halal food was provided. The troops would also slaughter animals themselves, cook curries and make chapattis. Heinz canned 37.5 tonnes of halal mutton for them. 'Each company therefore resembled a Punjabi village,' writes the academic and author of *The Indian Contingent* Ghee Bowman, 'transplanted into

French territory.'[5] King George VI visited Force K6 in August 1940 following their evacuation to rural Derbyshire, where they were supplied with live sheep to slaughter for food and a mosque was constructed for their worship. The soldiers presented the King with two chapattis, one for Princess Elizabeth and another for Princess Margaret. And as the King and Queen went on their way, the men of Force K6 waved them on with shouts of 'Allahu Akbar'.[6] This was history, British history, about which I had been ignorant.

I had not known that during the First World War India had sent 1 million soldiers – more than any other part of the Empire. They saw active service in France and Belgium, in Gallipoli and Salonika, in east Africa, in Mesopotamia, Egypt, the Persian Gulf and Aden. I had known nothing about the Muslim soldiers in Dunkirk or the contribution of men such as Mohammed Hussain. Hussain came to Britain with his two sons on 23 November 1960. 'There was a push to invite people to Britain,' says his grandson Ejaz, 'and people in the military area were among the first candidates. My grandfather also wanted to bring my father over and to educate him.' It was not just the pragmatic desire to educate his children that led Hussain to Britain. 'I think this is the best country in the world,' he tells me, 'this is our country. My four generations are here. If I say that this or that country is good then why don't I go there?' It was fascinating to me that Hussain, unlike my own father, felt a duty towards Britain. 'It's a general concept of loyalty, which was developed in the military,' says Ejaz, 'and it has transferred through the generations. You worked hard, you got educated and you were good with everyone because that is what your faith pushes you to do – a true Muslim is loyal to British society.' So how, I asked, do we persuade non-Muslims that they – Muslims – do not hate Britain? 'We don't fight fire with fire,' Ejaz says. 'In the stories of the Prophet, when a woman used to throw dirt on him, spit on him and when she was ill, he didn't say, "Oh good, she's ill", the Prophet made sure she was OK. So, you cure people, not with bullets and weapons but with love and kindness.' Mohammed Hussain is a living testament to what Britain owes to those of us whose origins lay in the Indian subcontinent. 'My grandfather's story is the antidote to the narrative that we Muslims are trying to change Britain,' Ejaz tells me. 'Britain is what it is because of the sacrifices we made – otherwise we would all be speaking German today.'

I was really struck by the word 'sacrifice'. When I began thinking about this book, my starting position was that Muslims were, for many Britons, a problem. My Muslim identity was also problematic because it was associated with habits, attitudes and practices that made me uncomfortable. The longer I have worked on it, the more people I have talked to and the deeper I have delved into British Muslim history, the more I have seen that there is an alternative narrative about British Muslims that is less appreciated. The story of Muslims in Britain is also one of sacrifice and service to this country and Mohammed Hussain's experience embodies this. I know very little about my grandfather, but I do know that he, like Mohammed Hussain, fought in the Second World War and was stationed in Burma. I have no photographs of him, no possessions that used to belong to him, nothing to help bring him to life for me. My own father died before I got the chance to ask him any questions about my grandfather and so he remains almost entirely unknown to me. If I knew more about his army days and what prompted him to sign up to fight alongside Britain, might that have made me more confident in asserting my British identity? I will never know but it does make me think it is incredibly important that both Muslims and non-Muslims, and particularly the young, are made aware of the Muslim contribution to both world wars.

Mohammed Hussain arrived into Britain in 1960 and settled with his family in Birmingham. Twenty-four years later, in the winter of 1994, Zeeshan Hashmi arrived from Pakistan with his brother Jabron and his father. Zeeshan was almost fifteen and Jabron was twelve. The family moved into a house in Small Heath in the heart of the Pakistani community. Zeeshan recalls that other Asians bullied his younger brother at school. To them he was an outsider – a 'freshie' who had only recently come from Pakistan. 'Jabron was very generous,' Zeeshan told me, 'very warm-hearted and loyal and also a very deep thinker.' The family had relatives who had served in the military and Jabron often talked about wanting to join the Special Forces, so it was not a huge surprise when he revealed to his family that he wanted to join the army. One evening in February 2006, Zeeshan and Jabron went for a long walk. They found a cafe, ordered tea and talked about what it would mean to join the British Army. 'We started talking about our role as Muslims and our duties as Muslims in the world that we live in,' recalls Zeeshan. 'What did it mean to be British and be a soldier?' The night before Jabron was deployed to Afghanistan in April 2006, the two brothers talked again. Jabron made the decision to not tell his mother where he was going. He feared it would only worry her, so he told her he was flying to Germany for language training. It was only with his brother that he could be fully honest. 'If you do your job right you can save a lot of lives,' Zeeshan told him. 'Make sure you pray and ask Allah to protect you, and make sure you that you stay on the right path and make the right decisions when you go.' Jabron flew to Afghanistan and was on the ground in the first week of June 2006, based in the south of the country in Sangeen.

Jabron had been in Afghanistan for three weeks and Zeeshan was at home in Birmingham. One night in late June, Zeeshan was in bed when there was a knock on the door. It was 1 a.m. He answered and there were a two people standing there. 'I saw a male and a female officer who were both wearing civilian clothes,' recalls Zeeshan. 'I invited them in, and they told me, "We are sorry to tell you but at 21.00 local time there was a rocket attack and as a result Jabron was killed."' Reeling from the shock, Zeeshan saw that his mother had woken up and was demanding to know the cause of the commotion. He made the decision to tell her that Jabron was not in Germany but in Afghanistan and that he was dead. 'As soon as I told her, she asked "Why are you lying to me?"' he recalls. 'I told her that I was telling the truth and I could see the pain in my mother's face. She broke apart.' Jabron Hashmi was the first British Muslim soldier to die on the battlefield since 9/11. What made the family's loss even more painful was that not everyone in their community considered him a hero. 'There were mixed feelings because he was a Muslim and had gone to a Muslim country to fight,' Zeeshan tells me. 'I remember standing in the front garden of my house and young British-Pakistanis would drive past and point to the house and say this is where that kaffir was from. I would read comments online saying he was a dog and he got what he deserved.' Some of his neighbours may not have agreed, but for Zeeshan there was no doubt that Jabron lived a life of service and sacrifice. His story is not widely known whereas everyone knows about the Muslims who detonated bombs in London on 7/7 or those who committed atrocities as members of the Islamic State. The question I keep coming back to is why do so many see those individuals as representing Islam rather than people like Mohammed Hussain and Jabron Hashmi? I asked Zeeshan whether he considered his brother a British patriot. 'Service in the British army or my brother's death whilst serving in the British army doesn't necessarily make us the only patriots,' he tells me. 'You can be a patriot by contributing to society, by being a doctor, being a nurse, being a teacher, paying your taxes, making sure the community you live in benefits from your existence. That makes you a patriot. Patriotism is not just about military service – it's about contributing to the society that one lives in and wanting it to prosper.'

Individuals cannot overcome systemic challenges faced by communities, but they can embody hope through their sacrifice and service to the community. Asiyah and Jawad Javed run a cornershop in Falkirk in Scotland. One afternoon in March 2020, Asiyah noticed an elderly woman crying outside a supermarket because she was unable to afford necessities. It was the week Britain went into lockdown due to the coronavirus pandemic and some stores were raising the prices of handwash to profit from the panic. Asiyah and Jawad made a decision to choose a different path: they spent £5,000 of their savings on masks, antibacterial handwash and other products to organise care packages for anyone that needed them. They donated 3,000 masks and delivered more than 1,000 food parcels to vulnerable people in four weeks. Anyone over the age of sixty-five was given free facemasks, antibacterial hand gel and cleaning wipes – they could either collect the bags in person or have them delivered for free. 'I can't say enough good things about Jawad,' William Welsh, seventy-three, told a newspaper, 'he's been doing it for weeks. The work this man has done will not be forgotten – especially by elderly people. He's doing a first-class job and long may it continue.'

There are currently more than 200,000 Black Minority and Ethnic medics working in the NHS and the first doctors who died from coronavirus were all Muslim with ancestry in regions including Africa, Asia and the Middle East. Habib

Zaidi had moved to the UK almost fifty years ago and worked in Leigh-on-Sea in Essex. He died aged seventy-six. 'He was a dedicated GP and that dedication cost him his life,' one of his patients told a local paper. The fifth Muslim medic to die from coronavirus was Areema Nasreen, a nurse and mother of three who worked at Walsall Manor Hospital. Who did she support in the cricket, and did it matter? When these doctors treated patients and Asiyah and Jawad spent their savings taking care of the elderly in their community, they were being good citizens but they were also being good Muslims. Their behaviour was a reflection of the values they found in their faith. These stories challenged an assumption I had when I started working on this book – that to be a good citizen meant, in effect, dialling down religiosity. The less outwardly religious folks were, I reasoned, the more we could find common ground. That was not necessarily borne out by the stories I uncovered – in fact the more religious someone was, the more that could propel them towards being a better and more engaged citizen. Religion is not inevitably a wall between communities – it can be a bridge.

Nusrat Ghani grew up in Small Heath, the same part of Birmingham as Zeeshan and Jabron. In the winter of 2013 she applied to represent the Conservatives in the seat of Wealden after the sitting MP announced his intention to retire at the next election. The open primary attracted 400 applicants. Nusrat had grown up supporting the Conservative Party. 'We loved Margaret Thatcher at home,' she recalls, 'my mum couldn't understand a word she was saying but we knew she was strong. She was doing the right thing by the country and my parents were allowed to buy the council house I grew up in. Margaret Thatcher was a huge, powerful woman figure in our home and I've always voted Conservative.' It is one thing to vote Conservative and quite another to believe, as a working-class, British-Pakistani Muslim woman, that you have a chance of representing the party in Parliament. 'I never thought they would select me,' Nusrat says, 'so I didn't put any pressure on myself to get selected. I thought all I'm going to do is be myself in the interviews. I'm going to have a good time and I want them to have a good time experiencing what I've got to offer.' When she learnt that she had been selected – and to represent a seat with an overwhelmingly White electorate – it was a total shock. 'I couldn't sleep that night,' she recalls. 'I've never felt shock like it ever since because it was the last thing we expected. I remember the interview was in a hotel and my husband was on the sofa and when they came out and said I'd won, he sort of jumped off the sofa, flung his arms in the air, and was like "What the fuck have you done?" And I said, "I don't know."' The seat was a safe Tory seat but Nusrat knew not to take anything for granted. When she was elected MP in May 2015 it felt like another shock. 'It was hard to explain that we'd won,' she says, 'so when I heard it and I was told I was the MP for Wealden it was one of those "How has this happened? What the hell?" moments – it was just was incredibly hard to digest.' I asked her how it felt to step inside Parliament and take a seat in the chamber where Margaret Thatcher and Winston Churchill – not to mention Enoch Powell and Norman Tebbit – had once sat? She told me she heard her own voice in the chamber and felt shaky. 'You're in this place surrounded by green benches, hearing your own voice in the chamber, in the mother of all parliaments,' she says, 'none of it makes sense. There was nobody I could say, well this person was ahead of me and they've done what I've done. There was nobody else. How have I ended up here? What do I do next? And for my parents it was the same thing. They did not expect it. I did not expect it. And I have colleagues who always wanted to be here and mapped out their journey to be here. This is purely accident – I spent most of my youth just trying not to be married to a cousin.' If becoming an MP was hard for Nusrat to process, it was near enough impossible for her parents. 'They never thought I would be elected because they thought the system would never allow it,' she says. 'They genuinely can't understand how this has come to pass. They keep thinking someday someone's going realise I'm Asian.' She laughs. 'There is always anxiety when you arrive in a country that at some point you'll be asked to leave. There always is. My family had always been anxious about being accepted and belonging, this was a moment they thought, "We're OK. We are British – we are here. This is our future." And my brothers would wind up my dad and say, "She's a Tory MP, I'm not sure you're OK."'

I don't share Nusrat's politics, but I find her story to be filled with hope. The fact that someone from her background can be elected to Parliament and serve in government says something hopeful about the story of British Muslims. I was not surprised that her parents remained wary about the notion of belonging, but my hope is that that sense of fragility will gradually harden to a more secure sense of belonging with each successive generation. In the current Parliament there are eighteen British Muslim MPs, which is undeniable progress given that the first British–Muslim MP to be elected to Westminster was Mohammed Sarwar only twenty-two years ago.* The 2019 intake also included Apsana Begum – the first MP to wear a headscarf. When I look at the faces of these, and other MPs of minority ethnic backgrounds, I am reminded of the words of the Conservative PM Lord Salisbury in 1886, when he warned that 'however far we have advanced in overcoming prejudices, I doubt if we have yet got to that point when a British constituency will take a black man to represent them.' Progress may be slow, it may be painful, and it may be opposed, but it is possible.

In Chapter 2 I introduced the story of Shafayat Ali, who arrived from the subcontinent in the 1940s and found work in a plastics factory in Birmingham, where he met and married a local girl called Betty. The couple had a son they called Munir, who also grew up in Birmingham. He lived through the National Front marching through the city and skinheads chasing the Asian lads, but even though Munir was

---

* In February 2021, Mohammed Sarwar's son Anas became the new Scottish Labour leader. He was the first non-White leader of a major political party in the UK.

mixed-race he was treated as just another Asian. He went to school, trained as a psychiatric nurse and in the late seventies he had an arranged marriage to a Pakistani woman. 'I had no choice,' he recalls, 'my parents just arranged it and that was it.' The couple had four children – three boys and a girl. 'As soon as they were able to hold a bat in their hands we would go down and play cricket in the garden,' he recalls. 'They were very young – about six or seven years old.' All three boys were gifted but there was something particularly special about their middle son. 'From the age of eight he could hit the ball very hard, and he was a stylish player,' recalls Munir. 'He could hit the ball and he could play with boys older than his age.' Munir took his son to under-eleven county trials when he was still eight and he ended up playing for Lancashire under-elevens. 'I remember him scoring a hundred in every game,' he says. 'People in the county started to talk about it. He was the golden boy.' Cricket was the family obsession. 'We talked about cricket twenty-four hours a day – at breakfast, cricket for lunch and cricket in the evening,' he says, 'cricket was the theme in our house. It was all about cricket.' And, inevitably, it was Pakistan that the family all cheered on. 'I was supporting Pakistan,' says Munir, 'all we did at home was talk about the Pakistan cricketers. I was supporting Pakistan cricket and our loyalties were with Pakistan.' Munir realised if he was going to support his sons, he would need to leave his job in nursing so he could take his sons to their cricket matches. 'I left that job and became a cricket coach,' he says. 'I did like an Open University sports psychology course called

How to Win.' Munir learnt how to set goals, how to instill confidence and how to turn failure into success. 'I said to my son: "I want you to be the number one. Number two – nobody remembers."' History is filled with ambitious parents who dreamt extravagant dreams for their children, but Munir's boys were not just good at cricket – they were outstanding: in their twenties all three would play cricket professionally – the oldest at county level for Worcestershire and Gloucestershire and the youngest for Shropshire. It was the middle son that everyone predicted would end up playing for England.

On 12 June 2014, Munir Ali's son Moeen made his debut for England against Sri Lanka. 'It was a dream come true,' recalls Munir, 'the family was so happy.' Moeen Ali would go onto become one of England's most respectable, and recognisable, players. 'When he first started to grow a beard, I was a bit hesitant,' says Munir. 'A lot of people said it could affect his England career, but Moeen said to me, "Dad, if I make it, I'll make it as what I am. I'm not going to change. I'm not going to shave my beard off. God will help me."' The contrast with Imran Khan could hardly be starker: Imran Khan exuded glamour, was often photographed alongside women the newspapers could only identify as 'mystery blondes', and told an interviewer meeting women was chief among 'the very decadent pleasures in life' which he enjoyed.[7] 'Moeen doesn't go to nightclubs or pubs. He doesn't do anything which is haram,' says Munir. 'He changed all the family when he converted back to Islam. His beliefs became so strong. If you follow the faith in a straight way and read it and study, success will come. God will be with you. He still has a very strong belief in that. If you're on the right path and you believe in God, it will happen.' In September 2020, Moeen Ali became the first British Muslim to captain England in a T20 International.[8] 'Considering my background and where I am from, I think it's quite an achievement to have captained England,' he told an interviewer. 'Young Asian cricketers can look and see that playing for England is not impossible, it's a realistic prospect and that anything can be achieved if you really put your mind to it.'[9]

Moeen Ali is not the only British Muslim cricketer to play for England in recent years. Adil Rashid, Haseeb Hameed and Zafar Ansari have also all played for the national team. Zafar is the son of Humayun Ansari, author of *The Infidel Within* and whose story I have featured in this book. I wanted to ask Munir Ali how having his son playing for the England team impacted his support. Did he still fail the Tebbit test? 'When they played Pakistan and he scored a hundred, I was very, very excited,' he says (note how he uses 'they' to denote England). 'I also wanted Moeen to do well. I wanted Pakistan to play well but I wanted Moeen to win the match for England.'

Moeen Ali was named England captain thirty years after Norman Tebbit first suggested his cricket test. In those thirty years British Muslims have gone from having their loyalty to England questioned to representing their nation at cricket at the very highest level. I have two young children and it makes me reflect on the question encapsulated in the Tebbit test.

When Pakistan next play England, who should I support? I have to confess it is not so easy to answer. Habit would suggest Pakistan for all the reasons I outlined earlier, but now it is not so easy to portray England as the enemy; when the England cricket team features players whose heritage and history mirrors mine more closely than the Pakistan team, is it time to think of them as 'they'? The prospect of supporting England and not Pakistan when the two teams meet feels like a mild betrayal, it suggests that I have sold out, that I am burning my bridges with my past and trying a little too hard to fit in. It does not sit easily with me. Perhaps the most truthful thing to say is that these days I am more of a neutral than a partisan, happy to cheer whoever plays the best cricket and able to see myself in both teams. That is me, born in Pakistan and made in England. My children were born and made in England and I know this about them: should Laila and Ezra excel enough at anything to represent their country, I would want them to represent England, and I would cheer them on.

EPILOGUE

FATHER, PART TWO

I am searching for my mother. It is a warm August morning, and I am wearing a light summer jacket sat on a train I boarded at London's St Pancras station that is heading to Luton. I have not seen my mother for five months due to the lockdown imposed to control the coronavirus pandemic. I get off the train and hail a taxi. The Muslim taxi driver asks me where I'm from. I tell him Luton. 'Yes, but where are you *really* from?' he asks. I stare out of the window in anticipation and guilt. I do not visit my mother often enough. The taxi reaches its destination, and I take a deep breath and step out. My footsteps are heavy as I walk towards the front door. My brother answers. I take off my shoes, walk into the kitchen where my mother is sat. I look at her and say *'As-salāmu 'alaykum Ami-ji'*. Hello, Mum. I hold my breath, tense and waiting. She smiles in recognition. I secretly exhale: my mother still remembers me.

My mother is in her late eighties and suffering from vascular dementia. Her short-term memory is shot, and her long-term memory is fading. The last time I brought Bridget, Laila and Ezra to Luton she waited for them to step into the garden before asking me who the White woman and children were. It would be painful to witness my mother slowly fading in front of my eyes in any context, but what makes it particularly hard is that my mother is the last woman standing: the last living survivor of an entire generation. My father and his siblings and their partners are long gone, as are my mother's siblings and partners. She is the last keeper of stories, including the story of who I am and where I came from, but she is no longer able to share this story. My father's death and my mother's disease were partly why I wanted to write this book. My mother's entire life has been defined by sacrifice and service. Her story is ordinary and yet extraordinary, but women like her are rarely given the respect they deserve. My mother's journey has been epic: born in pre-Partition Pakistan, married to my father who promptly left for Britain. I picture her coming to Britain in the early 1970s, the years of toil and sacrifice that provided me with the opportunity to gain an education, leave Luton and pursue my dreams. I picture her at my wedding, embracing a White, Scottish, blonde Christian woman, soon to be her daughter-in-law. I wanted to write this book in part to honour the journey my father made in coming to this country, and the journey my mother made to come to my wedding. My present life is, in many ways, very White: I am the only fully Pakistani person in my own family and there are times when I feel disconnected from my Pakistani past. That was also why I wrote this book – to understand my place in the world and to tell a larger story about Muslims in this country.

In the best sense there is nothing special about the Muslims – they are no better nor worse, no more virtuous nor blameworthy than any other community. They are, however, too often singled out for criticism and blame but too rarely accorded praise and respect. Muslims have fought and died for this Britain; they have represented this country in sport and politics; they have served you meals in Indian restaurants and driven you home in taxis; they have worked in mills and factories; they have kept their stores open when everything else is closed; they own corner shops and Asda;[1] they have tended the sick in surgeries and hospitals. Some, like my mother, have blamelessly worked hard and raised children. This is not to say that challenges do not exist. Muslims need to accept that Britain is no longer a foreign country where they happen to live, it is home, but integration is a two-way street and too often we focus only on what Muslims have done and are doing wrong. Writing about the aftermath of the Rushdie affair, Sayeeda Warsi writes that 'the government failed to recognise that if Britain didn't hold its Muslims close, if it didn't show them that they mattered and treat them like they belonged, then there would be others more than happy ... to befriend them and shower them with concern and moral support.'[2]

I started this journey because I wanted to know why relations between Muslims and non-Muslims were so bad. My own assumption was that it was largely the fault of the Muslims; I suspected that a combination of culture and religion conspired to hold Muslims back. The reason Muslims had not progressed as far as other communities was that too many had not really left behind the village mentalities of their ancestral homes, too many continued to wish to live among their own, hoping to hold on to their culture and fearing the world beyond. It is clear to me now, having spent the last few years travelling around the country meeting and talking with hundreds of Muslims and hearing their stories, that I was guilty of simplistic generalisations. I had, without fully appreciating it, absorbed myths and stereotypes about Muslims. I had not fully recognised that what I had assumed was intentional behaviour of Muslims was in fact also the result – sometimes accidentally, sometimes not – of the policies and actions of both central and local governments.

I have come to appreciate how much of what I have been apprehensive about Islam was in fact the specifics of migration from the subcontinent. Put simply, many of the issues I have spent this book exploring have much less to do with religion and more to do with class and geography: where immigrants came from in the subcontinent and where they settled in this country. The question I have struggled with is the competing significances of culture and religion – why is the Islam that has developed in Britain among the south Asian communities so fearful and inflexible? There have been times in Islamic history when Muslims were pioneers in art and science and when religious scholars would study not only Islam but Plato, Aristotle, mathematics and philosophy. Critics of Islam sometimes use the words 'backward' to refer to the attitudes of British Muslims, but in fact if British Muslims went backwards they would conversely be moving forward. It would be more accurate to say that there has been a narrowing of influences and interpretations and the reason for that is, I believe, due to an emotion mentioned repeatedly throughout this book: fear.

The story of Muslims in Britain is a story of a community living in fear, and not only the fear of racism, violence and discrimination. It is the fear that their culture, traditions and heritage will be diluted and later disappear: the fear that integration will lead to assimilation, which will lead to extinction. It is fear that explains why my family so opposed my marriage to Bridget – the fear that the world they came from was under mortal threat. That fear, rooted in ignorance, leads to insecurities that harden into defensiveness. The more the Muslim community felt targeted and threatened, the more it withdrew and retrenched because it felt it was locked in a battle for its very existence.

My daughter Laila was still a toddler when I started thinking about this book and my son Ezra was yet to be born. When Bridget was pregnant with Laila, I remember feeling anxious about our unborn baby's skin tone. There was a part of me that, selfishly, hoped she would have a skin tone similar to mine, as I felt I would more easily bond with her. I also knew that darker skin might prompt questions about identity and belonging, that others might see such a child as different in a way they would not a fairer-skinned one. I also wondered, and frankly hoped, that my worries might be more the product of my past rather than the world today. There were, however, moments when I was reminded that things are rarely so simple. The times when Bridget would be mistaken for Laila's nanny because Laila has brown skin and she is White; the time when a stranger asked Laila where she came from and Laila, only three years old, replied 'from a hospital, of course'. I took these incidents mostly in good humour and did not worry about the internal impact they might be having. Ezra was born in late 2016 and he has fairer skin than Laila and me, but the fact he has a mop of curly hair means strangers still say he resembles me despite having a skin tone closer to his mother.

Throughout nursery, kindergarten and school, I rarely worried about whether my daughter felt British. She just *was* British. I did not fully appreciate how much any of this mattered to my daughter until the time, when she was eight, when she started talking about how she didn't like having brown skin and how she wished she had white skin. I put it down to the fact that she wanted to look more like her mother and tried not to feel rejected. It was not an isolated incident and often it was at night, particularly when Bridget was putting her to bed. Sometimes Laila would cry, and it left Bridget and me feeling helpless. How was it possible that my daughter was expressing the same apprehension today about being brown that I had felt four decades earlier? I remembered the White boy who would spit in the faces of the Asian boys at my school; I remembered that feeling of helplessness I felt when reading about the murder of Ahmed Ullah; I remembered the evenings I would try to convert my impotent frustration into teenage poems; I remembered the feeling that people like me could not hope to expect as much from the world as those born with white skin. I thought I had consigned all this to the past.

Laila was not, as far as I knew, suffering any overt racism at school. I doubted she even knew the meaning of the word before she started learning more about the Black Lives Matter movement. One evening, after an afternoon when Laila had again talked about not wanting brown skin, I decided I would talk to her about it. She was tucked up in bed and I was about to start reading *The Little White Horse*, but I began by telling her that I was really hurt by her saying that she didn't like her brown skin. I told her that in saying that I felt she was rejecting not just me but also her grandparents. 'But *you* look good with brown skin Daddy,' Laila said. I told her that she looked good in her brown skin too. She said nothing. I asked her what it was about having brown skin that made her feel so bad. She told me that no one who was brown had ever done anything all that great. The books she read at school and the individuals whose lives she studied were, she said, all White. I was stunned. 'Did you know that Jesus was brown?' I asked. She did not. 'So, you think brown people have not achieved anything?' I asked. She said yes. Laila and I had a running joke where she would always say I was not from Luton – I was from Pakistan and just happened to have grown up in Luton. I had taken it as a joke but now I recognised that for Laila belonging and being British were bound up with having white skin. She thought she was disenfranchised by her brownness.

I asked Laila what would help her feel less bad about being brown. 'Maybe if I knew about some heroic brown people,' she replied. That felt like a challenge I could meet and the next day I ordered *Amazing Muslims Who Changed the World* – a children's book by Burhana Islam I thought she might enjoy. I had tried to find a book about amazing brown people but no such book existed. Laila's discomfort sprang specifically from being brown rather than her Muslim heritage, but in her mind 'Muslim' and 'brown' were fairly interchangeable – even if she was still protected from the specific challenges that came with having Muslim heritage. The book seemed to do the trick. For the next few days, whenever I saw her she was immersed in it, learning about the Muslim scientist whose work preceded Charles Darwin and other inspiring stories. It seemed to work, for a while.

It was not long, sadly, before Laila started complaining again about her brownness – about how her brother had fairer skin and how she wanted Daddy's family to be 'more normal'. She would say that brown skin was not beautiful. When she had gone to bed Bridget and I would sit around the kitchen table wondering and worrying. It was strange, to say the least, to be confronting this question in my family life at the same time I was working on this book. When I was a boy, I worried that I was not fully British and would not be accepted. I no longer have those worries and the reason is that, regardless of what some bigots on both sides might argue, my British identity is baked into who I am. I had assumed that my children would grow up in this country without needing to fight those old battles; I had hoped that their sense of belonging would have been baked in at birth. I fear that I was too optimistic – perhaps nothing can be taken for granted.

In 2013 David Goodhart published *The British Dream*, in which he explores whether there is such a thing as a British Dream, what it looks like and who best embodies it. I had talked to him for his book and so, when I was reading it, I was naturally looking to see if he had included any reference to me. It is not until six pages from the end that he writes: 'There is a British dream and I want to give almost the final word to someone who exemplifies it.' And then he mentions me: I was, he suggested, the living embodiment of the British Dream. I was rather gobsmacked. It was deeply flattering, and it made me reflect on the journey of my life. It was a life that had begun rather unpromisingly in the village of Paharang in Pakistan, and it has led me to a terraced house in Bury Park and then to a somewhat nicer house in a decent corner of London. It is also a journey that has led me to marry a woman born in Scotland and to have children whose can trace their ancestors back to Limerick and Lahore. It has been quite the journey.

I began this book thinking about my father and his story; I end it thinking about being a father and my own children's story. I wanted to write this book to see if there were valid reasons for feeling hopeful about the state of relations between Muslims and non-Muslims in this country. What I have come to realise is that the journey towards a more hopeful land depends not only on politics and policies but also on people. Hope lives and dies in the hands of individuals and the choices they make. It is illuminating to notice how often change is the result of individual actions: the Muslim teacher who decides he wants to teach music to the children in his school, the Muslim woman who defends a Jewish father on the London underground, the Muslim woman who decides she will not consent to marrying her cousin, the Muslim man who helps his local Jewish community. These are all individual actions that proved to have far-reaching consequences. The power of the individual to make a difference is what connects my father making the choice to leave the world he knew for a farther shore with his son who also chose an untravelled road when he married the woman he loved.

I feel more hopeful than I did when I began this book, but I am also painfully aware of the work that remains. I want Laila and Ezra and their generation to grow up to be women and men who feel confident and comfortable as British citizens, for whom the traumas and turmoil that preceding generations endured will feel like history. If anyone truly embodies the beautiful rewards for love and faith in love, if anyone fully represents living proof of how great Britain *can* be, it is not me, it is my children and their generation.

I hope that this new generation emerges as adults into a nation where the mutual fear and ignorance between Muslims and non-Muslims, which scarred the lives of those in this book, have been consigned to history.

I hope they will grow up in a Britain where Muslims and non-Muslims no longer see the other as 'they'. I hope for a nation that can embrace a simple truth – that *they* are *us*.

ENDNOTES

The full list of the books and journals consulted during the writing of this book can be found in the below endnotes but I wanted to first highlight five books from which I quote extensively:

Muhammad Anwar – *Myth of Return: Pakistanis in Britain*
David Goodhart – *The British Dream: Successes and Failures of Post-war Immigration*
Sayeeda Warsi – *The Enemy Within: A Tale of Muslim Britain*
Rozina Visram – *Asians in Britain: 400 Years of History*
Humayun Ansari – *The Infidel Within: Muslims in Britain since 1800*

Prologue: Father, Part One

1   Elif Shafak, 'We need to tell different stories, to humanise each other', *Guardian* [online], 13 August 2020.

One: They ... Don't Want to Live Among Us

1   Humayun Ansari, *The Infidel Within: Muslims in Britain since 1800* (London: C. Hurst & Co. Publishers Ltd, 2004), p. 147.
2   David Goodhart, *The British Dream: Successes and Failures of Post-war Immigration* (London: Atlantic Books, 2021), pp. 116–118.
3   I wrote about the legacy of that speech in an article for the *Observer* in 2008. Sarfraz Manzoor, 'Black Britain's darkest hour', *Observer* [online], 24 February 2008.
4   Ibid, p. 134.
5   Jeremy Seabrook, *City Close Up* (Middlesex: Penguin Books, 1973), p. 50.
6   Muhammad Anwar, *Myth of Return: Pakistanis in Britain* (London: Heinemann Educational Books, 1979), p. 46.
7   They can be viewed at: https://rogerbracewell.com/news-blackburn1970s/. 'Black and White Photos of Blackburn in the 1970s', Roger Bracewell Photographer [website], 1 June 2019.
8   1976 was also the year when Eric Clapton declared support for Enoch

Powell in comments that would inspire the creation of Rock Against Racism the following year.

9   Muhammad Anwar, *Myth of Return: Pakistanis in Britain*, p 153.

10 The *World in Action* documentary 'The National Party' is viewable at https://player.bfi.org.uk/free/film/watch-the-national-party-1976-online.

11 Dervla Murphy, *Tales from Two Cities: Travels of Another Sort* (London: John Murray Publishers Ltd, 1987), p. 87.

12 'The Struggle for Race Equality: Ahmed Iqbal Ullah Murderered', Runnymede Trust [website], https://www.runnymedetrust.org/histories/race-equality/106/ahmed-iqbal-ullah-murdered.html.

13 Muhammad Anwar, *Myth of Return:Pakistanis in Britain*, p. 167.

14 Zamira Rahim, 'In the Latest Sign of Covid-19-related Racism, Muslims Are Being Blamed for England's Coronavirus Outbreaks', *CNN* [online], 6 August 2020.

15 Stephen Bush, 'British Muslims Are Being Scapegoated for the Government's Coronavirus Failures', *New Statesman* [online], 31 July 2020.

16 'Covid: London's Orthodox Jews have "one of highest rates in the world"', *BBC News* [online], 2 February 2021.

17 'UK riots blamed on ethnic division', *CNN* [online], 11 December 2001.

18 Anushka Asthana and Peter Walker, 'Casey Review Raises Alarm over Social Integration in the UK', *Guardian* [online], 5 December 2016.

Two: They . . . Don't Marry Outside Their Own

1   Chelsea Ritschel, 'European Royal Family Tree: How Prince Philip and the Queen Are Related', *Independent* [online], 29 April 2021.

2   Rozina Visram, *Asians in Britain: 400 Years of History*, (London: Pluto Press, 2002), pp. 35–43.

3   Ibid, p. 68.

4   Ibid, p. 274.

5   Photographs from the Belle Vue Studio [collection], Bradford Museums and Galleries [website], https://photos.bradfordmuseums.org/collection?key=T3siUCI6eyJoeXBlIjoxLCJpZHMiOlsyN119fQ&WINID=1621009065335.

6   Photographic portrait from Manningham's Belle Vue Studio, the Belle Vue Studio [collection], Bradford Museums and Galleries [website], https://photos.bradfordmuseums.org/view-item?i=206046&WINID=1621005315824.

7   Sarfraz Manzoor, 'Ode to Rome, a City of Passionate Pilgrimage . . . and Roses', *Guardian* [online], 22 November 2009.

8   Anonymous extract from Islam Question and Answer: https://islamqa.
     info/en/answers/45645/a-realistic-look-at-marriage-to-women-of-the-
     people-of-the-book.

9   The song that had brought on the tears had been 'Walk Like A Man'.
     Tunnel of Love is a 1987 album from Bruce Springsteen.

10   'Leamington Spa Sikh Temple Protest: Fifty-five Arrested', *BBC News*
     [online], 11 September 2016.

11   Sunny Hundal, 'The British Sikh men trying to stop women marrying
     outside their religion', *Independent* [online], 4 October 2015.

12   Ibid.

13   Sarfraz Manzoor, 'My family said they would boycott my wedding',
     Guardian [online], 29 September 2010.

Three: They . . . Don't Treat Men and Women as Equals

1   As quoted in Humayan Anisari, *The Infidel Within*, p. 283.

2   Matthew Taylor and Rowenna Davis, 'EDL Stages Protest in Luton',
     Guardian [online], 5 February 2011.

3   David Cameron, 'PM's Speech at Munich Security Conference' [tran-
     script], Gov.uk, 5 February 2011.

4   'Passive tolerance' of Separate Communities Must End, Says PM' [press
     release], Gov.uk, 18 January 2016, https://www.gov.uk/government/
     news/passive-tolerance-of-separate-communities-must-end-says-pm.

5   Muhammad Anwar, *The Myth of Return: Pakistanis in Britain*, p. 166.

6   Ibid, *The Infidel Within*, p. 253.

7   Ibid, p.258.

8   Ibid, p. 277.

9   Shaista is now fifty-one and, only days before our conversation, she had
     dyed her hair blonde.

10   'Sexism in the Qur'an', Wikipedia [website], Wikimedia Foundation, 29
     April 2021, https://rationalwiki.org/wiki/Sexism_in_the_Qur%27an.

11   Anonymous, '12 Things I Can't Reconcile About Islam as a Muslim
     Woman', Amaliah [website], 23 July 2020.

12   Policy Bristol, '"Cultural transformation" as Muslim Girls Out-perform
     Boys Academically, Research Says', Bristol University [website], 4 April
     2016.

13   DEMOS 'Rising to the Top' [report], 9 October 2015, https://demos.
     co.uk/project/rising-to-the-top/.

14   Lizzie Dearden, 'Islamophobic Incidents Rose 375% after Boris Johnson
     Compared Muslim Women to "letterboxes", Figures Show', *Independent*
     [online], 2 September 2019.

Four: They . . . Follow A Violent Religion

1   'List of terrorist incidents in Great Britain', Wikipedia [website],
    Wikimedia Foundation, 8 May 2021, https://en.wikipedia.org/wiki/
    List_of_terrorist_incidents_in_Great_Britain.
2   Aya Batrawy and Lori Hinnant, 'Leaked Isis Documents Reveal Recruits
    Have Poor Grasp of Islamic Faith', *Independent* [online], 26 September
    2016.
3   Barbara Bradley Hagerty, 'Is The Bible More Violent Than The Quran?',
    NPR [website], 18 March 2010.
4   Qasum Rashid, 'Anyone who Says the Quran Advocates Terrorism
    Obviously Hasn't Read its Lessons on Violence', *Independent* [online], 10
    April 2017.
5   Karl McDonald, 'Britons Massively Overestimate the Country's Muslim
    Population', *i newspaper* [online], 14 December 2016.
6   Sayeeda Warsi, *The Enemy Within A Tale of Muslim Britain* (London:
    Penguin Books, 2018), p. 79.
7   Lizzie Deardon, 'More White People Arrested over Terrorism Than Any
    Other Ethnic Group for Third Year in a Row', *Independent* [online], 4
    March 2021.
8   'Mohammed Saleem Stabbing: Man Admits Murder and Mosque Blasts',
    BBC News [online], 21 October 2013.
9   Maz Saleem, 'When my Muslim Father was Murdered by a Terrorist in
    Birmingham, I Realised Something About the Way we Label Killers',
    Independent [online], 16 February 2016.
10 James Gibbons, 'The End Game', *Los Angeles Times* [online], June 22
    2008.
11 Ed Pilkington and Jessica Elgot, 'Orlando Gunman Omar Mateen was a
    regular at Pulse nightclub', *Guardian* [online], 14 June 2016.
12 Peter Beaumont and Sofia Fischer, 'Mohamed Lahouaiej-Bouhlel: who
    was the Bastille Day Truck Attacker?', *Guardian* [online], 15th July 2016.
13 Gareth David and Peter Allen, 'Police question Bastille Day Killer's
    73-year-old Male Lover as it is Revealed Murderer was a "sex maniac"
    who Searched for ISIS Beheading Videos Online', *Daily Mail* [online], 19
    July 2016.
14 Sayeeda Warsi, *The Enemy Within*, p. 99.

Five: They . . . Follow a Religion That Hates Jews

1   Joe Middleton, 'Leader of Britain's Largest Muslim Charity Quits after
    Labelling Jews "grandchildren of monkeys and pigs" and Calling Egypt's

President a "Zionist pimp" in Anti-Semitic Facebook Posts', *Mail Online*, 24 July 2020.

2 Dr Rakib Ehsan, 'British Muslim Anti-Semitism', Henry Jackson Society [website], 4 August 2020.

3 ISGAP, Günther Jikeli, 'Antisemitic Attitudes among Muslims in Europe: A Survey Review', *ISGAP Occasional Paper Series*, May 2015, https://isgap.org/wp-content/uploads/2015/05/Jikeli_Antisemitic_Attitudes_among_Muslims_in_Europe1.pdf.

4 Melanie Phillips, 'We Must Call Out the Muslims who Hate Jews', *Jewish Chronicle* [online], 11 April 2019.

5 'British Muslims Twice as Likely to Espouse Anti-Semitic Views, Survey Suggests', *Jewish Telegraphic Agency* [online], 12 September 2017.

6 Ibid.

7 Mehdi Hasan, 'The Sorry Truth is That the Virus of Anti-Semitism has Infected the British Muslim Community', *New Statesman* [online], 21 March 2013, https://www.judaism-islam.com.

8 'Similarities between Judaism and Islam', Judaism Islam website, 21 August 2013.

9 Heather Stewart and Ben Quinn, 'Labour Suspends Three Councillors over Alleged Antisemitic Remarks', *Guardian* [online], 2 May 2016.

10 Samantha Lock, 'Rising Labour Star Mohammed Pappu, 26, Accused of Spreading Antisemitic Conspiracy Theories over Social Media and to Children in Troubled Areas', *Daily Mail* [online], 11 October 2018.

11 Susan Sachs, 'Anti-Semitism is Deepening Among Muslims; Hateful Images of Jews are Embedded in Islamic Popular Culture', *The New York Times* [online], 27 April 2002.

12 Ben Zehavi, 'Rise of "Jews of No Religion" Most Significant Find of Pew Study, says director', *The Times of Israel* [online], 3 Ocotober 2013.

13 Saif Rahman, 'What is a "Cultural Muslim"?', *New Humanist* [online], 3 May 2013.

14 Brian Whitaker, 'The rise of Arab ableism', *New Humanist* [online], 29th June 2015.

Six: They . . . Believe Homosexuality is a Sin

1 I wrote about daytimers in this *Guardian* article from 2012. Sarfraz Manzoor, 'Strictly Bhangra: How Daytimers Got Young British Asians Dancing', *Guardian* [online], 10 April 2012.

2 Max Bearak and Darla Cameron, 'Here are the 10 Countries Where Homosexuality May be Punished by Death', *Washington Post*, 16 July 2016.

3 Frances Perraudin, 'Half of All British Muslims Think Homosexuality Should be Illegal, Poll Finds', *Guardian* [online], 11 April 2016.

4 Andy Dangerfield, 'Residents Tackle East End "gay free zone" Stickers', *BBC News* [online], 22 February 2011.

5 'Video: East London Man Suffers Anti-gay Abuse from "Muslim Patrol" Gang', *Pink News* [online], https://www.pinknews.co.uk/2013/01/22/video-east-londonman-suffers-anti-gay-abuse-from-muslim-patrol-gang/.

6 The first known public appearance of the term homosexual in print is found in an 1869 German pamphlet.

7 Khaled El-Rouayher, *Before Homosexuality in the Arab–Islamic World, 1500–1800*, p. 125.

8 I came across this story in Scott Siraj Al-Haqq, *Homosexuality in Islam: Critical Reflection on Gay, Lesbian, and Transgender Muslims* (Oxford: Oneworld Publications, 2010), p. 39.

9 Quoted in Stephen O. Murray and Will Roscoe, *Islamic Homosexualities* (New York and London: New York University Press, 1997), p. 16.

10 Declan Walsh, 'Pakistani Society Looks Other Way as Gay Men Party', *Guardian* [online], 14 March 2006.

11 Flora Drury, 'The Secret Shame of Afghanistan's Bacha Bazi "dancing boys" who are Made to Dress Like Little Girls, then Abused by Paedophiles', *Mail Online*, 7 January 2016.

12 Quoted in Stephen O. Murray and Will Roscoe, *Islamic Homosexualities*, p. 36.

13 Quoted in Stephen O. Murray and Will Roscoe, *Islamic Homosexualities*, p. 17.

14 Sayeeda Warsi, *The Enemy Within*, p. 34–35.

Seven: They . . . Look Down On White Girls

1 'Revealed: Conspiracy of Silence on UK Sex Gangs', *The Times*, 5 January 2011.

2 'Independent Inquiry into Child Sexual Exploitation in Rotherham (1997 - 2013)', Rotherham Metropolitan Borough Council [website], https://www.rotherham.gov.uk/downloads/download/31/independent-inquiry-into-child-sexual-exploitation-inrotherham-1997---2013.

3 Nick Sommerlad and Geraldine McKelvie, 'Britain's "worst ever" child grooming scandal exposed: Hundreds of young girls raped, beaten, sold for sex and some even KILLED', *Mirror* [online], 11 March 2018.

4 'Oxfordshire Grooming Victims may have Totalled 373 Children', *BBC News* [online], 3 March 2015.

5 Ella Hill, 'As a Rotherham Grooming Gang Survivor, I Want People

to Know About the Religious Extremism Which Inspired my Abusers', *Independent* [online], 18 March 2018.

6   Girl A, *My Story* (London: Ebury Press, 2013), pp. 76–77.

7   Charlie Moore, 'Police Rescue Child Bride, 10, who was Sold to a 50-year-old Man by her Mother to Pay Off a £3,400 Loan In Pakistan', *Mail Online*, 21 December 2017.

8   Human Rights Watch, '"How Come You Allow Little Girls to get Married" Child Marriage in Yemen' [report], https://www.hrw.org/sites/default/files/reports/yemen1211ForUpload_0.pdf.

9   Mohammed Jamjoom, 'Yemeni Child Bride Dies of Internal Bleeding', *CNN* [online], 9 April 2010.

10   Reza Aslan, *No God But God* (London: Arrow Books, 2011), pp. 64–65.

11   Jean de Wavrin, 'The Wedding of King Edward II and Isabella of France' [collection], British Library [website], https://www.bl.uk/collection-items/the-wedding-of-king-edward-ii-and-isabella-of-france.

12   Myriam Francois-Cerrah, 'The Truth About Muhammad and Aisha', *Guardian* [online], 17 September 2012.

13   'Muslim Religious Leaders Condemn Child Sex Grooming', *BBC News* [online], 28 June 2013.

14   David Batty, 'White Girls Seen as "easy meat" by Pakistani Rapists, Says Jack Straw', *Guardian* [online], 8 January 2011.

15   Jessica Elgot and Graham Ruddick, 'Sarah Champion Distances Herself from *Sun* Article on British Pakistani Men', *Guardian* [online], 16 August 2017.

16   Martin Williams, 'EDL Supporters Attack Police During Rotherham Sex Abuse Protest', *Guardian* [online], 13 September 2014.

17   'Plea to Ban Repetitive Rotherham Protests Rejected by Home Office', *BBC News* [online], 22 February 2017.

18   Ibid.

19   Josh Halliday, 'Rotherham Muslims Launch "guardian" Group after Far-right Threats', *Guardian* [online], 29 January 2020.

20   Rev. Ben Johnson, 'What Did the Christchurch Mosque Shooter Believe? Inside the Mind of a Collectivist Killer', Acton Institute [blog], 15 March 2019.

21   Barnaby Kellaway and Chris Kitching, 'New Zealand Shooting: Rotherham Child Abuse Victim Condemns Killer's "tribute"', *Mirror* [online], 16 March 2019.

22   Matthew Jackson and Adam John, 'The Sickening Crimes of Richard Huckle and How his Parents Begged Police to Take Him Away', *Kent Live* [online], 14 October 2019.

23 Martin Saunders, 'Christian Paedophile Richard Huckle: Why the Whole Church Must Respond', *Christian Today* [online], 2 June 2016.

24 'Paedophile Richard Huckle Stabbed to Death at Full Sutton Prison', *BBC News* [online], 14 October 2019.

25 Peter Stubley, 'Richard Huckle: Man Arrested on Suspicion of Murdering "one of worst paedophiles" in Britain', *Independent* [online], 13 January 2020.

26 Jayne Senior, *Broken and Betrayed* (London: Pan Books, 2016), pp. 78–79.

27 Lara McDonnell, *Girl for Sale* (London, Ebury Press, 2015), p. 308.

28 Joe Watts, 'Sajid Javid Suggests There Could be "cultural reasons" for Pakistani Grooming Gangs', *Independent* [online], 26 December 2018.

29 Jamie Grierson, 'Most Child Sexual Abuse Gangs Made up of White Men, Home Office Report Says', *Guardian* [online], 15 December 2020.

30 Dan Hodges, 'The Sex Gangs Whitewash: Home Office Report into Abuse of Young Girls Found Attackers were "most commonly white" Despite Evidence of Mass Grooming by Asian Men ... but DAN HODGES Reveals the Inside Story of a Politically Correct Cover-up', *Daily Mail* [online], 19 December 2020.

31 Girl A, *My Story*, p. 61

32 Sarah Wilson, *Violated* (London: HarperElement, 2015), p. 61.

33 Holly Archer, *I Never Gave My Consent* (London: Simon and Schuster, 2016), p. 95.

34 Shaista Gohir MBE, 'Unheard Voices, The Sexual Exploitation of Asian Girls and Young Women' [report], *Muslim Women's Network UK*, September 2013, http://www.mwnuk.co.uk//go_files/resources/UnheardVoices.pdf.

Eight: They . . . Want to Take Over Our Country

1 Sam Lock, 'Hook-handed hate preacher Abu Hamza was a bodybuilding ladies man who worked as a strip club bouncer for a Soho kingpin before turning to Islamism', *Mail Online*, 26 August 2018.

2 Andrew Anthony, 'Interview: Anjem Choudary: the British Extremist who Backs the Caliphate', *Guardian* [online], 7 September 2014.

3 Robert Lambert, 'Tackling Islamophobia: Time for a Proper Debate on Anti-Muslim Violence and Intimidation', *New Statesman* [online], 5 December 2010.

4 'Guard Dumped Pigs' Heads at Mosque', *BBC News* [online], 6 August 2002.

5 'Pig's Head at Cheltenham Mosque: Simon Parkes Jailed', *BBC News* [online], 30 August 2012.

6   Josh Halliday, 'Manchester Mosque Left Gutted after Suspected Arson Attack', *Guardian* [online], 17 July 2017.

7   Ben Beaumont-Thomas, 'Morrissey Denounces Halal Meat as "evil", and Attacks May, Khan, Abbott and More', *Guardian* [online], 17 April 2018.

8   James Bloodworth, 'Meet Annie Waters – the UKIP Politician Too Extreme for Nigel Farage', *New Statesman* [online], 18 August 2017.

9   Euro-Islam, 'Islam Should have a "quintessentially British" Version with Minoret-less Mosques and No Burqas, Warsi Says', *More Bham – Euro-Islam* [website], 21 December 2015.

10   Mohammed El-Gomati, 'How to Tackle the EDL', *Guardian* [online], 31 May 2013.

11   Lizzie Deardon, 'Two-thirds of Tory Members Believe UK Areas "under sharia law", as Poll Reveals Scale of Islamophobia in Party', *Independent* [online], 24 June 2019.

12   Sayeeda Warsi, *The Enemy Within*, p. 236.

Nine: They . . . Don't Believe in Our Values

1   David Cameron, 'What I Learnt from my Stay with a Muslim Family', *Guardian* [online], 13th May 2007.

2   'Conform to our Society, Says PM', *BBC News* [website], 8 December 2006.

3   David Cameron, 'PM's Speech at Munich Security Conference', [transcript], Gov.uk, 5 February 2011, https://www.gov.uk/government/speeches/pms-speech-at-munich-security-conference.

4   IPOS, 'A Review of Survey Research on Muslims in Britain' [report], February 2018, https://www.ipsos.com/sites/default/files/ct/publication/documents/2018-03/a-review-of-survey-research-on-muslims-ingreat-britain-ipsos-mori_0.pdf.

5   Frances Perraudin, 'How Politicians have Struggled to Define Britishness', *Guardian* [online], 10 June 2014.

6   'Tony Blair's Britain Speech' [transcript], *Guardian* [online], 28th March 2000.

7   'Full Text of Gordon Brown's Speech' [transcript], *Guardian* [online], 27 February 2007.

8   Theresa May, 'A Stronger Britain, Built on our Values' [transcript], Gov.uk, 23 March 2015.

9   David Goodhart, *The British Dream*, p. 301.

10   'Britain Threatens to Flout International Law', *Economist* [online], 9 September 2020.

11 Lizzie Dearden, 'Islam is Reviving British Values, says Former Archbishop of Canterbury Rowan Williams', *Virtue Online*, 2 August 2014.

12 Judith O'Reilly, 'State Primary School of the Year: St Stephen's Primary, East Ham', *The Times* [online], 19 November 2017.

13 Sian Griffiths, 'St Stephen's in Newham Bans Hijabs for Girls Under 8', *The Times* [online], 14 January 2018.

14 I tried on multiple occasions to talk to Neena Lall – who is still head of St Stephens School – but although she replied to my emails she declined to talk on the record.

15 Centre for Media Monitoring, 'State of Media Reporting on Islam & Muslims' [report], *Muslim Council of Britain* [website], Quarterly Report: Oct – Dec 2018, https://mcb.org.uk/report/state-of-media-reporting-on-islam-and-muslims/.

16 Simon Cottee, 'Flemming Rose: The Reluctant Fundamentalist', *Atlantic* [online], 15 March 2016.

17 'Most British Muslims "oppose Muhammad cartoons reprisals"', *BBC News* [online], 25 February 2015.

18 Human Rights Watch, 'Questions and Answers on the Danish Cartoons and Freedom of Expression – When Speech Offends' [report], 15 February 2006, https://www.hrw.org/report/2006/02/15/questions-and-answers-danish-cartoons-and-freedom-expression/when-speech-offends.

19 John Rex and Robert Moore, *Race, Community and Conflict*, pp. 122–123.

20 Sayeeda Warsi, *The Enemy Within*, p. 47.

21 'State of Media Reporting on Islam & Muslims' [report], Centre for Media Monitoring, *Muslim Council of Britain* [website], Quarterly Report: Oct – Dec 2018.

22 Oscar Williams, 'British journalism is 94% White and 55% Male, Survey Reveals', *Guardian* [online], 24 March 2016.

23 John Twomey and Cyril Dixon, 'Muslims tell British: Go to hell', *Express* [online], 4 November 2010.

24 Sayeeda Warsi, *The Enemy Within*, pp. 36–37.

Ten: They . . . Don't Love Our Country

1 David Rosenberg, 'The Racist Killing of Altab Ali 40 Years Ago Today', *Open Democracy* [website], 4 May 2018.

2 '"You could set up as chai wallah in Piccadilly Circus!" It Ain't Half Hot

Mum' (14 August 2017), YouTube video, added by Seann Black [online]. Available at: https://www.youtube.com/watch?v=ViNDoQzeGBQ.

3   Javed was the name my family used for me.

4   Ghee Bowman's *The Indian Contingent* is the definitive book on the role of Muslim soldiers in Dunkirk.

5   Ghee Bowman, *The Indian Contingent* (London: The History Press, 2020), p.14.

6   Jane Goddard, 'Fabulous Photos Show Indian Troops at their Derbyshire Camp During Second World War', *Derby Telegraph* [online], 5 August 2019.

7   Alison Boshoff, 'From Swaggering Playboy to Pious Politician: Legendary Cricketer Imran Khan Used to be London Society's Premier Ladykiller . . . Now he's on the Brink of Becoming Pakistan's PM Following a Blood-soaked Election', *Daily Mail* [online], 25 July 2018.

8   Nasser Hussain was the captain of the England team for forty-five Test matches, from 1999 to 2003. He was the son of an Indian father and English mother and is reported to be non-practising.

9   Saj Sadiq, 'Moeen Ali: "Considering my Background and Where I am From, I think it's Quite an Achievement to have Captained England"', *i newspaper* [online], 3 October 2020.

Epilogue: Father, Part Two

1   Howard Mustoe, 'Who are Asda's New Owners the Issa brothers?', *BBC News* [online], 2 October 2020.

2   Sayeeda Warsi, *The Enemy Within*, p. 25.

ACKNOWLEDGEMENTS

This book exists because of everyone who placed their trust in me and the story I wanted to tell.

I had been musing about the ideas in this book for many years, but it was only after meeting my agent Andrew Gordon that I was able to distil those ideas down to their central themes. I want to thank Andrew for his wise counsel, faith and encouragement.

The first person to demonstrate faith in this project after Andrew was Shoaib Rokadiya – then at Wildfire – and so I owe a particular debt of gratitude to him. I also want to thank Alex Clarke, also at Wildfire, with whom I worked closely from treatment to publication.

I spent more than three years travelling around the country conducting interviews for this book and I am incredibly grateful for everyone who took the time to speak to me, often about deeply sensitive personal experiences. Those conversations so often left me stimulated, inspired and hopeful, and I am so very grateful to everyone who shared their stories with often painful honesty.

I want to give a very special salute of thanks to Ella Gordon, Katie Packer and Louise Walsh, who did the vast bulk of transcriptions of my interviews – their assistance was invaluable, and I am hugely grateful.

This book was largely written at home during the 2020 lockdown. The reason I was able to deliver it only slightly late was because my wife Bridget enabled me to work while heroically multitasking – doing her job as an autism specialist as well as most of the childcare during the daytime. This was particularly challenging during lockdown and without her allowing me the space and time to work this book simply would not exist. I love you, Bridget, thank you for everything.

When I was childless, one of the things I feared about parenthood was the awareness that it would inevitably impact on my work: it would, I worried, leave me exhausted and distracted, with less time to think and to write. These fears turned out to be entirely justified. It is no accident that my last book was published the year before I met my wife. Fatherhood may have afforded me less time to write, but it also gave me a reason to write at all. I wrote *They* because I wanted to believe the world my children were growing up in could be a kinder and more tolerant one than the world into which they were born. And so I want to end by thanking my children, Laila and Ezra: I hope you feel I did what I could to make a difference, to be a helper.